DISCOVER YOUR CREATOR CONTACTING YOU

Alan Fraser Bell and Heather Louise Bell

DISCOVER YOUR CREATOR CONTACTING YOU

Alan Fraser Bell and Heather Louise Bell
Published by **Peacock Quill**

Ⓒ Copyright Heather Louise Bell & Alan Fraser Bell 2002

Contact address:
Heather Bell, 26 Ottery Close, Southport PR9 9GE
Email: heather.bell7@btopenworld.com

Published by PeacockQuill
Printed by Printfine, Gibraltar Row, Liverpool.

The entire manuscript has been created by Heather and Alan Bell, including the text, photographs, sculptures, paintings, poems, designs and format.

Final Proof Reading: Alison Matthews.

Hand Crafted in:
The Healing Garden, 56 Andrews Lane, Formby,
Near Liverpool, L37 2EW, ENGLAND.
(Contact address)

All rights reserved.

No part of this book may be reproduced or utilised in any form or by any means, electronic or mechanical, without prior permission in writing from the Authors.
(Except for the usual review procedures)

The moral right of both authors has been asserted.

The information given in this book is not intended to be a replacement for medical advice. Any person with a condition requiring medical attention should consult a qualified practitioner or therapist so that the best treatment is utilised from all disciplines.

ACKNOWLEDGEMENTS

We wish to thank the following for their kind permission to reproduce the articles about our research work:

WOMAN'S OWN   AMERICA'S NATIONAL ENQUIRER
SUNDAY PEOPLE   AMERICA'S NATIONAL EXAMINER
DAILY POST   FORMBY TIMES
PSYCHIC NEWS   REVEILLE

Permission has also been granted to include scenes and references from National Television appearances associated with our work in the following programmes.

EXCHANGE FLAGS . . . . . . .with Gordon Burns
ALLSORTS . . . . .with Chris Kelly
GARDEN PARTY . . . . .with Paul Coia
MARGINS of the MIND . . . . .with Brian Inglis

ISBN 0-9542341-0-3

MEET the Scientists who stepped back in time to change the future. . .

Alan Fraser Bell Ph.C., M.R.Pharm.S., M.R.S.H.
(Health Consultant)

Qualified Chemist, Scientific Researcher, Health Consultant in a wide variety of fields: vitamin deficiencies, herbal remedies, purified water analyst. Married to Brenda, with two children, Heather and Paul.

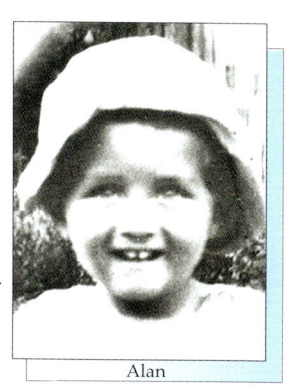

Alan

Heather Louise Bell F.G.A.
(Gemmologist)

Qualified Gemmologist with distinction. Writer, poet. Works closely with her father in many aspects of his research. Pre-press Supervisor, employed by Liverpool Daily Post & Echo, producing local weekly newspapers.

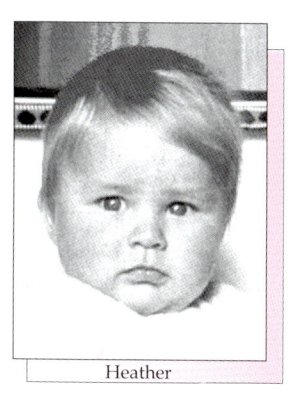

Heather

With the simplicity of a child and ability of an inquisitive mind, you will feel . . .

OUR CREATOR'S PRESENCE

"It's an Experience of a Lifetime You'll Have Forever"

A BOOK OF LIFE

EVIDENCE OF THE CREATOR

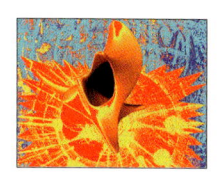

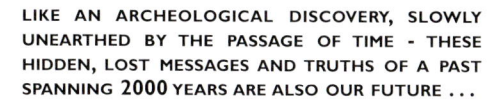

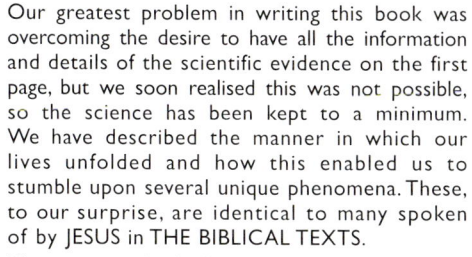

LIKE AN ARCHEOLOGICAL DISCOVERY, SLOWLY UNEARTHED BY THE PASSAGE OF TIME - THESE HIDDEN, LOST MESSAGES AND TRUTHS OF A PAST SPANNING 2000 YEARS ARE ALSO OUR FUTURE ...

Our greatest problem in writing this book was overcoming the desire to have all the information and details of the scientific evidence on the first page, but we soon realised this was not possible, so the science has been kept to a minimum. We have described the manner in which our lives unfolded and how this enabled us to stumble upon several unique phenomena. These, to our surprise, are identical to many spoken of by JESUS in THE BIBLICAL TEXTS.

There is so much of value we need to take time, even read a page again before we move on. It is a discovery of our Creator's Presence in and around all of us.

WE ARE NOT ALONE

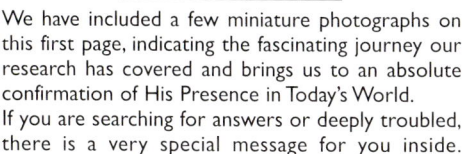

We have included a few miniature photographs on this first page, indicating the fascinating journey our research has covered and brings us to an absolute confirmation of His Presence in Today's World.

If you are searching for answers or deeply troubled, there is a very special message for you inside.

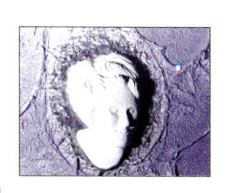

FOREWORD

By BRIAN QUINN MBE

When Heather and Alan asked me if I would write a foreword to their book, I was surprised and taken aback. It was later, the words privilege and honour came to mind.

My wife Hazel greatly admired the work Heather and Alan do in their Healing Garden at Formby. It was in 1976 that I met the Bell family, at Hazel's insistence; I approached them with the balance problem, Meniere's.

I had lost confidence as well as my balance, I walked away that day with a smile on my face, convinced that I could live a life with Meniere's. I did, I played Rugby and then refereed, until I was sixty-two years old.

I wasn't looking for proof, but I got it.

The friendship and admiration has lasted over the years. I'm a Sixty Herb anticancer man and a user and believer in the benefits of Colloidal Silver.

My one wish is that Hazel could have read through Heather and Alan's book with me, but I can see her lovely smile and hear the words: "I told you so."

Thank you Heather and Alan, you taught me to reach out and ask for help and understanding.

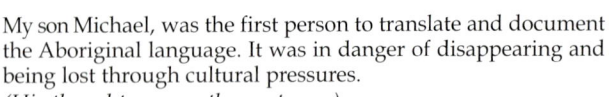

Brian

My son Michael, was the first person to translate and document the Aboriginal language. It was in danger of disappearing and being lost through cultural pressures.
(His thoughts are on the next page).

In a similar way, Heather and Alan are perhaps the first to interpret the true meaning of Jesus' Sayings - after 2000 years of mystery, doubt and continuing conflict.

'Sayings' that had been selectively edited, forgotten in the dust of generations and hidden beneath new doctrines. These are now brought back to life.

The first to recognise a real communication and its encoded message that could give the answers mankind has sought, since life began . . .

(II)

From MICHAEL QUINN in Australia

Anthropologist and Aboriginal Linguist

Extends beyond cultural and religious boundaries

The Healing Garden is a "Special Place" .... Alan Fraser Bell, is an unassuming, modest kind of man, who gave up his Chemist shop and Dispensary in 1975, to devote himself to full-time healing and research into creativity.

The book you are now embarking upon has grown out of this pursuit. It is the product of an unusual mind: that of a man with a scientific training and an almost contrary disposition to practice therapies designated by an often sceptical world as "psychic". In this he is something of an enigma.

Yet Alan Bell's healing powers have been attested by many. He has helped my father overcome certain life-threatening ailments that have afflicted him during the last thirty odd years, and helped him learn strategies to cope and fight against these debilitating conditions, and live a full and rewarding life. And when a specialist told my father that he would have to live with intense back pain for the rest of his life, whether walking or sitting, Alan Bell occasioned a total cure, either through the pharmaceuticals he suggested or the laying on of hands, or both!

He discovered this power of healing when his own daughter recovered from a very serious double curvature of the spine through the simple act of laying on of hands and asking God for help. Since then, working with his daughter Heather, also a healer, they have set many sufferers on the road to recovery and helped others reach their full potential in life.

In a certain sense he is a prophet awakening the world to the fact that the eternal is not something to be experienced after we die, but present within each moment. Our attitudes and habits, our worldly personalities can, and do obstruct the view.

Immortality can be experienced as a present fact. "It is here! It is here!"

Although Alan Bell's message is decidedly Christian there is a sagacity in his thinking that extends beyond cultural and religious boundaries.

The refreshing fact is that Alan Bell cannot be subsumed under any label. His knowledge of modern pharmacology and the healing herbs of antiquity provides him with remedies for the body, whilst his belief in the efficacy of the laying on of hands allows him to address the full person, body and psyche.

Heather has taken on her father's mantle, and with no more ado I suggest you read on and benefit from both of the authors' unique perspective on life.

Michael Quinn

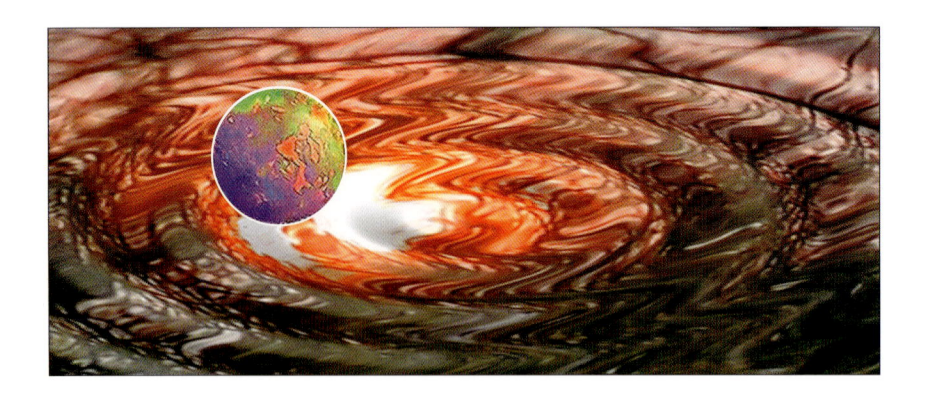

THE PATH

MEET THE SCIENTISTS
A BOOK OF LIFE - Evidence of The Creator .... (I)
FOREWORD - Brian Quinn MBE .... (II)
FOREWORD - Michael Quinn .... (III)
CONTENTS - The Path .... (IV/V)
"YOU ARE NOT YOUR OWN"- said Jesus. (We belong to Our Creator - We Are Not Alone) 1
SEA OF GALILEE - Dedication - To everyone in search of Truth 2
INTRODUCTION - People we had Healed insisted, we must write about God's Presence ...... 3 - 6
THE EAR - Some of Jesus' strange Sayings - All absolutely true .... 7 - 8
FORMATIVE YEARS - As a child you know! - Then it fades, and needs regeneration .... 9 - 12
SELF DESTRUCT - Or Live Forever .... 13 - 15
HIGH SCHOOL YEARS - History of our Future .... 16 - 21
THE CONSTANT BACKGROUND - God designed us not to notice Him - But why? .... 21 - 24
AIR FORCE YEARS - Choir Out In Space - We are not alone .... 25 - 27
THE ELEMENTS - Hidden for a Reason - No. 113 could be from another dimension? .... 28 - 31
OBSCURE MESSAGES - Brave new world .... 32 - 33
"THE WORLD IS A BRIDGE - Become passers by" - to a better place .... 34 - 35
NEW LIFE - Another Choir - Miracles .... 36 - 39
SILVER - MORE PRECIOUS THAN GOLD - From Bible Times to Spoon and Pusher .... 40 - 41
COLLOIDAL SILVER - Unbelievable Properties .... 42 - 46
KITCHEN TABLE TECHNOLOGY - Return to health - Do it Yourself .... 46 - 48
BUTTERFLY PHENOMENON - Spaces between the air molecules 49
RELIGIOUS GENE 50
"I WILL SPEAK TO YOU THROUGHOUT ETERNITY" - God Speaks to Enoch and to us ... 51 - 52
ECLIPSE 1999 - Concentrated the minds of Four Billion people worldwide .... 53 - 54
MOVING METAL MEMORIES - How Odd? .... 55 - 57
NATURE'S SCULPTURES AND DESIGNS - Every shape is here - HE made them ALL ... 58 - 63
CREATIVE THINKING - Music, Laughter, Poetry and Art can change your soul .... 64 - 67
BELIEF EXERTS A FORCE - Thoughts can make physical changes in materials .... 68 - 77
HERBS OF ANTIQUITY - And Cancer Prevention .... 78 - 88
ACHIEVE POSITIVE HEALTH - Beneficial foods .... 89 - 91
NEGATIVE EFFECTS AND TOXIC ITEMS .... 92 - 96
SOME GOOD NEWS 97
UNIQUE VIBRATIONS OF NATURE - Frequency Generator inhibits human parasites ... 98 - 103
SILVER AND TISSUE REGENERATION 103

EVIDENCE OF JESUS' PRESENCE - Remarkable Revelations - Edge of Discovery........... 104 - 105
MIRACLE OF WATER - "All waters are Holy."... 106 - 111
LIFE SUPPLEMENTAL - Vitamins - Minerals - Health Check.. 112 - 115
PAGE 117 - MOST REMARKABLE EXPERIENCE OF A LIFETIME .... 116 - 117
CREATOR'S CHANGES - In The Healing Garden .... 118 - 119
JESUS MAKES CONTACT WITH US - He is here for everyone .... 120 - 123
YOU HEAR WITH ONE EAR - Instant Revelation 124
SAYINGS OF JESUS - And Their Special Messages .... 125 - 132
JESUS MAKES HIMSELF KNOWN - In the life of each one of us................................. 133 - 134
THE HEALING MUSIC - Cavern sounds Liverpool - Philharmonic Hall - Record .... 135 - 140
NEWSPAPERS - MAGAZINES - And TV examine our work.. 141 - 146
MIRACLES - Can be put in writing 147
JESUS TOUCHES YOU - More of His Sayings - Listen ! 148
HOW TO HEAR AND FEEL HIS PRESENCE .... 148 - 153
RECEPTIVE SENSES - Rejuvenated 154
SOUL AND SPIRIT - Component of life 155
LOST WITHOUT KNOWING - Expect to Hear Him and you will 156
POSITIVE THOUGHTS - And Miracles 157
CREATIVE THINKING OF CHILDREN - Needs nurturing and not ignoring 158
YOU ARE YOUR ONLY LIMITATION - Reach Out 159
ALTERED STATES OF CONSCIOUSNESS - TV Interview by Chris Kelly 160
SPONTANEOUS INSPIRATION - The mind at work on it's own .... 161 - 162
UNIVERSAL MIND - In touch with The Divine 163
KIND THOUGHTS AND DEEDS 164
GOOD WORKS - "I come because you need me."... 165
SCULPTURE RE-CREATED - Inspired Regeneration .... 166 - 167
TELEPATHY - Margins of The Mind - TV with Brian Inglis .... 168 - 170
COMMUNICATION WITH PLANTS - Pyramid shaped Pears .... 171 - 173
STILL TIME - We must get to know Him now - He makes order out of chaos 174
THE 5th DIMENSION - Cosmic Strings in Space - There may be more than Five 175
MEDITATION - Simple Ideas - Practical Uses .... 176 - 177
PREPARE TO BE MOVED - By God's Presence .... 178 - 179
NEGATIVE WORLD - Sceptical Doubt - Miraculous changes 180
A BEAUTIFUL VOICE ANSWERED MY PRAYER - Before Time Began 181
SCIENTISTS - Misdirected Power 182
"LET THERE BE LIGHT " - Energy E = mc^2 183
"GOD'S IMAGE IS HIDDEN BY HIS LIGHT" - Crookes Radiometer 184
JESUS REVEALS THE MYSTERY 185
OUR SPECIAL MOMENTS - Living Sayings - "Until We Meet Again." 186
SAYINGS OF COUNTRY FOLK - Could be derived from Jesus .... 187 - 189
ABILITY TO MOVE - "The Sign Of Our Heavenly Father."... 190
SHROUDED IN MYSTERY - An unusual photograph of our research .... 191 - 192
JASMINE AND HIS PRESENCE - In a perfume 192
SHROUD CONFIRMS THE NARRATIVES OF THE GOSPELS - Direct Communication 193
LIVING WORDS - Our book seems to have a life of it's own 194
"MAY YOU HEAR WITH ONE EAR" - The Mysteries of The Lord 195
RECENT RESEARCH - Listen to new Evidence.. 196
THE SAYINGS OF JESUS .... 197 - 200
GOD SPEAKS TO MAN 201
IDENTICAL OR PARALLEL SAYINGS FROM THE BIBLE 202
FURTHER READING 203
INDEX .... 204 - 210
WORLD PRESS, TELEVISION AND RADIO 211
A SPECIAL PERSON 212

(V)

SAYINGS OF JESUS

We wish to acknowledge that The Sayings of Jesus referred to in this book are derived from the translations of
WILLIAM TYNDALE

The Authorised King James Version of The Bible for which Tyndale's works became the basis.

THE GOSPEL ACCORDING TO THOMAS
Coptic Text established and translated
by
A. GUILLAUMONT, H.-CH. PUECH, G. QUISPEL,
W. TILL AND †YASSAH 'ABD AL MASĪḤ

THE GOSPEL OF THE ESSENES
The Original Hebrew and Aramaic Texts
translated and edited by
EDMOND BORDEAUX SZEKELY

and

THE GOSPEL OF PEACE OF JESUS CHRIST
by the Disciple John
translated by EDMOND SZEKELY and PURCELL WEAVER.

These books by Professor Szekely and many more are available from the
INTERNATIONAL BIOGENIC SOCIETY
P.O. Box 849, Nelson, British Columbia, Canada V11 6A5.

For the complete list of Jesus' Sayings referred to in our text,
see pages 197 - 200

JESUS SAID To His Disciples:
*"Thy Father in Heaven hath loved thee before
The Foundation of The World."*
John - Chapter 17, Verse 24.
These words are also from a fragment of the Essene Gospel of John.

So we were all in existence before the creation of matter.
Therefore we will continue, even when we no longer have a physical body.

BY FOLLOWING THE EXPERIMENTS AND INSTRUCTIONS
in this book your Creator will reveal Himself to YOU.
Although not hidden He has been obscured by our thoughts.
Even young children have enjoyed reading these pages and mature sceptics have been astonished.

JESUS SAID: *"You are not your own."*
(1 Corinthians - Chapter 6, Verse 19.)
In other words, we belong to our Creator - WE ARE NOT ALONE.

This book is dedicated to:
Everyone in search of truth.

Photo N. Dabell

The Sea of Galilee

Jesus walked along this shore of pebbles, which has remained unchanged for 2000 years, and by the ancient steps spoke to His Disciples, inspired by the peace and tranquillity of God's Presence. Following in His footprints today is a deeply moving experience.

The roar, the rush and ripple of the tide,
The pools are cool and the hollows in the caves inside,
Are filled with crystal water.
On the rocks and in the cracks and fissures,
The sea plants sway,
And round about the fishes play.
The air is fresh and pure,
What is there more to wish,
And pray it stays this way.

INTRODUCTION

AS REAL as the book in your hands

ONE of our friends said, "I need to know now, how to Feel God's Presence - my life depends on it, then I'll go back and read the whole book."

IT IS with this desperate plea in our minds from a troubled soul, that we suggest if you also are in need of immediate help, go straight to page 117 and travel the path. When you have followed the simple way to find Him, come back to the beginning and read about the experiences and experiments which led us to GOD's most remarkable gift - allowing us to feel HIS Presence in truly physical ways, as real as this book in your hands, the sensations are beautiful.

YOU CAN DEVELOP your ability to communicate and be aware of His replies by applying the detailed Experiments to your life, and not just reading about them.

EXPLORE the early days of your childhood or even later years and you will find special moments when God touched you, but you were not aware of what had taken place, or if you had noticed, it was not understood, but when you have completed this book - YOU WILL KNOW.

I HAD known Nancy and Derek for many years, helping them through difficult times with our own particular type of Healing. They are long standing friends now, rather than patients or clients. We had been chatting for an hour or more.

"Write a book," Nancy said, out of the blue.

"Oh! everyone writes books these days, I'm sure there are more books than people to read them," I replied, in a rather dismissive tone.

"You should, in fact you must," she said.

"Do you think anyone would want to read my words?" I muttered, using the same tone of voice.

"Why do you think people travel hundreds of miles to listen to your wisdom?" she threw back at me. "Call the book simply CONTACT," she continued.

"It is a lovely thought, but there are so many people in need of help, would I find the time to write it. Why don't you do it for me, we've chatted for hours during the past twenty years, you know all about our research work; would you do it for me?"

"No I couldn't," was her immediate response. "My words would not carry the same conviction as yours."

Inspired sculptures in the Healing Garden

"Well," I mused, "I only use everyday phrases to convey ideas and experiences."

"Ah yes!" said Nancy, "but you talk about God because you feel His Presence. You talk about Jesus - you've seen His Miracles. When you say we are not alone - He's trying to contact us if we would only listen - they're not just words, they are the truth. The belief radiates from you. You actually know."

THERE was a long pause here, while we each pursued our thoughts . . .
"Is there life after television?" I asked. "Most people would have put the book down by now and reached for the remote control. Talking or writing about God and Science, Healing and Jesus seems a big turn off for many. I know the time is coming, in fact it is very close, when everyone will have to consider these, but Heather and I are what you might call simple scientific souls. Someone in the Churches should be more involved in this work."

"But they haven't necessarily experienced God's Presence, like you," she said. "Some don't even believe in God, to many it's only a profession."

HEATHER and I are scientists not theologians and many years ago I began independent research into several unusual psychic phenomena, healing, telepathy and others. Not only did I find that Healing was real and it worked, but it took us over as a family - we became Healers. It wasn't something we had sought to do, it happened to us, it came upon us as you might say. We have experienced God's Works to such an extent that what was once a strong belief in God, is now beyond belief, it's KNOWING. We know HE is alive and well and cares for us all most deeply. HE is real, not just a belief, not just a hope, or a desire that He's here somewhere. He is here everywhere, in us all, a part of every living creature, in all the flowers, the vegetation, in every atom.

"There now, if anyone was still reading, they would have put the book down, wouldn't they?"

"No, you're wrong," said Derek in his own gentle way. "Yes, they are simple words, but they carry such profound belief - they are knowing words. We experience God's Presence when we're with you and He stays with us when we return home. It's an experience of a lifetime we will have forever. Nancy's right, do it, call it CONTACT, because it really is. Then it will become part of everyone's life, they need your wisdom - I'm sure they'll feel it through your words, just as we do when we talk with you. You could show people how to Feel God's Presence, but most importantly, so that they would know for themselves. It would become their experience. It would belong to them, not just something they had read about. Real phenomena they could see, hear and feel."

"The book wouldn't help anyone to enjoy their food more," I interrupted, "or their cigarettes or drinks. It wouldn't have any love scenes or sex or anything similar; isn't that what makes most books interesting."

The Healing Sanctuary where many people feel God's Presence.

"No," said Derek sharply, "all those are only filling empty spaces in many people's lives; they are searching, you have already told us that. They are looking for something real, but don't know what it is. You have found it - you can give it - you can show the way. Your work could show everyone how to solve the Deepest Mystery of LIFE for themselves . . . GOD'S PRESENCE."

"I prefer talking with those who need help, conversations, exploring ideas together. It seems rather lonely just writing words." I continued, "I am still trying to escape from putting pen to paper and I'm not doing very well."

Then Nancy chimed in, "Do it like that then. Talk to us and write it down later."

NANCY PUSHED on about our poems, paintings, healing music, sculptures and how they were inspired, and writing about all the experiments with Colloidal Silver, and its remarkable healing properties, and the sixty cancer prevention herbs.

She went on and on, but most important of all, she said: "Describe HOW TO FEEL GOD'S PRESENCE."
I finally agreed to start that night.

"GOOD," they said, both together and in harmony.

NOW the Millennium

NOW THE MILLENNIUM is upon us with very little thought of its true significance by those who should know better, there literally is . . . . **NO TIME LIKE THE PRESENT**.

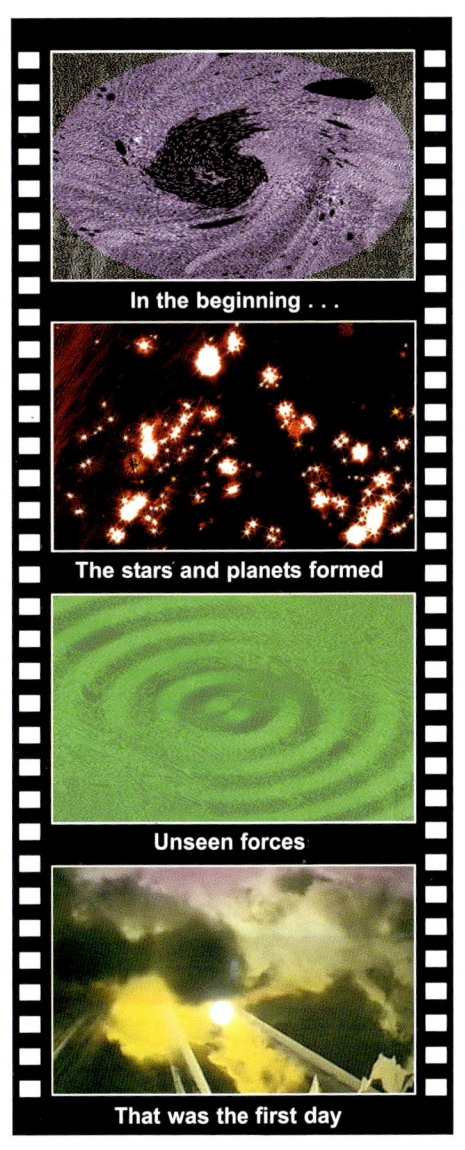

In the beginning . . .

The stars and planets formed

Unseen forces

That was the first day

MANY years ago Heather and I decided to prepare documents of all our research work because it is very important to us that they are not lost, especially now we have found Jesus' Presence as real physical experiences. After the passage of so many years, with people waiting for His return, He is here, as He said He would be in The Biblical Texts. Not as a physical man, as many people have expected, but as an overshadowing, (a coming into consciousness, an awareness without knowing its origin), just as He had described to His Disciples, when He said:

"I will give you what the eye has not seen, what the ear has not heard, what hand has not touched, and what has not arisen in the heart of man."

HE is telling US, not just the Disciples of His time, how He will make Himself known to future generations. The full miraculous significance of Jesus' message is highlighted in a later section.

I HAD seemed to be obstructive with Nancy and Derek, but I wanted to be absolutely sure that they were convinced it should be published as a book, and the need was as real as we felt. Many others have expressed the same thoughts, but we had to be sure; we pressed them also.

IT IS two thousand years since Jesus was here on earth as a real living person, with a remarkable Message concerning all mankind. In The Biblical Texts He tells us how, in the years following His Ministry, we will be able to experience God's Presence and His own, in real physical ways.

IT IS OUR PLEASURE TO HELP EVERYONE TO EXPERIENCE THESE

WE HAVE discussed many aspects with several friends, and I remember saying, it may have happened in The BEGINNING that our CREATOR found Himself in empty space, isolated and alone, a superb creative intelligence of such wisdom and power, His every Word became Reality.

Let there be light . . .

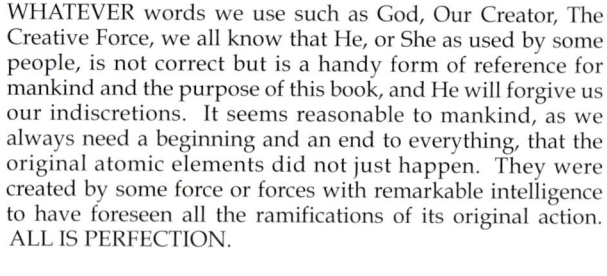

Creation of the solar system

WHATEVER words we use such as God, Our Creator, The Creative Force, we all know that He, or She as used by some people, is not correct but is a handy form of reference for mankind and the purpose of this book, and He will forgive us our indiscretions. It seems reasonable to mankind, as we always need a beginning and an end to everything, that the original atomic elements did not just happen. They were created by some force or forces with remarkable intelligence to have foreseen all the ramifications of its original action. ALL IS PERFECTION.

WE CAN ONLY experiment and hopefully understand material things and their interactions with known existing forces. Perhaps it is not within our Creator's programmed code for us to understand His creative processes, which brought into being all the elements and forces unseen.

WE do not understand the many hidden forces like Gravity; we only know they are there because of their effects on matter. Even light itself can pass through empty space unseen, until it illuminates something in its path, and can also be deflected by gravitational forces, yet neither appear to be there.

THERE ALWAYS has to be a scientific device, or some material substance to demonstrate their presence. Therefore, it seems quite reasonable to us that some of God's Forces exist, for which we do not have scientific detecting devices. But we do have THE HUMAN BRAIN which He developed as an instantaneous receptor for His messages and a two way communication with us all, if only we would listen. In later parts of the book we explore Jesus' constant references to the ear. The percentage of brain actually used is minimal, compared to its size/capacity . . . there are areas not used by US at all! But are they active? Who IS using them? GOD HIMSELF?

IN THE Beginning God said: *"Let There Be Light,"* and there was Light. Genesis, for instance does not say God Created Light, He said, *"Let There Be,"* and there was. His Word allowed it to happen, made it happen, such is His Power, and so it was with all His Creations. Although we think there's nothing there, He tore empty space apart, into equal and opposite components, Electrons and Protons, negative and positive fields of force, and He's kept them apart ever since, allowing the formation of all the Elements. The first being Hydrogen with one positive and one negative charge, then building all the other elements from this original structure with the liberation of vast amounts of His Energy as radiations.

IN THE present day, scientists have reported the creation of new atoms of hydrogen in interstellar space! He is not just at work out there, He is here also, and can reshape damaged or diseased tissues, if we would only ask for His help and believe it will be given, although He does not demand belief of us, but He wishes we would allow Him to Touch us in His own way, not having to prove His Presence.

THE MILLENNIUM should be a celebration of Jesus' Presence today, not historical discussions about a man who strode the earth 2000 years ago.

Who JESUS IS and what HIS LIFE MEANS
can only be appreciated by:
EXPERIENCING HIS PRESENCE TODAY

This book is dedicated to that purpose

WE ARE NOT ALONE

THE EAR

JESUS said His Heavenly Father had prepared a Maiden by the name of Mary to receive Him when He came to earth. Mary was overshadowed by The Holy Spirit and found to be with child. When it was time for Jesus to come to earth, when His Father had a 'thought' to send Him, He entered into Mary by 'The Ear' and He came forth by 'The Ear'.

VERY STRANGE WORDS these may seem to be, but many times during Jesus' Ministry He would say: *"Whoever has ears to hear, let him hear."* This is a special Message. We must listen.

HE WAS BROUGHT into the world as a physical birth by Mary, but the LIGHT that shone around her also enabled a Spiritual birth to take place involving The Ear in God's Presence. The LIGHT was so bright that no one witnessed This Miraculous Event.

JESUS said during the latter part of His Ministry that we would not see the Father, for He is concealed by His LIGHT. His message was always to show how everyone can experience our Creator, In The Ear, as a special sound, and in The Light, as little pinpoints of light hovering over someone who is being helped.

Jesus even said: *"You hear with one ear."*

THE SIGNIFICANCE of this remark is described in a later section, in an answer to one of His Disciples' questions. Remember His mission on earth. His purpose was to show us the way, to Find The KINGDOM of GOD. He has and He continues to do so.

IF YOU have an immediate need to feel God, Jesus and The Holy Spirit as we said earlier, then turn to **page 117** and follow the path, but if you have time, it would be even more beneficial to work through these early pages in the way that Nancy and Derek made their exciting discoveries. Then you also could rediscover and remember wonderful moments in your early years, which have been forgotten; for He Touches us all in many ways, if we would only pause long enough to listen and allow Him to be with us as a constant companion.

FOOTSTEPS IN THE SAND

THIS IS a beautiful story which we have seen presented in many different ways, so we are not sure about its origin, but briefly: A young man takes a daily walk to work along the sand, and if he looks behind himself he is always aware of two sets of footprints in the sand. One set is The Lord's and the other is his own. Once, when he was very ill but still struggling to work, he could see only one set of footprints, and he said out loud:

"Why O'Lord, when I need you most of all, have you deserted me?"

"No, my son," was His reply. *"You are not alone, I am carrying you."*

Etched in sand, the words *'Jesus said'*.

THIS IS lovely, and so true. It also happens to many people in hidden ways. For instance, if you have ever fainted and lost consciousness, the first words most people say, when they regain their faculties, are, "Where am I?" Even if they are still in the same place. They have all been somewhere else, and are still partly there until the strength of the worldly information and stimuli overwhelms their physical senses again, and then they are truly back with us.

A FEW very interesting phenomena occur before we faint, especially with the two most valuable senses, which keep us in touch with everything around us - sight and sound. Our sight begins to fade, often becoming shades of mauve through purple to deep violet, with little stars of light, then blackness. A high pitched ringing chord occurs in the ears, sometimes in only one ear.

During this time we are unable to look after ourselves, and we may have crumpled to the floor in the position of minimal energy expenditure.

OUR WHOLE survival has been taken over by subconscious processes; we have been in the care of our Creator. He made us this way, the mauve colour, the blackness, the high pitched chord in the ear or both ears, the experience of being somewhere else. In other words, the consciousness has continued without the usual full contact and control of the whole person. We have had an experience of another place, without the body. He has made Himself known to us, He is carrying us, but without footprints.

As Jesus said: *"The world is a bridge, become passers by."*

WE ARE PASSING through; maybe we have had a glimpse of where we are going, but we do not usually remember it when the reality of the world has taken control again, when the faint has passed. We will write in greater detail about the pinpoints of light, the mauve colour and the chord in only one ear, in another section. These have a remarkable significance in Jesus' communications with us.

IT IS of scientific interest that the last one of our five physical senses to be active when we die is the sense of Hearing, and the same seems to occur during loss of consciousness. We are being carried and the chord is His communication with us. He is increasing His care and so becomes louder. He is taking us over, we are returning to Him, briefly, for maintenance, and when it is complete we will be back, with work to do and time to pass. If it is His decision, we may stay with Him and discard the physical body, having completed our journey through this physical world.

The experience of being somewhere else . . .

FORMATIVE years

AS A CHILD of about two years of age, I can remember looking into a lovely deep purple pansy and, even at that age, marvelling at the wonderful velvet like surface texture of each petal, and the golden softness of a daffodil's trumpet with its curly serrated edge. I had a fascinating childhood, always very happy and encouraged by two gentle parents. I also had a brother a little older and seemed to be aware of not being much of a playmate for him as a baby, although we were a comfort for each other. It was in an atmosphere of freedom, caring and enlightenment by my family and relatives that I experienced an awareness of belonging to all living things, and I marvelled in my childlike way at the beauty and perfection of everything; the colours, shapes and movements, the sounds, the touch and taste of life. This feeling has been part of my soul ever since but now I KNOW WHAT IT IS!

Velvet perfection

ALL THE WONDERS of The Earth did not just happen by chance, they may indeed have evolved a little through time, but each one contains the Spark of Life, the Touch of Creative Genius; it is God's Presence. Especially when the tendency is towards chaos, or dust to dust, it is surprising that anything has arisen at all, let alone had the chance to evolve. He still has His Mind on the pulse of the universe with a gentle guidance and, as mentioned previously, is still creating odd atoms of Hydrogen in space.

WHAT JOY He must have had in perfecting all the lovely vegetation and beautiful living creatures; but what sadness must have followed at man's wanton destruction and lack of wisdom in the pursuance of greed.

Structured with such beauty

THE STRUCTURE of everything He created has such beauty, from the smallest living cells to the largest lifeless crystals, from the grains and colours of pieces of wood to the iridescent scales on the surface of the fishes. Jesus, as God's Earthly Representative, is everywhere helping us to overcome our wanton tendencies.

WE CERTAINLY are not alone. He is indicating here that work, involvement, doing things is an essential part of our life. It is God who moves us all, and we should not be acquiring everything for ourselves without returning more,

"Cleave the wood and I am there, lift the stone, I am there also."
Jesus said to His Disciples. (Amethyst quartz crystals)

to perpetuate the balance of creation, and helping evolution. We develop this remarkable thought in a later section; that it is God who moves us, without Him we would not move at all.

As Jesus said:

"If they ask you: 'What is the sign of your Heavenly Father in you?' say to them: 'It is a Movement and a Rest.'"

Think about it!

THIS IS quite a good place to start with your own development. Are there some wonderful memories you have, which are more than just existing in the physical world, but moments of being really moved by experiences? It is always something that happens inside you that changes your life. You do not necessarily know what the changes are or understand them but you may grow up being happier or with a different attitude. You will be able to see more than seems to exist on the surface of life.

CHILDHOOD DISCOVERIES

MY MOTHER was a very good artist but never had the chance to pursue her talent. With a few hasty pencil strokes, because she always felt she should be doing something else, she could capture the essence of a cat, for instance, and its smile, which clearly said that you belong to him and not the other way around; anyway, this is his house and how long do I have to stand by this saucer for supper. Sadly, this is the only sketch of mother's which we still have, as she spent most of her time bringing up her children, (there were three of us eventually, all boys;) also looking after father, his patients and business.

SHE FOUND time to make home-made bread and other wonders, such as seedless jam from the garden raspberries or mulberries when in season. As a child I would sit and watch the bread dough rising by the warm fire. It would start as a small sticky lump, sprinkled with flour, in the bottom of a very large bowl covered with a damp cloth.

MUM WOULD say, "In a little while there will be a surprise under there, see how long you can wait without looking."

Knowing smile

EVEN AT that tender age of three there were wonders happening, everything was an experiment, we never had time to be bored, we were never looking for things to do. Keeping us out of things was more the problem, every day exploring the simplest of tasks.

THEN I THOUGHT I saw the damp cloth moving slowly upwards in the middle and finally lifting itself off the edge of the bowl. What was that inside? Like a magician - she whisked away the damp cloth. The bowl was full with a creamy-white dome rising inches above the rim.

"Now," she said, "wash your hands - soap and water - then touch it."

IT FELT as if there was someone in there, it was soft and springy like pressing on your stomach.

"Press it down in the middle," was her next comment.

I DID and was so sad to see it gradually kneaded down into a small lump again. I thought the fun was over, but no; small pieces were then placed inside large metal tins; odd, I thought; such little bits of dough, but to my surprise, it rose up again to fill the tins. Then it was time to place them in the oven, with the lovely aroma of freshly baked bread for tea.

Round and round the Mulberry bush

ALL THIS IS NOT a diversion from our purpose . . .
For Jesus said that:

"The Kingdom of God is like a little leaven (yeast) *hidden in a lump of dough."*

IT GROWS and spreads, if given warmth, loving care and water, and nourishes the world, even if suppressed and kneaded down, it rises up again. The fresh baked bread with raspberry or with mulberry jam, as in Jesus' time, made this another special day.

HE GUIDES us in every simple aspect of life but He has a very special Message concerning water, and hopes that we will listen. We extend this aspect later when writing about purification.

He said:
"If you do not first understand water - you know nothing."

"Eat of all the fruits," He said, *"Except those which have bitterness."*

INFANT SCHOOL

MY FIRST school at five years was named The Convent of Mercy. Although I was brought up Church of England, this was the nearest to our home. I was terrified and intimidated by the tall black clad women I had not seen before, with black shiny boots which peeped out below their skirts. These billowed out like curtains in a breeze, as they swept along the corridors dusting all the floors. They seemed to wear white starched collars, not round their necks, but round their faces; as a child I assumed they had ears, for I had never seen them. I am not being disrespectful in any way at all; these are my childhood memories.

I WAS THANKFUL to find that the lady who taught us most of the time was a slim, elegant, sensitive person who wore normal clothing, had longish fair hair and a kind smile.

I WAS TOO young to know of anything other than her beauty but she taught us with compassion and looked after us all with a gentle attitude.

SHE HAD no trouble with discipline, she was able to reach us at our level, without expecting us to be anything other than who we were; children needing guidance and understanding.

Renewal of life

BUT WHEN Mother Superior, with fat bright pink cheeks came into the classroom, displeased by something that we had apparently done, the cheeks became fiery red with a touch of purple. To me she often seemed to be in a rage about our behaviour and I had not come across this at home. We always had things explained to us, rather than shouted at us with a telling off.

WHAT UPSET me most was to see our wonderful teacher, cowering behind her tall wooden rostrum, trying to hide. Mother Superior obviously had the same power to intimidate grown women as well as little children. It always took some time for our teacher to regain her composure when she had gone and I wanted to go home, having experienced enough for one day.

I HAVE OFTEN thought over the years why she was called the Mother Superior and the school the Convent of Mercy, as I found no motherliness in her and certainly no noticeable mercy. Yet all those of her calling, who I have met since then, have been wonderful souls. Perhaps we were all terrible children, but I think not.

THE MEMORY which brings most happiness, is that every year our gentle teacher would brush white paint lovingly over a tall statue of Mary holding baby Jesus. I would watch, transfixed at the beauty of the sculpture and the reverence with which she carried out the task. I should, of course, have been involved in the set work for the afternoon but I always wanted to paint the statue, and learned more from watching people do things than just talking about how to do it; they are so very different.

THE ONLY other joy that I remember from my days there, was again watching, this time one of nature's miracles; the re-emergence of life from a dormant structure. A very dried up, pinkish, scaly hyacinth bulb, almost the size of my closed up hand, was placed in the top of a colourless, transparent glass vase. The vase had a special shape, quite wide at the base, and as it sloped upwards and inwards it became narrower, about nine inches tall, then the top widened into a cup shape with a hole in the lower part. The hyacinth bulb was placed in here after filling the lower vase with water.

The white Madonna

NOTHING HAPPENED for two weeks, but the water kept disappearing and it was my job to always add a little more. Then one day a green circular pyramid emerged through the top of the bulb and translucent silky white roots began to reach deep down into the water. These fascinated me. They filled the lower vessel with swirls and curled round and round, like an inverted hair style, as the flower stalk grew on top. I was intrigued by the roots, which I had not seen before, when they were growing in the soil. This was my first experience of a plant life-form with all its structures exposed and once again, as a child, I marvelled at its beauty. The perfume of dozens of mauve, bell-shaped flowers on a tall green stem was exquisite.

The hidden angel of the flowers

SIMPLE THINGS and simple thoughts; but they reached my soul and influenced my life. How could these have evolved without our Creator? Such wonders cannot happen on their own. Each cell knows exactly where it has to be and what it has to do. They are all aware of each other and work together for a common purpose; but do we know what it is? It looked so perfect, only inches away from the white painted statue, and the perfume drifted around the classroom covering the musty smell of dusty wooden floors and ancient books. Water was the secret and so it is with everything that lives, and Jesus knew the secret.

Jesus walked on the water and calmed the storm. He said: "If you do not first understand water, you know nothing."

> **THE SECRET OF LIFE - WATER AND ENERGY**
> The Mystery is that both of these exist in many forms, and carry messages to and from everything they touch.

A SIDEWAYS GLANCE AT GENETICALLY MODIFIED FOOD

THE ultimate destruction may occur, now that some scientists have introduced an improper gene from animals into plants which are eaten by mankind, without knowing what the effects will be. Even more disturbing is the fact that once released into the countryside, we can NEVER return to the moment before it happened, God's Creations will have changed for ever, as we interfere immorally with His Works.

IT has taken mankind several thousands of years to know what is safe to eat, with many lives lost acquiring that knowledge. Will we have to start again? We have, until now, evolved in harmony with plant and animal life. Has science gone too far? Just because it is possible, should it be done? If it is, then it should be contained in a sealed environment, until we know it is safe.

ARE we really kept informed, could a Chemical Company control the world with a mind altering gene, hidden in the foods which they avoid? God may then be forced to intervene sooner than He intended and we may lose His most valued Gift; FREEWILL.

THIS book shows how to feel God's Presence NOW, so we can exert a positive effect on those who need more wisdom. Good research takes time, but there is no "going back to the drawing board," with this one!! WE NEED HIM NOW, TODAY. So make a start, it is very simple.

SELF DESTRUCT Gene

IT IS a very interesting thought to consider that, although everything God made is perfect in every way, mankind has what seems to be a flaw, a self destruct gene. This is not an error or a mistake, we are designed this way. For example, He could have made us incapable of sinning, incapable of temptation. It would have been simple for Him to do so but He did not!

EVERYTHING He has made and achieved since the beginning of time has a purpose; there is a reason. He also gave us freewill and an understanding of the difference between right and wrong, and the chance to choose between the two, and in so doing allowed the arrival of evil. But with the presence of a self destruct gene already inbuilt as a level of control in any eventuality, evil could never become dominant enough to overpower our Creator Himself, because we would destroy ourselves before this could occur.

THIS COULD be why mankind always insists on doing things that are intrinsically hazardous to life, not just their own but often everyone else's. We do not need to list these life threatening habits and pursuits, we all know what risks we take.

THERE IS A WONDERFUL POSITIVE SIDE to this odd situation. If we succeed in overcoming even one temptation or sin ourselves, during our lifetime, when we rejoin Him at the end of our individual physical existence, we will take with us something which He had not given us in the first place - an achievement of our own, overcoming a sin or temptation ourselves. This will strengthen His purpose. He will be capable of many more remarkable creative achievements, if we give Him something He had not already given to us. We would also have made a wonderful addition to our fragment of soul material which occupies this temporary Temple (our body).

THIS COULD BE THE ELUSIVE PURPOSE AND MEANING OF LIFE

GOD MAY HAVE placed us here on the Earth, not as an experiment, but for His own creative development. He may be using us so He can grow, as there is a part of Him in our souls and spiritual material.

HE MAY be allowing His thoughts and genius to be explored by some of us on earth, in perhaps developing a biological computer chip capable of receiving Him electronically, instead of always being hampered by the human mind, which is so frequently occupied with the gratification of human physical desires.

THE FUTURE IS BEYOND OUR SCIENTIFIC IMAGINATION. HE HAS BARELY BEGUN.

Jesus said:
"There is nothing hidden which will not be revealed."

LIVING forever ?

WE ALSO have a genetic make-up which does not allow us to live for ever. Many people who would wish to be immortal have missed our Creator's kindness in not leaving it up to us to determine when we have to go, as it would be the worst agony of existence to have to decide ourselves when we need to die. We may think that when we make love it is for our elation and pleasure, but we are really fulfilling a genetic biological process; we are in fact being driven to perpetuate our species then leave the offspring's space to occupy our place. So when HIS PURPOSE IS FULFILLED there will be humans here to greet Him and, in the meantime, He is making contact and has made Himself known to all of us. But many have missed Him.

OUR MIND and consciousness continues along with soul and spirit material, when our physical body ceases to function, and we return to our origin to be with Him in peace and tranquillity. We only have our life and being because of His Presence. I often think that when I undergo this transition, two or three days later I may say to myself, "I haven't had a cup of tea today," a trivial thought perhaps, but soon realising I no longer needed one. It will then be possible to think to myself - I want to be somewhere, anywhere, and instantly I will be there without any apparent mode of transport. This is surely how Jesus can be with each and every one of us all the time, for His time has no beginning or end, and the past, present and future are all one with Him. But we humans need these time spaces between the beginning and the end of everything, in fact they are essential. That must be why time stands still in His presence, as experienced during our Healing work, when we have asked for His help.

WE DISCUSS this passage of time later in the book. For example, when I was standing in the middle of an isolated wheatfield at night guarding an aircraft. Hours had passed by, but time had stood still for me. I had not moved, not been anywhere. I was fully conscious, wide awake and in an upright attention position. Then suddenly it was dawn. I had asked for God's help to ease me through the night and He had made Himself known. This is important.

HEAVEN AND HELL

MANY people ask about Heaven and hell. We have to point out that our work is really scientific research. This is our personal view and it has served our students well, over the years. There is not a particular place for Heaven or hell, it is not located anywhere. A point which interests us is the difficulty we have using a capital H when typing the word hell, it does not seem correct.

IF THERE were a location, it would occupy the same space we are inhabiting now. There is enough space between the electrons and nuclei, between the atoms and molecules for many other 'worlds' to exist. When we touch something it is not really solid, it is the electrons revolving round the atoms that push

The tranquillity of Heaven

The torments of hell

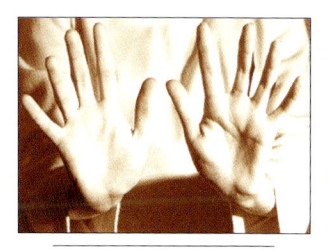

Reaching other dimensions

our hands away and the electrons on the surface of our hands have the same effect on the object, by pushing it away, so we experience the sensation of contact.

IF, FOR example, the position of the atoms in our hand coincided with the spaces between the atoms of a solid object, we would be able to pass through it, but would have to move at the speed of light to do so, or even faster, and that is questionable. Even then we would have to know which way all the atoms were moving, the effect of other forces, such as magnetic fields, temperature and the thickness of the material.

DO NOT try this experiment at home! Sorry about that comment, we couldn't resist it. Although the remark was flippant, the science is serious and has been over simplified to make the point.

BUT TO return to our thoughts of Heaven; this is not a place but a state of mind that comes upon us when we are forgiven all our sins by The Heavenly Father, at the moment we meet up with Him again after the transition. He knows if we have done our best and have remorse for our indiscretions, then we may be allowed to experience Heaven. Hell may be self induced at the same moment as a reasonably good person was forgiven, if he were to think in the free floating mind of after life that, having been forgiven, he could have done all sorts of dubious acts and got away with it. He plunges into a self induced hell, the same as if he had actually perpetrated those evil deeds. Hell could also be an evil person's realisation of the pain and torment they have caused during their lifetime.

IF, ON THE OTHER HAND, we have been evil at every possible moment during our life, we are remarkably still forgiven, but such a mind is plunged into a state of deep remorse at God's forgiveness and cannot return to earth to undo those dreadful deeds or to do the many things which were neglected and left not done. So a state of hell exists. It is not delivered upon us by God, it is self induced by His forgiveness. We have cast ourselves aside. We can meet with Him sooner, before the moment of truth, and experience Him now and welcome His forgiveness while we still have time on earth to make atonement.

DO IT NOW, TODAY, not tomorrow or later. Ask for HIS forgiveness. That is why Jesus died for us, that is why He is always with us to show the way to find The Kingdom of God. He has made contact with us and later we indicate how this will be A Special Invitation To Feel God's Presence, to Find Him for Yourself. It is a Spine Tingling Prospect of Discovering the Real You; not just the physical body you are occupying.

Sculptures created by guided hands

HIGH School Years

QUARRY BANK HIGH SCHOOL LIVERPOOL

YES! I did study there, but well before John Lennon's time, when the Headmaster was affectionately known as Bill Bailey (not of the song fame!) and had been depicted on the front cover of ASHLAR, the school magazine, as a Cheshire cat, with his mortar-board on his head. He was a wonderful person, strict but absolutely fair, a genuine Christian. It was a delight to have known him and a pleasure (looking back) to have studied under him; he influenced us all most beneficially. It would seem that all he demanded of you was the truth. He wanted students to think and explore their actions or inactivity and to explain and understand what they had done or not done.

BILL BAILEY succeeded in a teacher's most difficult task, helping people to 'think'. He was a very gentle, caring person who wanted us all to grow up as thinkers, to understand the basic principles of life, of science, of literature and sport, and to acquire sufficient knowledge to cope with the challenges of life ahead. He wanted us to understand Creation in all its aspects, not only scientifically but as the Original Miracle. He would discuss these with you in great depth, if he knew that you too, were searching for the Meaning of Life. He was always sad if you cycled past him as he walked to school in his misshapen hat, without saying, "Good morning," or "Good afternoon, Sir." I always felt he was a very lonely soul, who, I believe, lived by himself and needed the friendship of his flock.

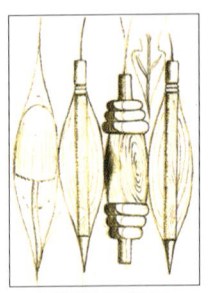

SPORTS AT QUARRY

I HAVE NEVER been very good at sports of any kind, so I eventually lost interest and, if I was forced into playing football, they always tried to find a place for me on the field in which I would cause the least number of goals for the other side. They preferred it if I stayed still, at least they knew where I was and they could get on with the game, because I always got in someone's way. In cricket it was more difficult; not for me, but for any captain who had the misfortune to have me in his team:

"Perhaps your best place," he would say to me, "is a sort of out fielder, right out over there in that lady's back garden."

And of course, as luck would have it, the Headmaster Mr. Bailey, on his little walkabouts to see how everything was functioning, had noticed that I seemed to be weeding someone's garden.

Cricket stumps

SO NEXT DAY I had to present myself at his study. "Come in."

"Good morning, Sir," I said with a false cheerfulness. He seemed to warm to that.

"Now Bell, what were you doing yesterday - the truth lad, the truth."

"Well, Sir," I replied, "they tried to find a place for me where I would do least damage to the match. So if I wasn't even there, someone else could run and catch the ball, knowing full well I'd only miss it if it came my way."

I quaked inside. I thought, this must surely be my last day at school, and I would have more explaining to do when I got home. But he roared with laughter, which was an unusual event.

"Well that's a new one," he spluttered. "So what do you really think about sports - football for instance?"

I remember thinking, that if the buttercup, convolvulus and daisy were very difficult to grow, everyone would want them!

16

MY HEART missed a beat, for I knew what I really thought, but would I get away with it this time, so cautiously I began.
"Well, Sir," it was almost obligatory to start with a "Well" in those days, in fact many people still do, especially during interviews on television. "I can't understand the purpose of twenty-two grown students kicking a little ball round a field in the middle of winter, Sir."

I HAD done it this time. I knew he would not settle for anything less than the truth. He seemed to know what you were really thinking, so there it was, no point in waffling. I did not hear his reply. It was quietly spoken, and my courage, of which I had very little, was not strong enough to ask him to repeat it - that would be asking for trouble.

HE WAS silent for a while, put his stick down on his desk, turned to look out of the window at the beautiful trees in the school gardens and said:
"Go away and study something that you consider will be useful for your future."

THIS WAS HIS way of converting a hopeless case into a benefit for the pupil; so I did, and became even more engrossed in the sciences, and will always be grateful for his advice, for he had allowed me to develop the subjects which deeply fascinated me, by not insisting that my formative years were consumed trying to do things that were not in my soul. He was a gentleman with the wisdom of a Saint. So where do you think I was during the sports period? In the laboratories.

Beyond the trees of the school gardens - All Hallows Church - It did not have a spire, but I always thought it should have, so I painted one. My wife Brenda and I were married there, long after the war.

THE SCHOOL CONCERT

EACH CHRISTMAS we had a school concert in the main hall on an excellent stage and many of us played instruments, performed little sketches, sang silly songs and I gave a monologue (or so it was listed). I was very nervous, having put it together myself. It was once again make or break time. I had studied all the mannerisms of the members of staff for years, all their peculiar sayings, attitudes, silly walks, ear tweaking, nose rubbing, and so it went on and on, but most important of all was The Headmaster, Mr. Bailey. He was a remarkable member of staff to impersonate and I had every twitch to perfection; months of practice, every little mannerism and saying. I also dressed up for the part as an exaggeration of his appearance. It was just before Christmas, two days to go before the end of term, at least they would have two weeks to forget all about it.

MY TIME came to go on stage, a lonely isolated dishevelled figure. I had managed to look about fifty years older than a teenager, so that no one would recognise me. In front of the curtains with vast empty space either side, I started:
"The Day War Broke Out," in a voice that was a cross between Mr. Bailey and Rob Wilton, a wonderful entertainer who kept us in good spirits on the radio during the war. Notice I did not say wireless, as this would pinpoint my age.

THERE WAS SILENCE for the first few seconds, which seemed like minutes, my heart sank and, like an earlier experience at my first school, I felt I should not be there. Had I made a mistake?

SUDDENLY the place was in an uproar. I could not really believe they were laughing at my antics and comments, or was there something else going on somewhere?
I know it is a much used phrase by stage professionals but, 'They wouldn't let me go.' I even began to enjoy it. I had forgotten about tomorrow. What if I had offended someone? Or should I break up for Christmas early and not come in at all? Apparently this had not been done before at Quarry Bank. "Was it satire?" someone said. I did not know; it was just exaggerated life, kindly performed with a touch of humour.

The Christmas break would allow time for them to forget, but . .

AFTERWARDS, everyone had enjoyed it so much I thought there may be a future for me in the theatre. But the feeling soon wore off, because next day a brief message came down to the classroom in the middle of a lesson: "The Head wants to see you now, in his study, about last night." I had a premonition it might be an error to be there that day. The History teacher was quite pleased to let me go because I had no leaning towards History either (along with sports). But the sciences, they really thrilled me.
"Now you've done it," he said, although he had enjoyed my send-up of himself.

I WAS OUTSIDE Bill Bailey's study, as I had referred to him on stage. What a terrifying thought! A timid knock on the glass panel.
"Come in, Bell, close the door, sit down." He had a very serious face. "Where did you get all that material from last night?"
"I put it together myself, Sir, from observations and moments of inspired intuition."
Then the serious face, which indicated he did not know he was such a lovable character, began to move, a smile crept across it and his moustache quivered, he laughed.
"I didn't know you had it in you Bell. It was superb, thoroughly enjoyed it. Don't tell anyone I said so. Keep on with all the sciences, with observations and research like that, you'll make it one day, even without cricket."

HE CHANGED MY LIFE by what he said because, although it was wonderful to see people laughing, especially during those difficult times, and it seemed so universal, so helpful, I stayed with the sciences. I felt that health and well-being were more important, we could all enjoy life more, achieve more if we were well, and I wanted to know all about what made us tick and how we have evolved.

SO I LEFT the humour to Derek Nimmo and other fellow students, who always did an act at these concerts, but I never knew what Derek thought of my efforts. It was good to know The Headmaster had realised he was a wonderful character and how much he enjoyed all my impersonations of his idiosyncrasies and mannerisms.

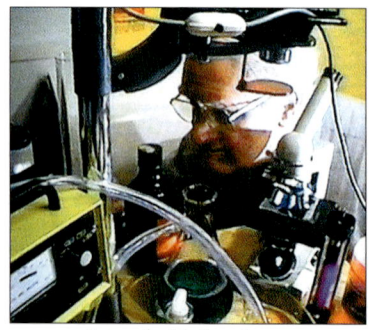

I stayed with the sciences

I BEGAN TO THINK even he was searching and wondered if he had found the Elusive Knowledge; for when we had talked together briefly there was a meeting of minds. He did not talk down to you, as so many people do, but was in fact reaching out to you, hoping that some of his wisdom had impinged upon your mind to help you to find yourself. He was allowing you space to develop, as long as he knew he could trust you.

HISTORY
of our future

IT IS ODD that I should have been in a History lesson at the time I was summoned to his study, for I had no interest in it, but there has always been one period of History which intrigues me. The years when Jesus was here on Earth. My interest was not in the details of the times, only in everything He did and said; in His Miracles and travels, His Messages, His Purpose. People have tried to live by His standards ever since.

Biblical times

Not only an historical memory

THE HISTORY MASTER wanted to know why I repeatedly obtained only twenty percent marks in his history examinations, when I was always in the nineties for the sciences.

THE ONLY WAY I could explain it was that, once science discovered something, the knowledge was real, it changed the world and it could be used to benefit mankind. However, although the lessons to be learned from history are phenomenal, they were nearly always ignored by countries and their politicians, who continued to make the same mistakes. I know I may be wrong, but I could see no place for history in my vision of the future.

I COULD see a place for Jesus as a reality, a need in fact, not only as an historical memory, but of finding a way of experiencing His active presence in today's world. We have found Him and are working towards this in our writings, describing real physical experiences of His Presence.

NOW WE KNOW
WE ARE NOT ALONE

The conjunction of Jupiter and Venus on 18/2/1975; it will be 3,000 years before they are this close again . . . see you in 4,975 . . . We will all know Jesus by then.

19

EXPERIMENTS

WHILE STILL AT QUARRY BANK I began experiments, making plastics like 'BAKELITE', which everyone knows was one of the earliest synthetics, from carbolic acid and formaldehyde, and I used a solution of this nearly clear colourless resin to paint the 500 watt lamps that illuminated the stage in the hall where the religious assembly was held every morning before lessons. I used special dyes and painted some lamps blue, some green, yellow and pink, screwed them all back in the gantry above the stage, under which all the staff would stand to conduct the prayers next day.

THE COLOURS were lovely, different ones all over the place, and everything looked good, but gradually the brilliance began to fade and everyone became more yellow, then orange, then red; most of the teachers thought it was quite effective, but in another ten minutes everyone there would have disappeared into a dark brown oblivion because of an error in my research. This indicates why all research should be carried out before the final test (and that morning was the final test) and all experiments must be repeated by different scientists in several laboratories. I learned the lesson at a very early age and the reason everything takes such a long time is to be absolutely sure.

Solid piece of colourless plastic, but not 'Bakelite'

I WAS INVITED to give a lecture on plastics after this experience because no one knew much about them in those days (which I almost proved). The lecture, to my surprise, was to be for all the distinguished staff with multi-science degrees and the sixth form students; a formidable ensemble.

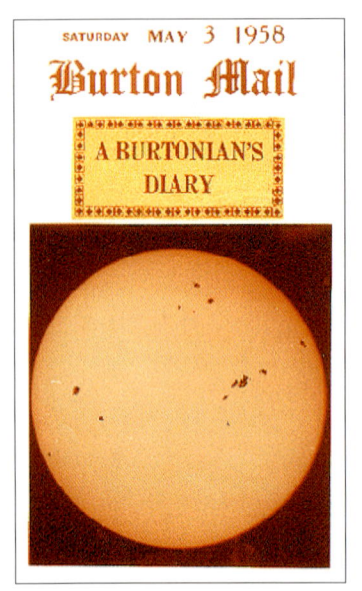

TO START WITH they all wanted to know how I had achieved the fascinating effects on stage, without touching any switches, (they had to wait). The lecture went very well indeed and the teachers wondered where I had obtained all the information, which was before its time and only available in obscure scientific papers, and some, not at all.

I HAD TO EXPLAIN that most of the knowledge came about by experimentation. I was in fact making various plastic materials at home in the attic (with the window open), and what they thought was a very interesting effect on stage was actually an experiment that went wrong. It took me five days scraping all the burnt resin off the bulbs. I explained that some plastic resins remain clear and colourless when heated, as they were with 500 watt lamps. All was now clear (or was it) because this plastic did not stay colourless, the bulbs baked it a dark brown, like all original 'Bakelite' products.

IT WAS SO DARK you could view sunspots through it; in 1958 I used the material for this purpose and supplied a photograph to the local newspaper. It does have other uses after all, such as eye protection during welding, as the thickness and colour density could be varied, but it was still transparent, so we can utilise the results of a scientific test for another useful purpose. It was back to the drawing board, or in my case the attic.

Sunspot viewing - newspaper cutting

ALL THESE LITTLE STORIES play a vital part in how it became possible to find Our Creator's Presence through scientific research and, not assuming we know it all already, without the experiments and mistakes. He allowed us to make mistakes so we could learn, whereas many people state that some line of action or thought is not possible without even trying. Heather and I have frequently tried the impossible with astonishing results.

Brenda and myself, early years

CALDER GIRLS SCHOOL was next door to Quarry Bank, the other side of a twelve foot wall. Brenda, my wife to be, was a student there and we have been together since we were fifteen. After going to the cinema on most Saturday evenings (before television) we would walk to the tramcar; these were steely, sparking, electrical trolly monsters, on rails built into the roadway, like a double decker toast rack, not as the modern ones are in Manchester, and I would take her home.

ON THE WAY up Queens Drive, as we walked from my home, we passed Jimmy Tarbuck's house (he was only a little boy then). Frequently he would hide behind his front garden hedge below the wall and shout out some of the cheekiest humourous remarks we have ever heard. He, of course, pretended he was not there, so we had to play the same game (it was his game really) and pretend we were not walking past either, otherwise he ran away. So we had to wait until we reached the tram stop, before we could burst into laughter.

I HAVE OFTEN THOUGHT since then, we should be thankful he was too young to play golf, like he does today, because there were lovely wide swathes of cut grass on either side of his part of Queens Drive, and our lives would have been in constant danger from flying golf balls, rather than flying insults. He was safer behind the hedge, although he did venture out when the coast was clear, and dash at full speed down the grass verge blowing strange trumpet noises through a cardboard tube which shall remain nameless.

HUMOUR and laughter is an essential part of life and its effects are miraculous. This is why we have included the Laughter Experiment in the details for extending the sensitivity of the mind, for these are special moments making us free to feel God's Presence.

THE CONSTANT background

THIS NEXT PASSAGE may take a few minutes to study but is very interesting, as it gives us an insight into how we have been created to be almost oblivious to His Presence.

THE BRAIN makes continuous adjustments in the presence of constant stimuli, so that the mind can be conscious of changes. In other words, if a noise or something else is going on all the time we tend not to notice it. THESE ADJUSTMENTS are in opposition to the stimuli to negate them. For instance - if the eye is viewing a RED object, the brain is opposing this with a PALE GREEN/BLUE object of identical shape and brightness and vice versa, a green one is opposed by a red one. The following simple test shows this very well.

(1) Stare at the black dot in the centre of the RED square with both eyes for about ten seconds.
(2) Then stare at the black dot in the centre of the white square.
This white square now appears PALE GREEN/BLUE.

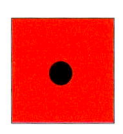

IN A SIMILAR manner, if the eye is viewing a YELLOW object, the brain is opposing this with a VIOLET object of identical shape and brightness and vice versa, a violet one is opposed by a yellow one.

(1) Stare at the black dot in the centre of the YELLOW square with both eyes for about ten seconds.

(2) Then stare at the black dot in the centre of the white square. This white square will now appear to be VIOLET.

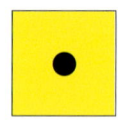

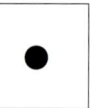

THIS EXPERIMENT may be extended to produce many interesting effects which reinforce the statement made on the previous page:

For example:-

IF YOU VIEW a red square with the left eye, and a green/blue square with the right eye, each having a black dot in the middle, and both at the same time, for about ten seconds, but not allowing either eye to see the colour viewed by the other one, what would you expect the brain to do?

EACH EYE would experience the opposite colour and the brain would superimpose one upon the other. So if you looked at the white square afterwards, with both eyes, there would not be an after image present at all, they would cancel each other out and you would only see a greyish/white dot in the centre of the white square.

THIS DOT is often surrounded by a darker grey edge and has come into being because both eyes were originally viewing a black dot, although the colours in the squares were opposite, and would need to be perfectly complementary to cancel each other out.

(1) Position these two squares about six centimetres from your nose or about seven to ten centimetres from your eyes.

(2) Hold a small strip of white paper on its edge, between your nose and this page, so you can only see the red one with the left eye and the green/blue one with the right eye.

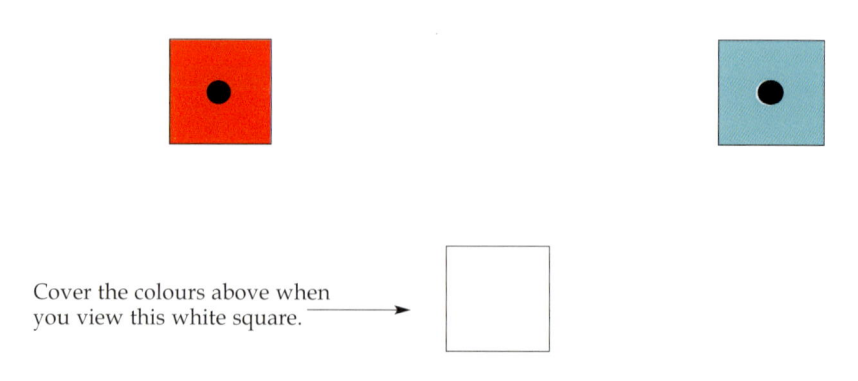

Cover the colours above when you view this white square.

MANY HOLD the belief that the opposite colours occur because the retina of the eye is being over stimulated and loses sensitivity to the colour being viewed, but it is very interesting that the after image is opposing the original visual material, so any changes in our environment may become more apparent, and this acts as an inbuilt biological survival mechanism.

THIS IS also in keeping with the fact that God always Creates an equal and opposite to everything, so His Constant Presence has initiated within us a constant opposition in some form, of which we are not aware, and makes us oblivious to His Presence. We need to penetrate this to experience His Reality, which we can all accomplish, because hidden in 'The Texts' Jesus reveals how it can be achieved, now IN THIS MILLENNIUM.

THE EXPERIENCE IS REAL NOW - FOR EVERYONE

MAKE IT YOURS
DO NOT ALLOW INNATE OPPOSING FORCES TO OBLITERATE HIS CONSTANT BACKGROUND PRESENCE

Allow God To Make Himself Known To You
Break Through The Human Barrier And Unite Your Soul And Spiritual Being With Your Earthly Body

Live forever with our Creator, become part of His unfolding future, all of us moving forward together with Him as one living consciousness.

NOW TAKE another step into the unknown; what would you expect to see if you stared at the yellow square for ten seconds and then squinted at the white square, so you could see two white squares.

The VIOLET coloured after image, which you have seen before in the earlier experiment, does not appear in either of the two squinted white squares, but only as one VIOLET square between them. You are seeing this in the brain; but if it were occurring because of an over-stimulation of the retina of each eye, would you see two VIOLET squares when you squint and not just one in between them? Think about it!

WE KNOW THIS is rather complicated but very simple once you have performed the experiment a few times and is well worth further study as the revelations are superb. You begin to feel you are not just a functioning piece of physical material.

ANOTHER INTERESTING NOTE before we continue. Acids and Alkalies are opposites and neutralise each other. Plant flower colours are often complementary in acid or alkaline solutions and these colours depend upon the concentration of Hydrogen ions, in other words a Proton, a single positive charge.

A PROTON is one of God's building blocks of the Elements, when He tore empty space apart into equal and opposite, positive and negative charges. Of necessity this is only briefly scientific but of sufficient interest for a few experiments of your own, followed by much thought.

Foxglove natural colour in acid solution

Foxglove in alkaline solution showing colour change

CONSTANT SOUNDS

ALSO a continuous sound, providing it is not overwhelming, is very often not noticed, for the same reason that the brain is trying to avoid hearing it, so as to be ready to hear a change. In other words a change gives us information which may be essential as a survival mechanism.

A SIMPLE experiment is the ticking clock, perhaps on the wall. You do not hear it ticking, it has been accepted by the brain as a constant background noise, but if it suddenly stops ticking, you know something has changed, but you may not know what has happened and it may take a while to realise what has changed. It is simple when a new noise starts. You listen to it because it is there. When a sound ceases, there is a change but nothing to listen to.

WE KNOW we have laboured this point a little but it is important, because we consider that GOD'S PRESENCE is a constant background, against which everything else takes place. It can be SOUND we do not hear, it may be LIGHT we do not see, it may be TOUCH we do not feel, and so on; HE may also be on FREQUENCIES that only communicate directly with the brain, or in other ways about which we have no scientific knowledge.

WE WOULD WONDER WHAT HAD STOPPED, IF HE CEASED TO BE WITH US.

AND THEN WE would also cease to exist. It would be just too late, and quite terrible to miss something just because it stopped, without knowing what it was. So get to know HIM now, make yourself aware, open up your soul and move on together knowing you are not alone.

THERE ARE WAYS WE CAN ACHIEVE THIS, NOW IN TODAY'S WORLD, in later sections.

GOD IS A CONSTANT BACKGROUND
THIS IS WHY MANY PEOPLE ARE NOT AWARE OF HIS PRESENCE. ONLY IF HE CEASED TO BE, WOULD THE UNBELIEVERS KNOW.

AIR FORCE years

AIRMAN SECOND CLASS BELL

UNIVERSITIES WERE FULL, when I tried to find a place to go after Quarry Bank. It was very difficult at that time. There are more places in the present day and they sent my call-up papers for the forces. The school records show I was called into the Army but this is not correct; it was The Royal Air Force, and when I pointed out the mistake to those in charge and asked for it to be corrected, "Oh no! they cannot be changed they are the School Records." So there we are; I am one of the few people who served in The Army and The Air Force at the same time but I was only demobbed once.

WHILST SERVING in His Majesty's Air Force at the end of the last war, stationed at R.A.F. Feltwell in Suffolk, my activities were communications, signals, teleprinters, cyphers and so on.

THE TRAINEE pilots spent their days and nights doing circuits and bumps, in other words, flying round, touching down and taking off again. It was often very noisy, especially during the dark hours, but we all knew they were doing a superb job protecting our lovely Island and we supported them in every way, with a wonderful purposeful comradeship.

SO IT WAS SAD, when one day I was detailed to go out into the countryside to guard a crashed aircraft that came down sometime during the night causing problems at the airfield.

"Don't smile Bell - you're here to chase people away."

Guard duty in the wheatfield. This plane landed safely, only damaging the propeller and cowl.

WE HAD a tent, a kettle, a can of corned beef, a tin of beans and a paraffin stove. I do not think we had any water or matches, which was odd because nearly everyone smoked cigarettes in the forces. They must have chosen three non-smokers, because we would be quite close to the aviation fuel of the aircraft. I would buy my ration of cigarettes at the 'NAFFI' and pass them on to someone in the queue, but why give us a paraffin stove if we could not use it?

YOU HAD to take it for granted that everyone had done their job properly, life depended on it, but if you queried what was in the survival kit, all you got was:

"Don't ask questions Bell - just follow orders, you're not supposed to think."

I HAVE missed out the unprintable words to keep the text readable by every age group. I always have thought about things and this has helped me survive many dangerous situations.

"Airman Bell couldn't even frighten the birds."

CHOIR
of the stars

I HAD accepted the night-shift guard duty standing by the plane. It was a cold open sky but a dry beautiful night, jet black with all the stars I knew and many more unknown to me. I would always face towards my home town and say a little prayer for my family and girlfriend's health, safety and happiness.

THE PEACE and tranquillity was astonishing, no cars, no planes, no lights or noise, standing in the centre of a deserted wheatfield in the middle of the night, can you imagine that? It would not happen often in anyone's lifetime. And No! I did not make the first crop circle.

Radiant tranquillity

MY EARS extended their sensitivity out into space. I was alone, isolated, my two companions were fast asleep a fair distance away in the tent.

I BEGAN TO HEAR something very faintly, I did not know what it was, I had not heard it before, and could not describe it then or now. It was above and around me, it was spatial, stereophonic, three dimensional.

I BECAME troubled, scared, scared stiff, and now I know what that means, being unable to move, so I prayed in a very silent voice:
"Please God help me through this night, be with me."

I MEANT IT. I was not capable of coping on my own and instantly the fear lifted, realising I was not alone any more. Our Creator had touched me in some way and made Himself known. I could still hear the indescribably faint sounds, but now it was more like music played on unknown instruments and voices singing unknown harmonies.

THEN THE rabbits and mice started to make friendly little fidgeting noises in the field and the birds rustling in the distant hedgerows, as if they too had been listening to the same sounds as myself and they had also experienced His Presence.

OCCASIONALLY METALLIC clicks occurred as the plane cooled down, contracting, sinking a little deeper into the soil. I had, as it were, been allowed to return into myself. I had not been anywhere but hours had passed by, while standing at attention or at ease. I had been aware of everything happening around me but there were no time spaces between them. Then the first bird whistled a beautiful message to a friend in a distant field and she replied, followed by more and more fantastic songs; the sun was rising, the dawn chorus was superb and the mysterious choir of the stars had faded; the glory of the singing birds was heavenly. I knew that God was here. Maybe this happens every night, to those who are ready to receive Him, those in danger, and every living creature close to Mother Earth. This could be the reason for us all having to sleep. Not only does He regenerate our tissues but He rejuvenates The Soul.

JESUS SAID to His Disciples:
"I tell my mysteries to those who are worthy of my mysteries."
We continue to try and make ourselves worthy, but the closer you get to God, the more difficult it seems to become. But if He is with you, as we know He is, then nothing can be against you.

THE ENCOUNTER in the wheatfield to me is really one of His Mysteries, for to this day my life would not have been the same. Some sceptics have suggested I HAD BEEN ABDUCTED BY ALIENS, but no, I would feel it was surely the other way round, that those who think they have been abducted, have probably experienced God's Presence, and they may have misinterpreted the experience or even added imaginary ideas to their story, having heard it somewhere else. Heather and I have no personal research data on the abduction phenomenon, so we may be doing them an injustice or they may be happier if they were to think as we do, that any encounter with aliens is less important than Feeling The Creative Force which brought us all into existence.

JESUS ALSO SAID:
"What thou shalt hear in thine ear, and in thine other ear, (stereo) *that preach from your housetops."*

WE REFER to this again later, as we continue to pass on His Message, that our Creator can be felt if we allow Him to touch us, or if we are in a situation in which we may be unable to cope, as I have described, or during unconsciousness, illness or a faint, as mentioned in previous pages.

THE DAY WAS WARMING UP, my companions could now be heard snoring, it was time to awaken them, to change the guard. We were all hungry and thirsty, so two of us wandered off over the fields in search of signs of life. We came upon a friendly looking Tavern and, before we even asked, he offered to bring us some food.

"Yes we all knew you were there," he said, "but didn't know if we should approach."

He had hastily prepared several cheese sandwiches and a glass of shandy each. I have never been so thirsty in all my life, and really enjoyed that drink, although I would have liked a cup of tea. The country folk were kind and caring and looked after us very well. As we left to return to the fields I heard for the first time, one of those lovely one line phrases used by farmers and those in the country, as a parting comment to a friend:

"May the road ahead rise up to greet you."

ALWAYS said with a raised wave of the hand, a slightly louder voice and almost a Shakespearian feel to it. This simple phrase was so genuine it moved me, and from someone we had only just met. He did not even want us to pay for his life saving sustenance. I wrote the saying down, lest it be forgotten in the chaos.

DURING the years I have collected several more and hope to link them all together further on. The experience of the previous night, the kindness of the country folk, the cheery wave goodbye made beneficial changes to my life and greatly increased the sensitivity of my soul. I still cannot remember sleeping that day, to make up for what was lost during the night, or even if it was needed.

Time stands still where sunsets meet the dawn and the mysteries of the night reflect in deep waters.

WHENEVER I think of my Air Force days, I often remember one rather strange thing they tell you, which you cannot be sure is correct until it happens to you, and then most people perpetuate the story. When you joined up, your cap and uniform were apparently given to you by His Majesty and the Government of the time, under the direction of the War Ministry and its financial advisers. Now is this a joke or not? If you lose anything, perhaps your Air Force cap, you have to pay for it three times. Once for the one they gave you in the first place, again for this new one, because you cannot be seen without it, and the third time to replace the one in the stores, that they have just given to you. It almost makes sense, but is it true?

I GAVE UP this research as there was more important work to do. Although even to this day I still go hot under my collar when I think; 'what if we had lost the aircraft we were guarding?' If I live to be one hundred would I receive a Telegram from the Queen with a little note on the back, stating how much I still owe her father, the King at the time, and has the aircraft come to light yet? Sadly I have no recollection of ever receiving an answer to my question concerning the well-being of the pilot.

A WELL KNOWN celebrity, Quentin Crisp, due to his television play, one man stage shows in London and his tendencies, now lives in New York. I understand he holds audience with his public in a coffee bar and constantly eats bowls of mashed potatoes. The reason I mention him is that he was in the R.A.F. at the same time as myself and, although he was from London and I from Liverpool, we were stationed at the same centre in the Midlands. He was always a perfect gentleman and I was not even aware of his tendencies, nor have we communicated over the past fifty or more years since our 'demob,' so it came as a surprise to hear about him.

HE IS very intellectual, a deep thinker, with an hilarious laugh a sparkling sense of humour and a unique slant on every aspect of life. We spent hours in the 'NAFFI' drinking coffee and discussing, theology, science, politics and many other subjects. His ability to understand complicated scientific processes was exceptional for a literary mind. He is one of the few people who knows about some of my early research work into the natural elements of the universe. It was quite a simple experiment that anyone could do and makes it possible to divide all the existing elements into four groups.

Memories of Service life

THE ELEMENTS

THE FIRST THREE groups contained twenty-eight in each, the last group ceased of course at element No. 92, Uranium, and was therefore incomplete. They were all the naturally occurring ones which existed in the 1940's. There were only 92 elements in those days. When I said that 4 x 28 equals 112, that was fine, but when I predicted that the total number of elements which could exist within Our Creator's atomic structures is 112, it was treated as a huge joke in scientific circles.

HOWEVER, in recent years with mankind's interest in atomic power and nuclear research, several more elements have been artificially produced with increasingly shorter life spans, due to their instability, and some have only briefly indicated their presence. But we have reached 109 elements now from the original 92 and there are only another THREE to go to complete my predicted 112.

QUENTIN is probably the only person who will remember my research, as all the others who thought it was such a joke, the masters, lecturers and boffins, have long since gone. I know how intrigued he was by the experiment and he may even have mentioned it to his audiences, in that New York coffee shop.

POST SCRIPT: Quentin returned to Britain in November 1999 to give a one man show in Liverpool. I was arranging to meet him on the 24th, to check if he had remembered my research concerning the 112 elements, as he was the one remaining living person outside my family who knew about the work. He was the only independent witness to my prediction, but regrettably he died when passing through Manchester just two days before we were to meet again, after 55 years.

AN EXPLANATORY NOTE:

ALL THE Elements are either a solid, a liquid, or a gas and the solids can be a metal or non-metal. Some gases such as Hydrogen and Helium are lighter than air, so they rise upwards, in a balloon for example; and some are heavier than air and sink downwards. Hydrogen is the lightest and simplest Element with one electron and one proton.

ALL THE metals conduct electricity, some better than others; only one metal is liquid under normal everyday conditions, Mercury. One non-metal is also liquid, Bromine. Most non-metals do not conduct electricity, with a few notable exceptions such as Carbon, which is an excellent conductor.

Carbon Arc Lamp. Element No. 6 - C

Diamond also pure carbon

THEN there are semi-conductors, often requiring an altered environment to conduct. Silicon is one of these, without which computer technology would probably not exist as it is today. Selenium is another remarkable non-metal, (with metallic properties) as it does conduct electricity in the presence of light. Silicon, as the oxide silica, plays a vital part in many tissues of the human body in terms of elasticity and rigidity. Selenium has an active role in the enzymes' system also. Many other metals and elements have vital duties to perform in our functions and well-being. Each of these is really a separate subject and the above notes are not properly scientifically presented but are a rough guide concerning what the Elements are, to help those who are unfamiliar with them.

Horsetail Silica Supplement

THERE IS A PERIODIC TABLE OF ALL THE ELEMENTS which classifies them in relation to their properties and Atomic Weights, but we have listed them all below by Atomic Weight only to show the groups of TWENTY-EIGHT and where the transition takes place. The meaning of this is still part of our ongoing research and we would be delighted to hear of any constructive suggestions as to why this should be. What does actually occur at No 28, No 56, and No 84 which makes that group so different from the next?

Sodium metal is soft. Can be cut with a knife. No.11 - Na

FOUR GROUPS OF TWENTY-EIGHT - First period of 28

Element No.	1	2	3	4	5	6	7
Symbol	H	He	Li	Be	B	C	N
Element No.	8	9	10	11	12	13	14
Symbol	O	F	Ne	Na	Mg	Al	Si
Element No.	15	16	17	18	19	20	21
Symbol	P	S	Cl	Ar	K	Ca	Sc
Element No.	22	23	24	25	26	27	28
Symbol	Ti	V	Cr	Mn	Fe	Co	Ni

Sodium in water

Sodium Flash

Phosphorus smouldering

Phosphorescence at night No.15 - P

SECOND PERIOD OF 28

Element No.	29	30	31	32	33	34	35
Symbol	Cu	Zn	Ga	Ge	As	Se	Br
Element No.	36	37	38	39	40	41	42
Symbol	Kr	Rb	Sr	Y	Zr	Nb	Mo
Element No.	43	44	45	46	47	48	49
Symbol	Tc	Ru	Rh	Pd	Ag	Cd	In
Element No.	50	51	52	53	54	55	56
Symbol	Sn	Sb	Te	I	Xe	Cs	Ba

Copper - 29 - Cu

Iodine vapour

Iodine Crystal - No. 53 - I

THIRD PERIOD OF 28

Element No.	57	58	59	60	61	62	63
Symbol	La	Ce	Pr	Nd	Pm	Sm	Eu
Element No.	64	65	66	67	68	69	70
Symbol	Gd	Tb	Dy	Ho	Er	Tm	Yb
Element No.	71	72	73	74	75	76	77
Symbol	Lu	Hf	Ta	W	Re	Os	Ir
Element No.	78	79	80	81	82	83	84
Symbol	Pt	Au	Hg	Tl	Pb	Bi	Po

Thorium mantle - No. 90 - Th

Gold Nugget - Au

Uranium cabouchon No. 92 - U

Mercury - 80 - Hg

FOURTH PERIOD OF 28

Element No.	85	86	87	88	89	90	91
Symbol	At	Rn	Fr	Ra	Ac	Th	Pa
Element No.	92	93	94	95	96	97	98
Symbol	U	Np	Pu	Am	Cm	Bk	Cf
Element No.	99	100	101	102	103	104	105
Symbol	Es	Fm	Md	No	Lr	Unq	Unp
Element No.	106	107	108	109	110	111	112
Symbol	Unh	Uns	Uno	Une	?	?	?

Radium glow - No. 88 - Ra

(The last three were still missing when we started the book; they have recently been created by scientists, which completes my prediction.) (But there are unconfirmed reports of at least two other possible elements.)

WE HAVE OMITTED the details of our Experiment to allow intuitive thought and research into what occurs at the 28 Element intervals; for those who are interested.

Uranium glass fluoresces in UV light No. 92 - U

REFLECTIONS

I HAVE ALWAYS BEEN FASCINATED with the beauty of all the metals, particularly copper's wonderful colour, and have enjoyed designing and making copper items. Silver and Gold are equally spectacular when finely polished; you can see into them. The surface of these objects ceases to exist and you see only its shape and the reflected shapes of other things. There is so much more to Silver than wealth, as we will see later; and Jesus knew its secrets.

WHAT REALLY troubles Heather and I now is exploring what may be revealed having reached element 112, and what may lie beyond.

Jesus said to His Disciples :
"Have you then discovered the beginning, so that you inquire about the end?"

Some of my useful copper creations

WE have mentioned this before because it applies to so much of what we do in this life; where one thing finishes, another is already in place, it is not the end. 'Something' is there after No. 112.

HIDDEN FOR A REASON ?

THE AMOUNT of energy involved in producing element 112 and any beyond could be so large that WE may be impinging upon Our Creator's Presence, instead of Him reaching us, and certainly, without wisdom or knowledge of what lies ahead, we may have even reached one of His lower energy levels. God may be forced to reveal more of Himself than He intended at that time, but it may only be to those who performed the possibly forbidden experiment, and no one else would know, as they may not survive to tell the tale.

SHOULD WE really be achieving such creations ourselves without deep thought, just because they are now possible to perform? We may not always be able to return to the moment before it happened. We have insufficient wisdom to attempt to produce element No. 113. It could even be the first element of another world and should not be here at all. This last paragraph could be the basis of another cause for humour by scientists who have a reputation to protect, but we only seek the truth, even if it hurts our image as genuine researchers.

SOME PEOPLE have suggested you could prove that God exists by jumping off a tall building and asking Him to save you. It would be proved to the one who jumped, but he may not live to tell anyone, and meeting his Creator is for certain, with great displeasure for taking his own life. He would be forgiven but cast himself into hell by experiencing the remorse of God's forgiveness.

QUITE APART from never putting God to the test, we should not be seeking proof but allowing Him to make contact with us, as He has done. The path to follow is contained within these pages, as spoken of by Jesus in The Biblical Texts. We reach out to Him, not demand that He shows HIMSELF. Jesus told us how, but many have ignored Him, and some of His sayings have been misunderstood or interpreted to mean something He did not say, or that they were only relevant to His time on Earth, but they are for us all, NOW.

MANY BRITISH
brains hidden in the woods

STEPPING off a very old steam train at Bletchley Station, Buckinghamshire, in the early hours, perhaps from the Milk Train at 3am or the Mail Train at 6am, it was always wonderful to see little wisps of smoke coming out of a slightly open window, in the Canteen run by the Salvation Army, and the satisfying smell of hot toast and tea drifting along the platform. This little hut was looked after by a few young and elderly dedicated women. Nothing was too much trouble for them, when caring for members of His Majesty's Forces, and other mysterious Boffins who disappeared into the bleak Bletchley countryside to Station X. This had nothing to do with the railway and I do not think I would be allowed to say much more.

IT WAS not part of the Forces either, but was a special place, known only to a few people, where creative minds of genius were working day and night to crack the Enigma code, to help us overcome the aggressors in World War II. It was in this wonderful atmosphere of being looked after in the Canteen and the mystery of the woods that I came upon another of those lovely one line sayings.

Hut 126 somewhere near Station X

AFTER MANY long working shifts, sometimes through the night, I would wander along the country lanes, well away from the chattering teleprinters, perforated tape machines, morse code and telephones.

BETWEEN Bletchley Park and Chicksands Priory, sometimes by bus, I came across small layers of golden yellow clay which I took home to Liverpool, when next on leave, and made little pieces of pottery, fired in my homemade kiln.

THESE BECAME a lovely salmon pink when baked and not the usual terracotta. At another place close by, I collected a sparkling white fine sand which fused well with lead oxides to form a superb glaze, free from cracks and craze, even fifty years later.

Every clay contains a message from the past

THIS MAY SEEM strange to write about such things, but these were moments in the development of my soul. The peace and tranquillity of these natural areas, little outcrops of minerals, tall pines and other trees, fresh breezes, the sense of history being made not far away, where brilliant minds of great genius were evolving solutions to near impossible problems, to help us survive the war.

I WAS also glad to be away from the chattering machines expelling sheets of five letter cyphers; meaningless blocks of nonsense words, containing hidden messages, of vital importance to the well-being of all the folk in our green and pleasant land. Here, I painted the small, but spectacular flower of a conifer tree, and a scene of the fields towards the road to London, with the huts, camouflaged underneath the overhanging trees of the mysterious woods.

PEOPLE FLY and travel all round the world looking for something, without knowing what it is; but here it is, just stand still for a few minutes surrounded by God's creations, and you need go no further.

Quartz rock crystal (a mineral) Silica like the sparkling sand

MOST PEOPLE are always going somewhere, always passing through, they have to be there as quickly as possible, time is of the essence, but did they really need to go at all? They miss the joy and beauty of His Presence by not pausing for a while.

THE ISOLATION was delightful, only nature's creatures came to see what you were doing. It was as if the birds would sing for you and there was always a robin, each one it seemed had its own territory, occasionally landing on the corner of my painting as if to lend a hand, or in his case a foot. They have such a wonderful affinity with us, often resting on something we have held, as if to warm their feet.

The robin is only small but has everything he needs.

REMEMBER ONE stayed with Jesus on His Crown of Thorns, for there was a reason, which should remain unspoken. Such friendly little birds, for they would not see many people out there in the wilds.

ONLY one person passed by. He chatted briefly about the skies looking ominous and rain imminent, while viewing my painting of the ploughman's art, then plodded on with stick in one hand and odd boots on his feet. He raised his stick up in the air and called out:

"May the rains fall gently on your fertile land."

THIS WAS getting curious. I often seemed to be in a place where people used these friendly departing comments, and always with a dramatic gesture and a slightly raised voice. It made me feel at home, with a sense of belonging, not feeling alone, a sort of inner happiness at being in God's Garden, as if it were necessary for me to be there at that time.

"May the rains fall gently on your fertile land."

ONCE AGAIN I was sharing HIS Mysteries. He was giving me another chance of experiencing The Presence in His Garden and perhaps to tell others what happiness we find by being close to His Creations.

BRAVE new world

I WAS FINALLY demobbed and well after the end of the war we were still rationed and many things were in short supply. I had been interested for several years in recycling processes and, although not considered economic, it was certainly necessary in those difficult days. My father was a Dental Surgeon so I had access to surplus plaster of paris, pink and white shades of dental plate plastics; the extra pieces left over because they were always mixed in excess to make sure there was enough for the purpose.

THE SAME occurred with silver amalgam tooth filling material, wax and impression compounds. I developed methods to recycle all these materials and use them for other purposes. I destructively distilled the pink plastics to a pure transparent liquid to make thick sheets and solid shapes identical to "Perspex" (polymethyl-methacrylate), also buttons and magnifying lenses. I made furniture polishes and candles from the waxes, which contained bees wax along with many others. And so it went on, new plaster for models and household repairs to walls and other structures.

I DO NOT want this to be the story of my life, only if it concerns a special aspect of our purpose in writing the book, which is of course; How To Feel God's Presence, now in today's world. This comes later when we explore why and how it happened to us.

Jesus said: *"The world is a bridge.
Become passers by; but build not your dwelling here."*

Floral bridge - transition through this world to another . . .

THE NATURE OF MY SOUL has always been responsible for the difficulty I have in throwing anything away which may have another use, and this was reinforced by the shortages during the war. To me this IS part of our Creator's method; everything He made is recycled, dust to dust. If He does it this way, then who are we to be so careless? He made it like this from the beginning of time, and it will be so, until eternity, but remember, we are only passing through and should leave things as they are or make improvements.

THIS INDICATES (to repeat the point) that we have come from somewhere and we are going somewhere else, and where we are going will be a better place to dwell.

IN THIS PRESENT LIFE Our Creator has given us the special chance to touch and move things, to experience the reality of life itself, instead of only having thoughts or instantaneous mind experiences, as we would have in another dimension.

TIME COMES into play for an individual from the moment of conception, even though time may have been passing already for those who are here now. At that moment two half genetic codes fuse together and we are able to perpetuate the human species and prepare a physical Temple to receive a very small fragment of Soul, containing the directives of God's Presence. This is separate from His forces within each and every atom, which keep the charged particles in motion, without coming into contact with each other.

Sculpture: 'The Resurrection'. Jesus is even more active today as a Spiritual being than He was when on Earth, as mankind did not give Him a chance.

Jesus said: *"The sign of your Heavenly Father in you, is a movement and a rest."*

Sculpture: 'Mary holding baby Jesus' Saved a woman from suicide (See newspaper report, next page)

These two sculptures are made of the most remarkable recycled materials, which had been discarded - now brought back to life.

Psychic News

London, May 10, 1975

'Garden of Eden' saves woman who decided on suicide

THIS beautiful "Garden of Eden" is becoming a mecca for those in search of healing and peace.

Though our black-and-white reproduction does not do it full justice, it depicts another healing dimension. Even the sculptures completed by Alan Fraser Bell in semi-trance, seem to possess some unique quality.

"One woman who decided to end her life came to see us first. She was so filled with inner peace by looking at the large centre sculpture that she returned home a changed woman."

Now Alan's "healing garden" in Andrews Lane, Formby, Liverpool, has become a focal point in his life.

A chemist, he has had "so many desperate requests for help," he has decided to give up his pharmacy soon to devote the future to healing.

Alan and his daughter Heather, sent PN the picture "to thank all your readers for their kind thoughts on our healing garden's opening."

FORMBY TIMES

Wednesday, June 4, 1975

Woman says that healing method works

FORMBY'S psychic chemist, Alan Fraser Bell, deserves all the publicity he can get. That's the opinion of one of our readers, who claims her health dramatically improved after Mr. Bell's treatment.

Mrs. G. - she doesn't want to be identified for personal reasons was suffering from two serious complaints when she first read about the Elson Road chemist in the Formby Times some months ago.

She had been receiving traditional medical treatment for the complaints - a bowel disease and a phobia - for many years. Yet, she feels, little progress has been made.

Then came the visit to Andrews Lane "Healing Garden."

"I'd read about the place in the Formby Times," she said. "I have to admit I was tense at first - I didn't know what to expect. But once I was inside, I could sense this wonderful peace.

Cleared up

"Both Mr. Bell and Heather (his daughter) were very gentle and kind. She held my hand as I closed my eyes, and he laid his hands on my head. I really felt the tranquillity I'd read about."

Mrs. G. has been back a number of times to visit the chemist and his daughter. All the time, she says, she has been improving. The bowel complaint has cleared up, and the phobia is "definitely on the way out."

Sunday People

MARCH 9, 1980   No. 5,121   18p   LL

Here is your 'healing music'

CHEMIST Alan Bell, whose mystical "healing wavelength" offered instant cures to thousands, has put his powers on record.

And already sales of his disc - recorded in his "healing garden" to the background of a dawn chorus of bird song - are booming.

Mr Bell, has been besieged by the sick and infirm since the Sunday People revealed his claims of amazing powers nearly four years ago.

He came across his healing wavelength - he describes it as a single note an octave higher than top A flat - while meditating.

Mr Bell has been using his powers on the sick in the "Healing Garden" of his home in Formby, Lancs, ever since.

WE OFTEN point out that the sculptures, the garden, and ourselves do not possess any unique power, IT IS GOD'S PRESENCE that heals those who asks for help. OUR ROLE IS SIMPLY TO ESTABLISH A LINK.

INSPIRED meditation

Jesus said: "The sign of your Heavenly Father in you, is a Movement and a Rest."

WITHOUT HIS PRESENCE we would not move at all. The first cell formed at conception divides into two, then to four, then to eight, and on and on it goes; each time there is a movement, they fidget and reshape. HE has made Himself known to the mother and baby, by moving the newly formed cells. The rests are the pauses in between the cell divisions. This is the sign of The Heavenly Father in all forms of animal and plant life, as this short poem shows, which was written during an inspired meditation many years ago:

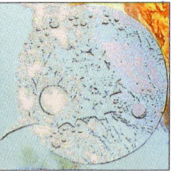

Beginning of a new life

WHICH PEACH?

When the beauty of the blossoms fade,
  And the bees in all the flowers have played,
And buzzed as bees must,
  Carrying particles of pollen dust,

The leaves grow long, thin and green,
  The winds blow strong and clean,
While the pollinated fruits begin to swell,
  The tree extends its roots as well,

Each little cell it seems,
  Contains a message in its genes,
It knows exactly what to do,
  Each cell dividing into two,

Then two to four, and four to eight,
  At such a rate, and more and more,
It forms a seed, a fruit, a core,
  A peach with delicate perfume,

So subtle yet so different from the bloom,
  Such perfect textured tissue contained within,
Smooth shaded coloured skin,
  A human female is indeed the peaches twin.

Television
Review of early research

Allsorts
Allsorts
ALLSORTS

Chris Kelly
was enchanted by
ALAN FRASER BELL'S film:
"WHICH PEACH"
"A superb Creation of Futuristic Music, Poems and Colour Movement."

● Chris Kelly with his producer, sound and camera crew were the first to film and record a fragment of the Healing Music, while Mr Bell was in a meditational state.

● Several of his musical compositions have been used in Television and Cinema films.

RECYCLING

IT SEEMS A SHAME to drift away from those lovely thoughts, but what follows does relate to the health and well-being of the lives so formed. It was of great interest to me to be able to recycle the excess silver amalgam from the Dental profession. I would heat it to distil off the mercury vapour and collect the tiny droplets which coalesced together to form a lovely liquid metal with a mirror finish. It was, of course, valuable for scientific and many other purposes but very harmful to humans and most life forms. The residual hard metal left behind contained all the silver and trace elements. I purified the silver content and used it in my research into its remarkable Colloidal properties. This has a unique contribution to make to human health, from babies onwards, if it is properly prepared, but can be useless if contaminated. More about this later.

QUALIFIED

I CONTINUED with my education, which was difficult after being in the Forces and away from the scientific environment for so long, although I was able to study human nature, in the raw as it were, and had many experiences which I value and would not have had as a civilian. My studies in Pharmacy and associated disciplines took many years to culminate in qualifying as a Pharmaceutical Chemist.

I MARRIED the beautiful young woman whose safety and good health I had prayed for, even from the centre of that Norfolk wheatfield. We have been happy together ever since and have shared the enlightenment of our souls.

Wedding day

WE BOUGHT a small village Chemist shop in Derbyshire, only because it was all we could afford, and developed the business, moving to larger premises. One thinks of the countryside as being healthy and life supporting with fresh air and other benefits, but we noticed many unusual aspects, which were quite surprising. We could reach out with our hands and catch a fly on its way past, because they were travelling so slowly, even the birds looked lazy in their flight, what few there were.

WE MISSED the fresh air which blew in from the sea, as we lived near the coast back home. The wind or even a gale would have to blow for a couple of days in Derbyshire before you could smell the sea. It was brief but beautiful and suddenly we could remember that we lived on an island surrounded by turbulent tides. It was only then we realised the odour and taste of herbicides and pesticides had gone and, although the birds and flies speeded up a little in their flight, it was only for a day if we were lucky. It was sad that the villagers had lived with these chemicals for so long and many had not noticed.

OUR DAUGHTER Heather was born there, our Chemist shop and Dispensary were flourishing, we enjoyed caring for the folk, not just the villagers but also those from around the countryside. They were wonderful people and we heard many tales from the local farmers, enough to fill a book.

AS BEFORE we seemed to be in a place where someone was bound to use one of those one line descriptive phrases sooner or later, and of course it had to be a farmer, as they are nearer to Mother Nature than anyone else.

I WOULD discuss a farmer's needs for medication of a sick animal that had fallen into a ditch; our Dispensary cared for animals as well as humans. Satisfied and happy with his purchase, he waved his cap and said with a flourish: "May your family's health and wealth abound," and left the shop.

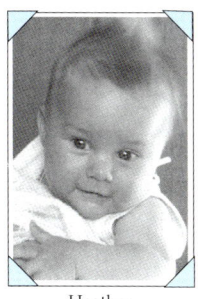

Heather

I thought it was a lovely gesture, for he had already lifted his cap to my female assistant and asked to speak to the Master Man. I had just helped one of his lambs, only recently born, and he knew my wife had given birth to our daughter the day before.

ANOTHER heavenly choir

I WOULD OFTEN make the late night or early morning feed for our baby, to give my wife a little more rest. I was downstairs in the kitchen one night mixing the feed when I heard again a vast stereophonic sound of choirs music and voices, so beautiful but so faint I had to pause to listen to it.

AGAIN, as in the wheatfield of years ago, I was transfixed and my wife Brenda was wondering why I was taking so long. She came down to find me quite still and I was overjoyed that she too could hear it. We listened together, it was all around, and high above us as if there were no rooms upstairs, and the roof had gone.

IT FELT LIKE empty space above; truly an experience of the soul and mind. It was real enough for us to share and I am certain we were sharing it with our Creator.

Jesus said:
"What thou shalt hear in thine ear and in thine other ear, that preach from your housetops."

MANY THEOLOGIANS suggest that Jesus was telling the people of His time to listen to His Words. But we know He is telling all the future generations to listen for Him in the ear. We could certainly hear a wonderful sound but the house top and roof seemed to have gone, although the two were definitely associated. So I feel compelled to talk about it, not to preach but to indicate what can be so easily dismissed and cast aside as an aberration of some kind. Yet when two people hear the same it can never be forgotten or dismissed.

IT OCCURRED on several nights over the following months. We intuitively knew that there was a purpose for what we had heard but had no idea of its meaning. It was not real in the sense that there were any choirs or music being performed or played anywhere nearby.

SHORTLY AFTER I had experienced this for the first time, when guarding the crashed aircraft several years ago, a large area of East Anglia was flooded, field after field and wide lakes of water surrounded Ely Cathedral.

Storms and floods

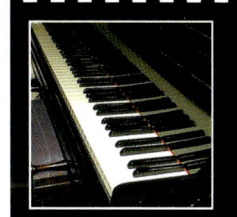

Jesus said: *"Let the fields be joyful, let the floods clap their hands; leave off your moans and lamentations." "Everything that happens is good."* The piano dried and played again, the garden blossomed with abundant fruits.

A FEW months after we had experienced this music, the whole Village, our Chemist shop and home were flooded. It came up through the floors, several feet deep, swirling round, musty muddy water; a very distressing time. Heather was only a young child and remembers looking down the staircase at the rising chaos, wondering how deep it was going to be, which was quite terrifying for her.

THE RIVER Dove, close by, had been very much wider in ancient times and was now reclaiming its identity, regardless of who had inhabited the widened riverbed since then.

THE NEXT YEAR everything in the garden grew wonderfully well, using all the nutrients which had been deposited when the flood subsided. A peach tree we had grown from a stone only a few years earlier produced dozens of delicious large fruits.

WE WERE FLOODED again only a year later, at Christmas; the piano fell through the water sodden floor. Before we bought the property our solicitor assured us from his documents that the whole area and house had never been flooded, because we did ask. This was very sad, for when we refurbished the premises to make a new shop and dispensary we could see at least two water tide marks three feet up the walls, from previous floods, as we moved away all the old fittings. My wife and I did most of the work ourselves with the help of a couple of wonderful villagers who became our firm friends.

FROM THIS experience we vowed that not only would we continue to do most things for ourselves, but we would also have to double check everything, being sure to ask the right questions and to continue probing until we got the answers we needed. There is always a huge difference between the replies people give and a genuine answer to your questions.

ALL JESUS' answers are always absolutely perfect and can be relied upon.

SO WE MOVED, having had enough floods. We came back up North, where our families have their roots, and found a wonderful house being built in Formby. Our son Paul was born, making our family complete and we have lived here happily ever since. We brought the peach tree with us, which continued to be very fruitful.

THIS IS WHERE OUR LIVES REALLY BEGAN AND THE MIRACLES TOOK OVER

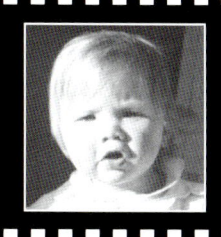

New home   Heather   Our son Paul   My wife Brenda

SILVER - more precious than gold!
Element No. 47 Ag

THIS IS NOT an obscure thought but is of vital importance. Silver is a remarkable metal, not as a symbol of wealth but one of health, so really health equals wealth; we will explain this a little later. We have already written about silver as element number 47, symbol Ag, which occurs in the second group of twenty-eight. We are always intrigued by the way in which the figure twenty-eight recurs:

(1) The number of elements required for perfect health of the human body is about twenty-eight, when you include all the many trace elements, such as selenium, chromium and others.
(2) The female fertility cycle is twenty-eight days.
(3) The path of the moon round the earth is the same.
(4) Most animals require twenty-eight elements and many actually receive these in supplements and are better nourished than most humans.
(5) This figure is also 4 x 7, God's special unit.
"Six days shalt thou labour." The seventh is God's day of rest.
(6) The sun spins on its axis in about 28 days, the bands at its middle spin faster.

THIS THOUGHT can be extended even further in relation to life on earth but we must return to silver. From the results of our research it seems that Silver is an essential micronutrient, necessary to maintain the immune system of the body, combating bacterial and viral infections.

Photographic processes

PHOTOGRAPHY & SILVER

AS A CHILD of about twelve years old, I was fascinated by photography and the chemistry involved in the process of producing a picture, and this interest has been with me ever since, leading to much research in many diverse directions.

I MANAGED to obtain a small amount of silver nitrate, which took a lot of pocket money and a very kind Chemist.
"What do you want that for," he said.
I told him, somewhat nervously, I wanted to make my own photographic plate to take a picture of the leaded light window in the front door.
"You'll never do that," he replied. "Anyway have a go; be careful with all chemicals, never put any in your mouth or touch them."

SO I PUSHED my luck and asked him for potassium bromide as well.

"I know," he prompted me, "you want to make some silver bromide."

HE WAS, of course quite correct and then threw in for good measure, that I should tell my parents what I had bought, which was sound advice. He also knew who they were, otherwise a note would have been required.

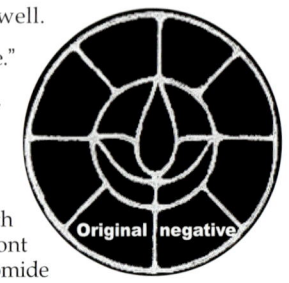

I DID MAKE my own photographic plate using a piece of glass with a jagged edge, about two and a half inches in diameter, from a front cycle lamp. I prepared solutions of silver nitrate and potassium bromide separately and, as I did not have a dark room, had to wait until night time to mix the two together to make silver bromide, because this compound is sensitive to light and slowly goes black, even without developing.

WORKING IN THE DARK was difficult so I used some deep red cellophane paper over the cycle lamp, because silver bromide is not very sensitive to red light. Even so I scratched my finger with the glass I removed from the lamp and also spilled some of the dilute silver nitrate solution on my hand, over the scratch, and generally made a mess of things in the gloom. I used some warm gelatine and finally made a plate with the gelatine-silver bromide set like a stiff pale yellow jelly on the surface of the glass. To cut the story short I took my photograph in a homemade cardboard camera using a lens from a Woolworth's sixpenny magnifying glass.

SUCCESS - I developed it in what was called M.Q. (Metol Quinol) in those days, fixed, washed and dried the plate. I took the photograph to school to show the science teacher, to fit in with a previous lesson about films. At first he could not believe it but after he had cross questioned me for quite a while we became firm friends and he helped greatly in my scientific studies.

THE SPECIAL POINT of this experience is that the scratch on my finger, from the piece of glass, over which I spilled some of the silver solution, DID NOT become septic or inflamed, as would normally be the case if I cut myself in those days. It felt comfortable and it healed rapidly without a plaster dressing. Even to a child of twelve, this was fascinating and may have induced me to study Pharmacy and Medicine, which I did in later life.

BIBLICAL TIMES

SILVER has been of great interest to me ever since and I am astonished by some of its properties dating back to Biblical Times. When water or milk was carried across the desert or on long journeys over the hills, a silver coin or other silver item was placed in the vessel and the movement of the fluid over its surface, along with changes of temperature, dissolved some of the metal. These few atoms killed bacteria, viruses, fungi, moulds and yeasts, or inhibited their growth, so that all the liquids arrived at their destinations in fairly good condition, or were consumed along the journey in a satisfactory state.

Silver antique era

EVERYONE IT SEEMS had at least one small item made of silver; it was known as being health promoting, hence our earlier remark that Health = Wealth. You were very wealthy if you had good health. So the more silver items you had, such as cutlery, goblets and dishes, probably the more healthy you were. These items were passed down from one generation to the next, and when they became too damaged or unserviceable they were replaced and the old ones were used by the servants or bodyguards, so everyone had some silver in their diet.

THIS HAS CONTINUED from ancient times to the present day. Frequently a silver spoon and pusher set was given to each child as a Christening gift and usually passed on to future generations.

A SILVER teething ring, either solid or hollow depending on income, was always of great benefit to a baby. The gums would be more comfortable and less inflamed than using a bone or plastic teething ring and, most interesting of all, there would be fewer digestive disturbances.

Silver spoon and pusher

IN RECENT TIMES many of the population had knives, forks, spoons and other items made of silver, or at least silver plated, so we all had some silver in the diet, until the arrival of plastics, stainless steel and aluminium. Plastics contributed nothing towards health in this sense, and some contained chemical plasticisers (to make them more flexible), which are detrimental to health. Stainless steel is often of dubious chemical composition but may supply micro amounts of beneficial chromium. It may not be very scientific to say that since then public health and well-being seem to have deteriorated, especially in regard to immune deficiency conditions.

ALUMINIUM metal, its alloys and compounds (antacids and antiperspirants, for example) are entering into the human body systems, when it should not be there at all, as it has no known function in our life metabolism.

FORTUNATELY ANTIBIOTICS came upon the scene as the use of domestic silverware was decreasing. The presence of silver in the diet does seem to have a beneficial health effect. With antibiotics we began to control infections very successfully; we thought that we had at last overcome bacterial diseases. More and more antibiotics became available to kill a wider range of organisms but gradually, due to overuse and misuse, the bacteria fought back, developing resistance to many antibiotics. These mutant strains are becoming increasingly difficult to control but Colloidal Silver could do so.

COLLOIDAL silver

FOR MANY YEARS before the antibiotics arrived, Medical and Pharmaceutical minds had been experimenting with silver salts, such as nitrate, to control and kill micro-organisms. These were difficult to use and not very successful, as they also caused slight damage to living human tissues, and some were absorbed, then deposited in the skin causing a grey discolouration.

THE ARISTOCRACY and several Royal Families across the world, probably had an excess of silver in their food (hence the grey colour of their skin and their alternative name, Blue Bloods) not only because everything they used was made of silver, but also, and this is a point not often considered, the silver in use in years gone by was not pure. The other elements present would increase the skin colour but, what is remarkable, they survived many infections and plagues, along with their live-in staff, even when the surrounding farmers and villagers were dying of unknown diseases.

THERE BEGAN TO BE evolved several Colloidal Silver preparations, which were entirely different. The silver content of these was not a silver salt like a nitrate but a suspension of very fine particles of pure metallic silver, so fine in fact, that you could see through the liquid which had various colours, grey, red, yellow, but if you shone a narrow beam of bright light through it, the fine silver particles reflected the light, so when viewing it from the side you could see the beam.

THE VERY EARLY colloidal silver products were made by mechanical grinding processes, which reduced small pieces of silver metal to a very fine black dust, suspended in water. These were not very useful or stable as there were limits as to how fine the black dust could be made, and after a while it would all settle down on to the base of the bottle. From the records available and our own research, these particles contain too many atoms and did not carry an electrical charge. The medical benefits were a very random affair, sometimes successful but more often useless, and always contaminated with several foreign materials, which could be detrimental to health.

AN INTERESTING THOUGHT comes to mind here; if you have ever polished a silver item using a very fine silver polish, the cloth becomes very black; this is not dirt in the usual sense of the word, but a very fine silver powder, even finer than those produced in the paragraph above, almost a colloidal state if added to water, but not quite, because a true colloid needs to be made with water.

SIMILARLY, in *"posh"* hotels that have a full silver service, if you were present at the time of placing the cutlery on the tables before the guests arrived, each item is given a final polish, after they have already been washed. A spoon, for instance, is then held between the cloth, untouched by fingers, and placed on the table. This cloth is black and looks disgusting but a fine film of silver powder remains on the spoon, having a slight antibacterial action in the presence of water (or soup). But, and this is quite remarkable, if the spoon were to be tested bacteriologically, it would be found to be sterile, so hardly any cross contamination by germs occurs between guests, when silverware is used. This would also apply to silver plated ware, so we do not have to be rich to be protected, but plastics and stainless steel do nothing for anyone.

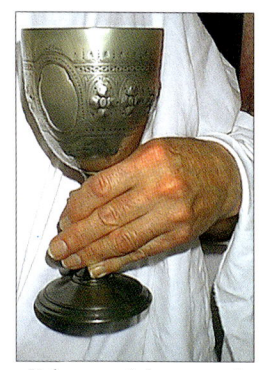

THIS BENEFICIAL EFFECT does not occur to the same extent when several people drink from the same silver vessel, even if it is wiped with a cloth or tissue between each individual's sip, as about five or six minutes would need to pass for any bacteria to be inhibited by the silver. It is not an instantaneous action and would depend partly upon the strength of any alcohol in the vessel and whether it was moved round between each sip, also the temperature, and amount of fine silver residue on the cloth or tissue.

THIS IS NOT so far removed from the purpose of our book as you might think, as a true colloid can only exist in the presence of water, and JESUS would know all about the special properties of water and silver. In His Miracles He converted it into wine, He would know how water reacted with silver in the presence of fruit juices, various minerals, and the effect of sunlight.

Unknown wisdom, passed down to prevent infection.

Jesus said: *"If you do not first understand water; you know nothing."* (Yes! It Is worth repeating).

He referred to water many times during His Ministry, He said:

"Why do you wash the outside of the cup?" (the body) *"Do you not understand that He who made the inside, is also He who made the outside."*

HE WAS SPEAKING of the cleansing properties of water; He was very health conscious and was stating how necessary it is to drink pure water, to remove toxic materials from the body; not just for use in Baptisms or washing the outside of the body.

IN HIS MIRACLES He was demonstrating the value of the most remarkable chemical compound on the Earth, - Water. He even made a wet paste to place on the eyes of a blind man, He told a group to apply the mud from the river bank for their diseases, and Miracles followed.

WATER DISSOLVES EVERYTHING to some extent, if only in parts per billion. This is very important, as it brings together substances which may never have come close to each other before, thereby giving a chance for atoms and molecules to interact. When Jesus told His Disciples to eat of all the fruits, except those which have bitterness, He was showing the way concerning all aspects of life. The human body should be a non toxic Temple for the presence of the Soul and Spirit material, which is our individual fragment of God, who initiates every movement within our physical electrochemical form. Without Him we would not move at all. *(A movement and a rest, the sign of our Heavenly Father within us.)*

We should be healthy, clean, properly nourished and with good thoughts.

FASCINATING facts

CONCERNING COLLOIDAL SILVER

● The true Silver Colloid only exists in the presence of water, as already mentioned. If the water is evaporated or removed, the silver atoms, which are in clusters of about fifteen, join together and are deposited as a very thin film of pure silver metal, which no longer has the remarkable properties of the electrically charged colloid which we will describe later. Neither can the colloid be reconstituted by just adding water because its physical nature has changed.

● SOME EARLY SAMPLES of colloidal silver were produced chemically by mixing together individual solutions of silver nitrate, sodium citrate and ferrous sulphate. They formed beautifully coloured liquids but were almost impossible to purify and most products were chemically contaminated, which restricted their medical usefulness.

● JUST BRIEFLY: another method loosely associated the silver with egg albumen or milk protein and once again was not consistently effective. It lost some of its benefits by belonging to protein molecules and could not be used for every purpose.

● FORTUNATELY the antibiotics had arrived, but sadly the silver colloids were abandoned and it would seem they were to be forgotten for ever.

● I CONTINUED TO WORK on the Silver Saga, it was far too interesting to abandon. I had always been intrigued by its properties, knowing there was something special we had all missed. It seemed very peculiar, because sometimes a few batches of these very early colloidal silvers produced spectacular results, while a preparation made by another laboratory was a complete failure.

● ONE DAY EUREKA! I had been experimenting with electrolysis, arcing and high frequencies, along with ultraviolet light and reverse osmosis, in the purification of water. We have drawn expertise from many branches of science and have succeeded in developing and perfecting an electrical method of making a golden yellow Pure Colloidal Silver in specially purified water.

● IT IS THE MOST REMARKABLE Healing Remedy I have prepared in over fifty years of Pharmacy, analytically standardised at 30 parts per million of Pure Silver 99.99%. It has been described as:

A MINIATURE HOSPITAL IN A BOTTLE.

● WE HAVE OBSERVED that all the healing processes occur more rapidly and with greater perfection (no scarring) if a wound, bite, sore, burn or any other condition, is kept constantly moist with the Colloidal Silver, rather than allowing it to become dry. Frequent applications are beneficial. When drying occurs the silver is deposited as atoms; not quite as active as the Colloid.

- IT DESTROYS bacterial, viral, fungal, and yeast infections, also single cell parasites. With the appearance and increase of antibiotic resistant organisms, this lovely golden yellow colloid could well be essential for the survival of mankind. These may sound lofty words for such a simple substance, yet even inferior samples have been known and used in simple ways for thousands of years, with no apparent bacterial resistance to its activity. It is the electrical charge on the groups of atoms and the purity of the silver in special water, which makes all the difference between this method and those early materials documented in Pharmacopoeias many years ago. It is not surprising they fell into obscurity.

- THIS NEW PURE FORM of Colloidal Silver may be taken by mouth and applied even to cut and damaged skin and scalp without stinging. It is odourless, almost tasteless and could save the lives of severe burn patients by taking doses internally and frequent applications to the burns, keeping them continuously moist with the colloid. It is comforting, soothing, healing and truly antibiotic, not just against bacteria, but nearly all invading organisms, and it has the wonderful ability to help regenerate underlying tissues, often without forming a scar. Use only for as long as needed, to avoid staining new formed skin.

- IT IS USED SUCCESSFULLY to cure acne, even for patients who have had no benefit from years of other treatments. Discontinue use when clear.

- IT HAS HEALED bites, stings, cold sores (herpes), mouth and internal thrush, pimples, gum boils, internal and external ulcers. Some arthritic and rheumatic conditions have also improved dramatically, although this is not fully understood, it is associated with the immune system.

- IT HAS BEEN of great value in the treatment of ringworm, fevers, colds, flu, and as a non-stinging spray for septic eyes, nose, throat and ears. Wonderful pain relief and clearing of shingles, athletes foot, allergic and itchy areas, for adults, children and pets.

- I HAVE SEEN HAIR REGROWING on a depleted scalp, although it remained grey, it grew very well. Each day we come upon new uses and continue to be amazed and overjoyed.

- AS WE DO NOT wish to turn this into a medical book, we have avoided the inclusion of photographs of all the health conditions mentioned and the beneficial effects, but you could soon gain the same insight for yourselves.

- IT DESTROYS OVER 600 PATHOGENIC organisms, its benefits are phenomenal, but no large Chemical or Pharmaceutical company would have much interest, because it could not be Patented; it is too simple. Once their research and clinical double blind cross over trials were completed, after spending millions of pounds, everyone could make it for themselves anyway and they would never recover their expenditure. So it is up to you! We understand that somewhere in the text we are legally obliged to state that all our research is for information only and is not advice, diagnosis or prescription for any human or animal condition, and qualified medical help should always be sought for every illness, especially for children.

CONSTANT RESEARCH

WE HAVE OBTAINED AND ANALYSED several samples of so called colloidal silver which have appeared on the market in recent years and unfortunately some are a remake of the old discarded formula or are not true colloids at all. After analysis, one sample was shown to be identical to tap water, from a known part of the country, so it would not be active for long, even if we had found any silver in it. It is these products of inferior quality which cast a shadow over the remarkable properties of the real material, just as in the past, almost preventing it from obtaining true respectability. There are further comments later concerning its storage and method of use, which you will find of great value. It is so easy to prepare it yourself.

WE PREPARE QUITE LARGE quantities of Pure Colloidal Silver using a special electrical method I evolved over many years and at quite a small cost but, because of the very high price and disappointing quality of other available products on the market, we have now made it possible for you to do it yourself at home. It would not be as active or as pure as we prepare in the laboratory and there would be difficulty knowing how much silver was present in your preparation, but it is worth trying and we have even made that last obstacle easy. Also the actual strength of your product is not critical, providing there is some real Colloidal silver present, as there does not seem to be any sign of toxicity, even in excess.

KITCHEN table technology

THE SECRET IS AS FOLLOWS . . .

PURCHASE :
■ Two Litres of Purified or Distilled Water from a Chemist; not so called purified water from a store or supermarket.
■ At the same time ask for Fifty Grams of PURE Sodium Chloride B.P. Do not use ordinary Table Salt, as it contains other chemicals.
■ One pack of Fine Cut or Powdered GREEN LEAF CHINA TEA.
■ 9 Volt Battery.
■ Two short pieces of wire (insulated copper is suitable).
■ A pair of six inch (15cm.) long Pure Silver electrodes (99.99%) about 2mm. in diameter, or a pair of three inch (7.5cm.) electrodes, to reduce the expense.

GREEN LEAF
CHINA TEA
200mg.
or as much as would lie
easily on this circle: ⟶

SODIUM
CHLORIDE
50mg.
or as much as would lie
easily on this circle: ⟶

USE a Pyrex glass or Teflon coated pan, well washed and then rinsed in distilled water. Do not use a metal uncoated pan of any type. Bring to the boil 300ml. of distilled water, then add the quantities of Salt and Green Tea stated above (to aid conductivity for the battery process), and boil gently for a further 30 seconds, then cover and allow to cool.

NOTE: Do not use sea salt for these experiments (only use pure sodium chloride). All sea salts are of course evaporated sea water from various parts of the world and are contaminated with many substances which should be avoided.

See facing page for step by step instructions.

THE PROCESS - do it yourself

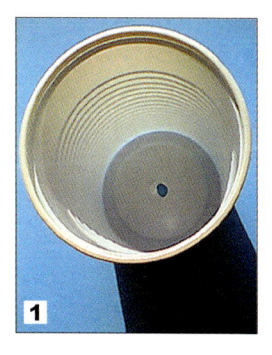

- *Picture 1:* When cool, filter this solution through a fine filter paper, previously rinsed, in the filter funnel with distilled water, or as shown in the photograph, filter it through a wet compressed pad of pure cotton wool, which has also been rinsed in distilled water. This pad may be pressed into the base of a white plastic disposable cup with a small hole made in it and, as we are using kitchen table technology, this cup will fit into the top of a jam jar.
- *Picture 2:* Pour the boiled, cooled solution into the 'cup' funnel containing the washed, compressed pure cotton wool. Collect the slightly coloured liquid in the jam jar.

- *Picture 3:* Separate the two Silver electrodes with pieces of plastic at the top and bottom. Keep them 5mm apart, they must not be allowed to touch each other. Ask a jeweller to obtain these electrodes. They must be pure 99.99% Silver.

- *Picture 4:* Connect each silver electrode to one terminal of the 9v battery. The liquid shows yellow/brown streaks reaching out from the darkened electrode; bubbles arise from the other one, which stays fairly bright silver.

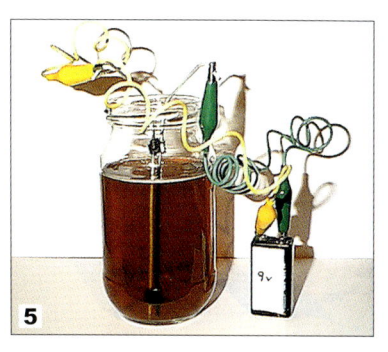

- *Picture 5:* Stir gently for a few minutes until the liquid becomes a darker colour, as shown in the photograph. It does not interfere if the wires become tangled during stirring, as long as they remain connected to the battery and the silver electrodes do not touch. Now disconnect.

- *Picture 6:* The enlarged view shows the negative silver is a bright metal colour. The positive silver is covered with a dark brown deposit. Gently remove this into the liquid by using a small, soft plastic handled artists brush. The deposit gradually dissolves after a little stirring.

NOW YOU HAVE MADE YOUR FIRST BATCH OF COLLOIDAL SILVER
Check the colour against those of the two spoons on the next page.

PURCHASE a few white plastic spoons about the same size as these, pour a sample of your product into one and compare it. One shows the colour of about 60 parts per million (ppm) that is 60 milligrams in one litre. The other spoon shows 30ppm. All you need to do is dilute your product with some boiled, cooled, distilled water to match the spoon containing the 30ppm. This can be used for all purposes in your own research. If paler than 30ppm, continue process for longer.

This spoon contains:
Colloidal Silver 60 ppm.

This spoon contains:
Colloidal Silver 30 ppm.

Place your spoonful here to compare the colour.

DO NOT continue beyond this colour, as it may become darker or greyish with a deposit on the bottom of the jar. The reason for using these two colour samples to compare with your product is that there are so many variables in the process that the colour is the best guide if the Green Tea and Sodium Chloride are used in the weights stated on the previous page. Some of these variables are: the strength (or age) of the battery, the temperature and purity of the distilled water, the purity of the salt, the distance between the electrodes and the length of time of the electrolysis, and many more.

MAKE IT freshly prepared (say each week) and do not store it for too long if you use this home method. It should be stored in an amber or brown glass bottle (not plastic) in the dark and at room temperature, not frozen or refrigerated. It must be kept well away from electrical or magnetic devices and equipment. It must not come into contact with any metal spoons or other metal objects, either during its preparation or afterwards, as all these would cause deterioration, which is not harmful but your product would not be as beneficial as the perfect material.

WE TAKE one 5ml. spoonful each day in a little purified water as a dietary supplement and apply it frequently for all the conditions already mentioned, if any should arise. For some time I have not used any antiseptic solutions or creams other than Colloidal Silver, nor have I used any other disinfectant, deodorant, bacteriological, fungal or other product. It may also be used diluted half strength, with distilled water, in all adult male and female body cavities.

PLEASE NOTE that all the information in this book reflects the personal experiences and research of the authors and are for educational purposes only, not intended as a prescription or medication for any disease or medical condition.

USE ONLY Pure Silver 99.99% or better. Do not use Standard 925 Silver, as this is for jewellery and contains other metals, such as copper, zinc and many more which could be unsuitable for human applications, and the copper and zinc are even in the wrong proportions for human metabolism.

WE HAVE EVOLVED a special mains electrical process for our own laboratory use, without the China Green Tea or the sodium chloride, but mains should not be used at home; it is too dangerous as it has to be D.C. current. So use the method illustrated above.

THE BUTTERFLY phenomenon

WE WERE in the garden about to photograph some items for the book; it was a windy day, leaves large and small were flying past us, up over the hedges and down between the houses, airborne bits of dried grass and feathers, all on the move, a constant stream. Then a lovely butterfly fluttered on its way, not being blown by the wind but apparently going where it intended, and even more astonishing, flying into the wind as if it were a calm summer's day. Does it not know that it cannot do this? It must have had immense faith in something. Does it have a special knowledge unknown to us, can it sense a space between the moving molecules of air, for it is even lighter than a leaf? We have observed this many times on different days and with several species of butterfly of varying sizes.

THERE IS ANOTHER little creature, he has no knowledge of his clumsiness; the bumble bee. It can be shown mathematically and with computer technology involving aircraft design that the bumble bee is a poor shape and cannot fly, but of course he does not know this, fortunately! If he suddenly became aware of aircraft design during his buzzing, he may drop out of the sky and wonder where his power had gone?

WE TOUCH upon this thought again later when discussing swimming, floating and riding a two wheel cycle. Maybe because the bee has such delight in all the flowers you can stroke his fluffy body, while he sips nectar, unaware of your presence. This could be a unique ability; not to know, rather than stifling possibilities by thinking we know it all. The lack of knowledge may allow the framework for unusual phenomena to occur. We are only aware of what things seem to be and how they relate to our present understanding, but really we know so little. Children have this superb ability; their innocence is vulnerable, yet filled with a moving eagerness to believe anything is possible. The imagination we are born with is a very precious gift. There are many colours to see between the shades of black and white of the adult mind!

BY ALLOWING the possibility for something to happen, you are not actively preventing it from doing so by thinking that you know the outcome or answer in advance. We extend these thoughts later.

JESUS said: *"Everything that happens is GOOD."*

HOWEVER, this is often very difficult to understand at the time of a tragedy or sadness, but is always correct. Even the two floods which we endured had a remarkable outcome, not only did we have prolific crops of vegetables the following year but, after the piano fell through the floor, we made a momentous decision, TO MOVE.

THIS IS WHEN THE MIRACLES BEGAN; we were just in the wrong place to begin our married life, and at the wrong time, but we were being guided . . .

THE RELIGIOUS gene

IF ONE PERSON of a pair of identical twins has a religious nature, then the other one is equally religious, even if they were brought up in different families and in different circumstances, rich or poor, and without either knowing the other twin existed; by separating them at birth. This surely indicates there is a gene for a religious nature, which we probably all have, because our Creator made us this way, to be able to seek out His Presence, particularly if there is a need or when we are unable to manage alone. So finding Him would be a wonderful experience when we succeed, and all our lives would be enriched, when we realise this is one of many genes that desires to be expressed in the real physical world. In the same manner an artist, a sculptor or musician, and many more would not know what their gene store held for them, if they did not at least attempt something.

DO WE ALL have a miracle gene, linked to our belief systems, which within God's framework of creation, unfortunately, also brings about an equal and opposite gene? Although this completes the perfect balance between all the things He created, this opposite gene tells our intellect that miracles are not possible, but regrettably, it expresses itself with more vigour than its gentle, creative counterpart. Only because we allow it to do so.

We should suppress this negative side and allow the apparently impossible to happen.

IS NOT THE FACT THAT WE ARE HERE ON EARTH ENOUGH OF A MIRACLE TO AT LEAST ALLOW FOR A FEW MORE?

JESUS would go up into the hills and commune with God, His Father, our Father, and drink the dew of pure condensed water from the mists, drifting in from the sea, dripping from the shiny leaves of the sparsely growing foliage. He would be instantly rejuvenated by the Purity of both.

JESUS said: *"I marvel at how this great wealth,* (God's Soul and Spirit material) *has made its home in this poverty."* (The Human body)

He was asking, how was it possible for the Soul and Spirit part of our being to occupy the people He met? He appeared to them in The Flesh but they were all drunken and debauched.

He said: *"My soul was afflicted for the sons of men."*

JESUS said: *"There is no power save that from The Heavenly Father; all else is but a dream of dust."*
He even makes the deserts bloom.

MANY PEOPLE SAY
THAT JESUS IS COMING BACK,
BUT HE'S NEVER BEEN AWAY!

Jesus said:
"The Kingdom of The Father is spread upon the earth, and men do not see it."

The Rose of Jericho dries, curls up and blows across the desert. Within an hour of rain it regenerates and grows. The desert lives.

SO IT IS up to us to find The Kingdom, and in very simple ways Jesus told us how to do this. His Presence is becoming stronger every day. It is even more insistent than it has been in the past. There must be a reason for HIS increased activity!

THE TIME IS APPROACHING, ARE WE GETTING VERY CLOSE TO SOMETHING SPECIAL? Not the end of the world but a spiritual renewal. He may manifest Himself to mankind in a truly modern manner using up to date science and technology, which is already in existence, and may only need a human living cell, from a person whose soul has experienced His Presence, to complete the ultimate electronic circuit.

"HELLO EARTH - WHY DO YOU NOT HEAR ME?"
**"I Wiill Speak To You Throughout Eternity.
Be Still, Know I Am God."**

STOP! Take a CLOSER look - now!

SOMETHING HAS JUST HAPPENED . . .

. . . as we are in the very process of putting this book together!
RE-READ this paragraph from the previous page and look at the meaning in it.

THE TIME IS APPROACHING, ARE WE GETTING VERY CLOSE TO SOMETHING SPECIAL? Not the end of the world, but a spiritual renewal. He may manifest Himself to mankind in a truly modern manner using up to date science and technology, which is already in existence, and may only need a human living cell, from a person whose soul has experienced His Presence, to complete the ultimate electronic circuit.

"HELLO EARTH - WHY DO YOU NOT HEAR ME?"

**"I Wiill Speak To You Throughout Eternity.
Be Still, Know I Am God."**

Then look at the last lines of text . . . there are two letter 'i's in the word 'Wiill'

. . . yet when I first keyed the text into the computer it had only one letter 'i' as shown below by a scan of our original printed page.

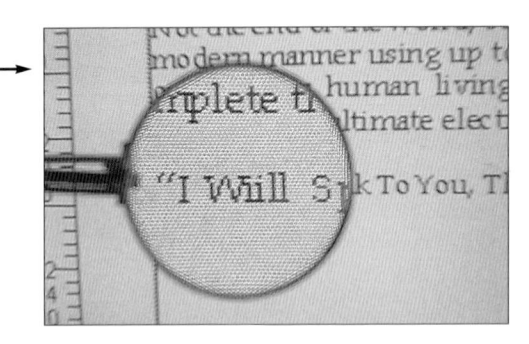

"I Will Speak

Can you imagine how the hairs stood up on the back of our necks when we noticed this subtle change? For neither Heather nor myself have altered this or re-typed it. After all, we have spent many hours reading these pages and trying to eliminate any errors or typing mistakes and no one else has access to the computer. We know the word WILL was spelled correctly, as we still have the original page and yet how could it have been altered so slightly but with such incredible meaning and implication?

The sceptics reading these last few lines will smile and assume that we are fabricating this to emphasise the purpose of our book: "Discover Your Creator Contacting You".

However, those who have faith will KNOW . . . That HE has included HIMSELF in this text as an additional 'I'. "I WILL SPEAK TO YOU." He has made Himself known to us once more. This has greatly increased our resolve to complete the book as soon as possible.

ECLIPSE 1999

A FEW DAYS AFTER THIS EVENT, in which our Creator included Himself in the text, we watched the Eclipse of the sun by the moon, on the 11th August 1999 from the garden at home. I just missed the last one in 1927 and I think we may also miss the next one!

IT WAS A WONDERFUL experience which I managed to photograph as a record of what we actually saw in the North West of England, as most of the pictures available were of the total eclipse filmed from a Hercules aircraft at over 30,000ft.

OUR VIEW HERE was only about 90% of the sun obscured by the moon and the sequence shows this by using frame capture technology from video footage; quite a simple set up, with crossed polarised filters and small aperture, but the main problem was tracking the sun across the sky through the haze and the cloud cover, hoping to record a little more when it appeared again. Some frames were actually photographed through the haze and thin cloud, so constant adjustments had to be made.

THIS SPECTACULAR natural event brought together the minds of over FOUR BILLION people worldwide. Seldom have so many concentrated on one of our Creator's remarkable happenings at the same time.

SIGNS OF THE CREATION

FOR MANY PEOPLE it was a very moving experience, touching the soul and perhaps reaching a part of us that has always sought signs of The Creation.

IT IS THOUGHT provoking for mankind that the sun is 400 times larger than the moon, yet it is also 400 times further away, so at 'Totality' the moon is almost the same diameter as the sun.

COULD THIS REALLY HAPPEN BY CHANCE?

COULD WE not allow our Creator to have a purpose for making it like this?

ECLIPSE AUGUST 1999

Jesus said, of
The Heavenly Father:
"He will manifest Himself and
His Image is concealed by His Light."

TO SEE the unseen

A sudden revelation

THE ECLIPSE IS a wonderful way of bringing together so many people, all watching the same place in the heavens, during such a short period of time. Not an overshadowing in the spiritual sense (not yet) but certainly in a physical way.

THE SHADOW passed over many countries and peoples of the World; no matter what language, what colour their skin or what Faith, He touched the souls of each and every one of us in HIS own special way. He moves in mysterious ways, either we see it as a demonstration of His Presence and control of His creations or as just another scientific phenomenon within the laws of physics; but surely these laws only describe the perfection of His creations because He made it so. The laws of physics apply to materials which are already in existence. Even before 'The Big Bang', at the beginning of time, the material must have been there, somewhere, or was it also the moment of Creation? Does science have any way of thinking about where the material came from and can any laws apply to 'something' that does not yet exist?

MANY PEOPLE were watching this beautiful event. They certainly could not be making war at the same time, so He does intervene. There are many more spectacular phenomena He would bring about, if or when He thought it were necessary. It may be a long time before we all live in peace and tranquillity.

JESUS' constant request: *"Peace be with you."*

JESUS said: *"While we are children, we will see the rays of the sun, but not the power which created it."* (He indicates here that we may grow up, gain more wisdom, and know The Father.)

Simple video camera setup for recording the eclipse.

JESUS said: *"With the Angels of the Heavenly Father, will you learn to see the unseen."*

OUR CREATOR IS OUT THERE, HE IS HERE, EVERYWHERE
Jesus said, of The Heavenly Father:
"He will manifest Himself and His Image is concealed by His Light."

WE HAVE TOUCHED on this before, when Jesus spoke of His own birth, which was concealed by The Light of The Father; we also extend this point later. Yes! we have said this before, because there is so much to come, it cannot all be written on one page. As you will remember, we have had this problem from the outset. We have such joy from what we have found that we need to say it all at once. But alas, we are only human and have to convey our experiences in lengthy phrases, page after page. Now Jesus can do this for you in an 'instant'. All you need is to ask Him and a sudden revelation may occur. So you could stop at this moment and read no further. But you will continue to read and as you become part of the book, it will be your experience, your life, not ours, then you will want to tell everyone what you have found. A glorious moment !

Clouds thinned sufficiently to capture a few frames using special filters.

MOVING metal memories

MY MOTHER AND FATHER always got on well and stayed together throughout their life and into a reasonable old age, giving us a very stable home and happy life, which enabled us to cope with all the problems of our future in a very responsible manner.

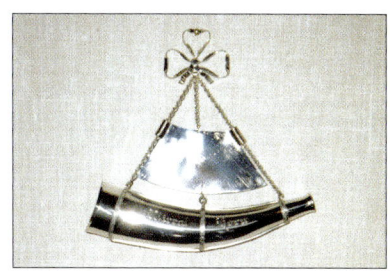

THERE WERE eventually three of us, all boys; six years after I was born my brother, Neil, arrived, who later became a well known Wirral Jeweller, designing and creating many wonderful pieces. One of these being a Silver Wirral Horn, which was presented to Prime Minister Margaret Thatcher by the local Conservative Party. My elder brother became a Chemist like myself.

Brother Neil and handcrafted silver horn.

BOTH PARENTS encouraged us to think, which is something very difficult to teach. Many people can accumulate a vast amount of knowledge and have the ability to remember it all, but it is an entirely different matter to be able to think creatively with what you know and bring together inspired ideas as a solution to a problem, or to originate something new.

I OFTEN RECALL what Albert Einstein is reported to have said: "I never commit anything to memory; it gives me more time to think but I know where I can find what I need".

DAD WOULD BE perhaps slightly pessimistic, he could see the pitfalls, difficulties and problems in doing something. He was always correct, because they were really there, and of course he could demonstrate it mathematically, legally, morally and in many other ways. Mum would come along, always an optimist, she could see a way forward, what if? Or could we try? Or maybe if it were upside down, or inside out, and she would get it done, with the help of one of the lads (as she called us), and of course, she too was always right. That is how they got on together and everything was always completed.

OF COURSE, there was the feeling that if Dad pointed out the pitfalls, he could safely leave it to us, Mum included, to get it done. And, because he had been to University, survived the First World War, complete with bullet holes and damaged knees, we knew he also must be right.

Mum and Dad, guiding hands.

ENCOURAGING US TO THINK STARTED EARLY

Father had a workshop and laboratory above his surgery and he stimulated our minds towards the sciences by some of the little 'tricks' he performed. They were not magic or conjuring as such, but the application of a known scientific principle to an alternative situation or everyday procedure.

Beautiful opal and silver cross, designed and crafted by my brother.

ONE DAY my elder brother and I were with him as he was working on a gold inlay for a tooth reconstruction. He filled a Pyrex glass beaker with very hot water, put a few drops of dark

Mystery metal rod melting at 71°C

blue dye in it, so you could not see the bottom, and secured it to the bench, so as not to knock it over. We thought it was part of one of his processes. Then he handed me a six inch long shiny metal rod, it was strong and heavy, and said: "Just stir that up for me."
Which I did, and to my surprise the rod got shorter and shorter, and in my astonishment I let go of it, and it disappeared altogether. I laughed: "Where's it gone?"
"Where's what gone?" Dad replied. "Oh! did I give you the metal rod? We'll find it in a minute."
He cooled the beaker and slowly poured away the blue water - nothing there! But when the beaker was completely empty, there was a flat sheet of shiny metal in the bottom.
"What do you think about that? What happened?" he said.
The real hidden 'trick' here was encouraging us to think; we continued to give him many explanations.
Then he said: "You're very close", and explained it to us.

HE HAD MADE the stirring rod earlier in the day out of 'Wood's Metal,' which melts at 71°C; well below boiling water at 100°C. It melted and sank to the bottom of the beaker as I stirred the liquid and, when cooled, became a solid flat sheet. The memory is with us for ever.

IN WRITING about these moments it is a shame we are not able to capture the smells and sounds that accompanied father's experiments, such as the hissing of the bunsen burner and the steaming pressure vessel for vulcanising some of the original dental plate materials, along with the smell of the sulphur vulcanising agent. The smell of old city coal gas, which was quite different from the North Sea gas of today; the smell of hot waxes and thermosetting plastics like 'Stellon' or polymethyl-methacrylate. (Yes! that name twice in one book). The strange aroma of wet Plaster of Paris as it warmed itself up while it was setting and in so doing expanded slightly to make a perfect cast.

ONE MEMORY evokes another and now, as adults, we realise that these are the memories upon which we have associated all our later acquired knowledge; so the more we learn in those early days from two years onwards, the more we remember, and the easier it should be to add to it.

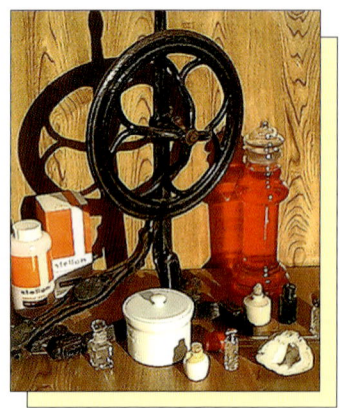

A corner of Dad's dental laboratory 1920's onwards.

THE SECRET for parents is to discover what their children can do well, then their whole future can develop around these abilities, rather than forcing them to achieve what is not within their make-up or our own aspirations for them.

THESE THOUGHTS and many more often come to mind when I see Uri Geller and others bending spoons, although I must point out that 'Wood's Metal' will not respond in this way, as temperatures near 71°C are too hot to hold. The URI phenomenon is quite different.

WHEN URI GELLER VISITED LIVERPOOL to appear at the Shakespeare venue, about the time of threats to his safety, I had asked the security personnel, who were there to look after him, if it could be arranged for us to meet?
"No it was not possible", was the reply.

I INTUITIVELY KNEW where he would be and I was there to greet him as he stepped from the car, well before the security people even knew he had arrived. I ushered him in through a side door of St. Georges Hotel, into the lift, up to Reception. The lift was like a steel box in effect with hardly any access to the lift shaft and had sliding sealed doors.

URI WAS VERY DISTRESSED, enclosed in this steel box, and I experienced the same sensations myself. It was as if we had been cut off from what we needed; we were very ill at ease and not happy until we reached the upper floor. I had booked a room for him in my own name for security reasons and we were almost there, when the security personnel suddenly realised he had arrived. We had time to chat briefly about mutual concerns; healing and creative forces, then 'security' demanded that I should leave, perhaps because they were embarrassed. I had been in the right place at the right time and they had not; but I had succeeded in discreetly looking after him and making an unseen entrance to the hotel.

WE WERE BOTH a little sad at this request, as there were many thing to discuss. So I set off for home and, before I arrived there, I understand Uri tried to telephone me, but to no avail. When I did finally arrive, it was late, so Uri had to reach me in another way, as I was chatting to my wife and family about the evening's events.

WE WERE STANDING by a small mirrored wall cabinet with two hinges on the door. This hinged mirror was opened and closed daily having been there for many years. While we were talking, the two stainless steel rods through the centre of each hinge began to slide downwards. We were able to observe this happening and a moment or two later they would have fallen to the floor, but with only one finger and a gentle push they were back were they should be and have stayed there, in their proper place, ever since. They cannot be pushed out; they fit too tightly.

FROM THIS EXPERIENCE and our brief conversations at St. Georges Hotel I know Uri Geller is absolutely genuine and is aware of many forces unknown to others.

THOUSANDS of years

I WOULD DESCRIBE his energies as being derived from our Creator's Presence. His work, demonstrations and abilities are possibly a test by our Creator to check if mankind is ready for truly unusual events, before the real spiritual overshadowing takes place, which will bring the revelations of The Holy Spirit and Jesus Himself to mankind.

• Top: Hinge in cabinet
• Bottom: Hinge centre rod

THIS MAY SOUND rather strange, but we believe that mankind has been tested many times over the years, in different ways, and has always been unprepared for the REAL EVENT and often quite antagonistic towards remarkable occurrences. God must be deeply saddened by this passage of thousands of years, for us to realise That We Are Not Alone.

WE SPEND most of our time seeking pleasure and escaping from pain, rather than experiencing the value of truth, because so few accept the REALITY of His Presence.

NATURE'S sculptures

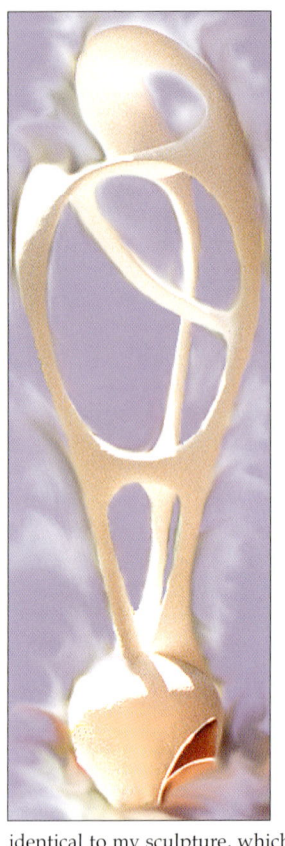

- Left: Large white sculpture completed in 1972.
- Top: Beautiful mauve Campanula flower, more variations below.

THERE ARE MANY paintings, sculptures, photographs and poems placed throughout the book which were created while developing Contact with our Creator.

THIS LARGE WHITE sculpture in the Healing Garden I completed in about 1972 while constantly feeling God's Presence, and twenty years later, in 1992, a group of lovely mauve, bell-shaped flowers grew close by it. The centre of these flowers, to my astonishment, had a structure almost identical to my sculpture, which indicates, there is nothing mankind can create which has not already had its origin in God's Mind, and it is far more beautiful and delicate than my structure. Part of my soul must have indeed experienced His Presence, before I had even seen the centre of His flower (a Campanula).

THESE FLOWERS had not been planted but probably grew from seeds dropped by the many dozens of different birds which visit our garden each year. We often feel that the public should be forgiven for thinking scientists create scares about many things, so they can seek funding for research into the situation, which they may have indeed created themselves, and seek even more funds to solve the problem. They look in the wrong places for the missing birds, animals, insects, and plant species. We all know many are not where they used to be, having moved away from the countryside because man has changed their habitat, forcing them to take up residence in the towns and cities, so why count those still left in the country? Then declare them nearly extinct, when many have merely moved home to a more hospitable place.

NATURE'S moving sculptures

THERE ARE many little creatures passing through our garden each day and the birds are too numerous to mention, including the diminishing species. All is well with God's Gardens of the World. He moves them to be in places where they are wanted, in a habitat that suits them.

THE SALT marsh plants grow in estuaries washed by sea salt waters, not necessarily because they thrive on salt but because very little else will grow there, so they have plenty of room. And if you are counting red squirrels, it is to no avail standing in the middle of a salt marsh and saying: "Alas they are extinct", for there are none there anyway and never have been. Obtaining funding for this research, looking in the wrong place, would be more than difficult!!

ULTRAVIOLET LIGHT is another interesting research project. Nearly everyone seems to be concerned about the levels of ultraviolet radiations increasing, due to ozone depletion in the upper atmosphere, and great sums of money are spent on new research into the protection of humans.

WE HAVE BEEN MONITORING ultraviolet radiations directly from the sun since May 1987, here in Formby at sea level, and contrary to popular scientific belief, we have found that ultraviolet light is NOT increasing, but DECREASING!! Very interesting !!

MISLEADING INFORMATION

WE HAVE the feeling we are only being told what someone wants us to know. We need to find out more for ourselves, rather like taking our health back into our own hands. This research has taken over twelve years and the results are not what we had expected. It also coincides with a period of great increase in the number of aircraft trails across the skies, each one of which absorbs ultraviolet light and spreads over many square miles of sky. Another coincidence is the abominable increase in the number of cars and other transport vehicles producing 'particulates', ozone and other chemicals by the activity of sunlight, which are all acting as ground level filters absorbing the ultraviolet light.

THERE IS NO NEED for numbers and graphs here, we feel the words explain it all quite well, and we all know that sometimes you have to hail a taxi just to cross the road.

SO IT IS NOT only the application of high 'Sun Protection Factor' creams we should be concerned about, but also the elimination of toxic pollutants in the atmosphere we breathe. This may be partly achieved by using air filtration systems at work and at home and installing negative ionisers. Thoughts should also be given to limiting the use of sunbeds.

NOT ONE
natural cloud in sight!

THERE IS NOT ONE natural cloud in sight in this photograph; only aircraft vapour trails against a beautiful blue summer sky. We had only one blue sky day this year. Usually the haze is even thicker than this and the ultraviolet levels reaching the surface of the earth can be reduced by as much as 25%, all year round. Where are all the ultraviolet levels increasing, we may ask?

THE CAR AND PLANE are here to stay, but business methods change and develop using science and technology, so fewer people will need to travel as we become more involved in the new digital future, where decisions will be made at the speed of light rather than the speed of sound. Perhaps in the future, at the speed of thought?

WHO WILL NEED TO GO ANYWHERE?

GOD's Garden

THEN THE AIR we breathe will purify the body and the water we drink will detoxify the tissues, with not having collected all the pollutants from the air on the way down. We may once again enjoy God's Garden and live our lives as He intended, if we use our new found sciences with wisdom and understanding to work with Him and not against Him. Then the future will be beyond all scientific imagination. We need to feel His Presence and have Him with us each moment of every day, as much more will be achieved in this way.

THIS LAST COMMENT becomes more understandable as we think about it, for we have already quoted:

"Six days shalt thou labour; the seventh is God's day of rest."

BUT IF WE think of it as one seventh of the week is God's day, then also one hour in seven is His, one minute in seven, and then one second in every seven seconds is His moment of rest, or at least should be a recognition of His Presence. This is still equivalent to only one seventh of the week. However, one second in every seven feels like all the time, so have Him with you always; do nothing for which you have to cut Him out of your life to do it. Pause a second longer and ask Him to help you avoid it.

MANY PEOPLE are constantly searching for a sign, a cross, a face of Jesus appearing in the trees or in the sky and other places. These in some way stimulate the ability to experience His Presence but should only be a guide, to bring us back from where we have strayed, so that once again we can truly Feel His Presence as a 'direct' communication with each one of us.

THIS BEAUTIFUL clover plant grew in the grass where someone stood, who had been touched by God's Presence and made well again. It produced just one stalk with four leaves. The next year it gave one flower with an extra three components opening at the top of a little stalk rising from the centre of the flower, in the shape of a CROSS. Unfortunately producing no seeds for its perpetuation, as it had no need to do so; having already achieved its purpose.

● Top: Clover cross
● Centre: Cross forming
● Lower: 4 leaf clover

61

MARK of the cross

Potato and starch

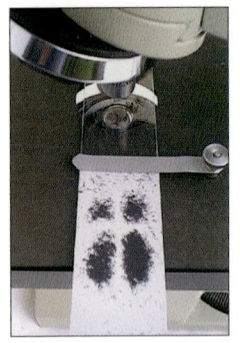

View of cross in one grain

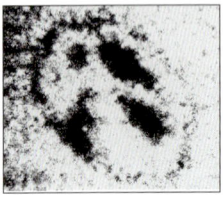

A cross in another grain

THERE HAS TO BE A PURPOSE for wanting to Feel His Presence, perhaps to benefit mankind; to prevent our destruction, by our own hand; to understand His Mysteries; to increase in true wisdom, not just worldly wisdom; to preserve and perpetuate future generations; to care for this wonderful planet and serve His Creative Purpose. All these, and many more, are strengthened by a loss or need, and superb creative work always follows suffering, but must never be inflicted upon any living creature, for this shrivels and closes up the special place within us, where our soul and spirit have contact with HIM.

EVEN THE STARCH grains of a humble potato show a cross under the microscope, in polarised light. The Cross is not just symbolic, because Jesus knew He was here on Earth to be Crucified on The Cross to save us all. We have been trying to obtain a few grains of starch from the genetically modified potato, which was toxic to mice, to check if the cross is still present, but we have not yet been able to do so!!

THIS STRANGE CROSS is produced within the starch grains, by differing degrees of rotation of polarised light, by its structure. Does this also relate in some obscure way to Jesus' reference to light and God's concealment, and that His sign within us is a movement and a rest? This is so with everything, for without movement and rotation even the elements would cease to be. The rotation of light is the movement and the rests are dark segments in between the cross. God is in all things; it is always up to us to find Him. It seems scientifically far-fetched but it may serve His purpose and return a few more souls to Him. Think about this when you next enjoy His hidden Presence in the most humble of foods.

BEFORE EASTER these beautiful Honesty flowers appeared, with a white cross at their centres, and all those that opened after Easter Sunday were the normal purple colour, and on the same plant; once again in the Garden where so many people have been touched by God's Presence and made well again. This has occurred a few times over the past years.

IT MAY BE possible to explain it away but, as God made all these wonderful structures, can we not allow Him to show His Touch from time to time, and at such a meaningful moment as Easter? But, as always, the belief or rejection is up to you. We find Him and know Him, or avoid His Presence altogether, often by pretending a scientific explanation is satisfactory, when really it only describes something He has already created in the first place.

HE HAS HIS PULSE in every living cell and can change it in an instant, or perpetuate the change through His DNA genetic codes.

Jesus said: "Even the hairs of your head are numbered."

SIGN of the cross

ALL WHO SEE IT . . . will remember

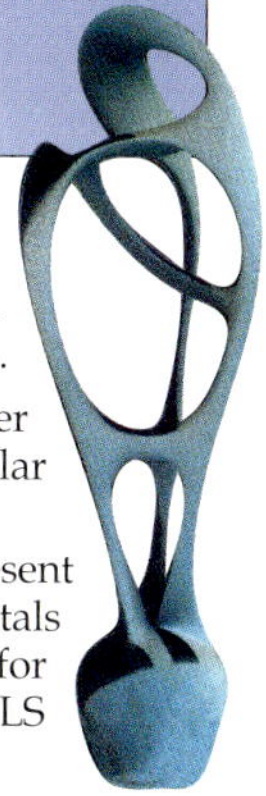

THE PASSIONFLOWER

ALTHOUGH there are many legends concerning the passionflower, not one appears to fit or belong. But it would seem very obvious from these beautiful photographs that it does contain a very powerful cross.

JUST BEFORE the flower closes, the centre comes together and forms this lovely sculpture, which is again very similar to the inspired sculpture in the Healing Garden.

SOME INTERPRETATIONS believe the ten sepals represent the Ten Commandments. The corona of blue-tipped petals indicate the Crown of Thorns, the five yellow stamens for Five Wounds and the divided stigma for the THREE NAILS of the CROSS.

THE DOGWOOD LEGEND

SO FIRM and strong was the dogwood tree that it was chosen for the wood of the Cross. This greatly distressed the tree. Jesus sensed the torment and, in His understanding of all suffering, said to it:

"Because of your regret and sadness, never again shall the dogwood tree grow large enough to be used as a cross. From now on it shall be slender and its flowers shall take the form of a cross: two long and two short petals.

ON THE outer edge of each short petal there will be nail prints, brown with rust and stained with red, and in the centre of the flower will be a crown of thorns, and all who see it will remember."

OPERA and rock'n'roll

OUR WHOLE FAMILY HAD BENEFITED greatly from our Creative Thinking Experiments, before the Healing took us over. My wife Brenda, qualified as a Chiropodist, well before I became a Chemist, and we married in 1953. She has always been a wonderful mother to our two children and became a superb pianist and opera singer. A genuine Christian, she has kept our feet firmly on the ground, helping us to relate Jesus' sayings to the real world of today.

OUR SON Paul spent his early years reaching audiences with his deeply moving interpretations, as a Cabaret singer in many Hotels and 'Nitespots' in different parts of the world. The youngsters would 'rock and roll' and enjoy all Paul's exotic rhythms, the Grannies and Grandads would waltz and sing to their special ballads and then there would be moments of moving tranquillity with some of his deeply spiritual songs.

Brenda - special talents

AT THE END of each evening members of the audience would go up to the stage to shake his hands but what intrigued us most of all was the number of disabled and perplexed people, who would also be up there, and they just wanted to hug him, with no words but sometimes with tears. He has a wonderful ability to reach everyone with his voice, a very precious gift indeed, but because of increased transport problems he gave this up to continue his life long research into chance phenomena and their relationship to a multitude of known and unknown variables.

DURING THE HEALING work of Heather and myself, Paul and my wife often presented us with deep searching questions. The answers were always in the Sayings of Jesus.

MY WIFE AND I would travel with Paul to most of his engagements, as we enjoyed listening to him sing, and with her special talents my wife often accompanied him on the keyboard. On one occasion we were trying to locate the venue for that evening and stopped the car in the suburbs to ask directions to the centre of the city. I leaned out of the window and enquired from a young man walking along on his own:

"How could we get there?" In a soft lilting Irish voice he said: "Well if I were you, I wouldn't start from here."

WE HAVE LAUGHED about this many times since then, even during difficult moments, as he has sung all over Britain and other countries of the world, often preparing for the evening show in a top class dressing room and even in the dingiest of broom closets. If you can laugh in one of these while you prepare to go on stage, you can cope with anything that life may throw at you.

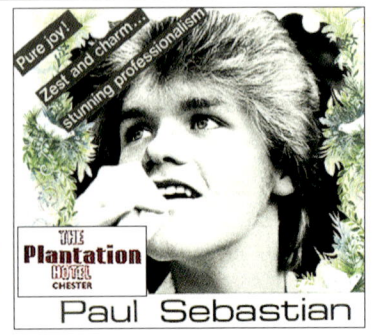

A few of the many locations where Paul has performed.

BENEFITS of laughter

DURING MY RESEARCH into the healing effects of laughter, when Heather and Paul were only small children, I was asked to prepare some humorous material for the Eamonn Andrews television show, which not everyone will still remember.

I SUPPLIED many items and found the audience responses were very interesting scientifically, as all my work was clean and simple.

THE surprise needed for a laugh to arise could be achieved without the use of any bad language, swear words or any references to bodily functions, devious human activities, and was enjoyed by all age groups.

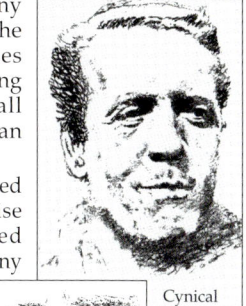

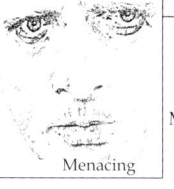

EAMONN ANDREWS talking on his programme about these drawings by Alan Fraser Bell

Spike Milligan
Woody Allen
Dawn Adams
Michael Bentine

Production Team
ROY BOTTOMLEY
TOM BRENNAND
TOM CLEGG
MALCOLM MORRIS

Cynical
Menacing

Drawings of Patrick McGoohan

THE EARLY creative thinking experiments

THESE HELPED me to sketch some of the 'stars' at that time, who appeared on the Eamonn Andrews show. They were drawn from the screen and, of course, were in black and white as we had no colour or video recorders in those days and Eamonn presented them on his programme.

EVEN EARLIER than this I had met Alastair Sim at The Little Theatre in Southport in the 1940's. He was in the audience watching a first night performance of Cyril Luckham in a play. He was even more remarkable to meet in person, only a small movement of his eyes or mouth could convey immense humour or sadness. He has added so much to the lives of everyone who has seen his work or met him.

LAUGHTER experiment

THIS IS VERY SIMPLE and will only take a few minutes to read, but is of great benefit to health and well-being, as laughter produces wonderful effects in the mind. As we all know, it is a joy, a happiness and a superb tonic with strengthening recuperative properties. Usually it is a spontaneous phenomenon but can be brought about in the following manner.

Ha! ha! ha!

HAVE TWO OR THREE friends with you; each person merely has to say the word - Ha! You all say it together, one - two - three - - - - Ha! Then a moment later you all repeat it, but this time say - Ha! - Ha! In other words, say it twice close together. Continue adding one extra Ha! each time you repeat them, so that the next repeat becomes - Ha! - Ha! - Ha! and so on. Sooner or later one of you will go out of step with one of the - Ha's. Then it sounds like real laughter, suddenly taking on reality and everyone is having a good time without a joke in sight.

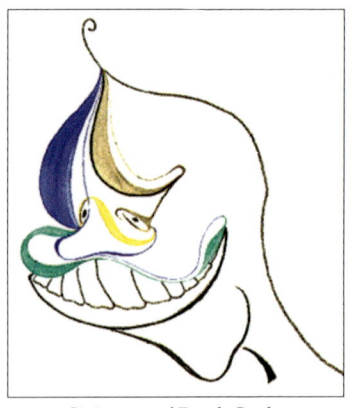

Caricature of Patrick Moore

Caricature of Derek Guyler

TO MAKE IT EVEN EASIER, you should exhale a puff of air when saying each - Ha! Try to analyse the state of mind existing during and after the laughter session; then try to experience the feeling without laughing first. In other words attempt to reach a state of happiness within the mind without any reason or cause. While you are in this condition it is impossible for you to think unkind, unpleasant or evil thoughts about anyone or anything, so it now becomes easier to to be aware of God's Presence and Jesus is happy to be with you.

DO NOT FORGET, all the experiments mentioned throughout the text are not just to read about, they should be performed and each successful outcome should be analysed to enable you to ease into that state, without always having to use the experiment.

LIKE FATHER like daughter

Early Morning

Millions of glistening droplets of dew,
Adorn the earth with a breathtaking view.
Emerald leaves shimmer in delight.
As another new day is born from the night.

The sun rises in a haze of gold.
Delicate flowers gently unfold.
Birds sing in melodious song.
One great and joyful throng.

Everything is fresh and new.
From pink apple blossom, to sky so blue.
It is on a day such as this,
That the world is perfect bliss.

God speaks to man:
"I speak to you through the dew of the morning. Be still, know I am God."

HEATHER has been brought up within a background of Creative Thinking and her sensitive soul has helped us all to experience God's Presence in the way we have. We are deeply aware of His continuous contact.

DURING our development Heather began writing many beautiful poems and superb stories with brilliant paintings and drawings. She also makes a remarkable scientist, by always asking one more question when others have given up the search, and the answers arise as if from another mind.

As she said, "Like father - Like daughter." Our wisdom and guidance comes from God.

HER WORKS have been presented to the various producers of Starsky and Hutch, Dr. Who and the many people in her drawings. Heather takes up the story on the next page:

LIVING words

MY BROTHER and I remember a childhood filled with imaginative games; awe and delight in God's creatures; the laughter and warm security of a close family. We remember watching Dad creating sculptures and Mum's 'Ave Maria' drifting up the stairs, as we fell asleep listening to her singing at the piano.

THESE MEMORIES interrupted by those days at school - when a free spirit tried to conform.
After the first day at school, I said to Dad:
"I've been to school, now what shall we do tomorrow?"
He forgot to tell me that this went on for years!

READING exercises of English Literature and Comprehension, long passages that seemed uninspiring and difficult to hold my attention. Then came the day of discovery; some unknown fictional adventure that suddenly absorbed and captured my imagination, transporting me into another world, creating places, characters and emotions where time and the surroundings blurred into the distance.

David Carradine of 'Kung Fu'

THE WORDS had come alive and since then, I've written many stories, including poetry, romantic fiction and dramas for favourite television heroes. Some drawings and an editor's letter are included here.

I ALSO gained typing/word processing qualifications and followed a typesetting and publishing career with the Liverpool Daily Post & Echo/Mirror Group newspapers as a Pre-press Supervisor.

ALL THESE achievements culminating in the creation of this book with my Dad. A most gentle, unselfish and kind man; his life's work has been unique and special, each step leading us along a path of discovery which is now encapsulated within these texts.

A BOOK that we feel has come alive in our hands, each page unfolding a part of the truth that will catch your breath and transport you into another dimension of belief. In much the same way as those early pages caught my childhood imagination . . .

BUT THIS TIME the
message and story are
SO REAL, SO SPECIAL,
SO ULTIMATELY MOVING.
Although we are in the
New Millennium,
The JESUS MESSAGE
Is TIMELESS . . .

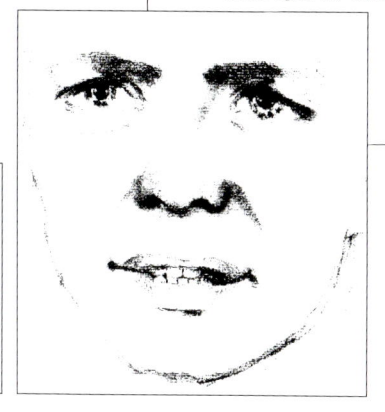

SGP
Spelling-Goldberg Productions • 20th Century Fox Studios • Los Angeles, California 90064

January 31, 1977

Ms. Heather Louise Bell
56 Andrews Lane
Formby
Liverpool L37 2EW
ENGLAND

Dear Ms. Bell:

Thanks you so much for your letter and script of December 4, 1976. I am sorry it has taken a while to get back to you, the mail tends to pile up faster than we can get to it around here.

Unfortunately, while I enjoyed reading your script and I appreciate all the effort and thought you put into it, company policy prohibits our using any material not submitted through an accreditted agent, by a member of the Writers Guild of America. I realize this must be disappointing to you, but I would like to congratulate you of a fine effort. I read many scripts and stories sent in by fans, and yours was certainly a cut above the rest.

Thanks again for thinking of us.

Sincerely,

Michael Fisher
STARSKY AND HUTCH
Story Editor

● Above: Letter from
Michael Fisher,
STARSKY & HUTCH,
Story Editor.

● Left: David Soul of
'Starsky & Hutch'

ULTERIOR MOTIVE - hidden agenda

DAD CONTINUES . . .

I KEPT IN TOUCH with one teacher from a previous school, who was very interested in my scientific experiments, but always seemed 'pushed for time.' On one occasion, during a visit to his home, we discussed some of the unusual plastic materials I had been working with, as they were quite new to him.

HE WAS VERY CLEVER, intellectual, brilliant in fact, and abruptly, after about fifteen minutes, he said he was going into town to do some shopping; he would come along with me, there was a bus in a few minutes.

WE REACHED the town centre and he said:
"Cheerio, let me know how you get on."

I MADE MY WAY towards the railway station, then stopped to look behind, to see which shop he was going into, and to my surprise he had crossed the road and was standing in the opposite bus queue to return home; he was not shopping at all. He was teaching me lessons even at that age, although he never knew it. This was the easiest way of saying my time was up, without hurting my feelings, and he had at least given me some of his valuable attention, but he had also learned something new about a synthetic plastic, which was not yet available.

THIS WAS THE FIRST moment I realised how brilliant people like himself always underestimate everyone else; I had rumbled his ploy, and this has helped me to find truth and reality in everyone I meet. With this knowledge I helped many people to survive the wartime years that followed and soon realised very few ever say what they really mean; there often seems to be an ulterior motive, or in modern terms a hidden agenda.

ONLY JESUS MEANT exactly what He said; we can believe Him and we have grown to rely upon Him. Although much of His wisdom has been interpreted in the present day to coincide with modern thinking, we still think of His words as He spoke them 2000 years ago. That is how He intended them to be.

WEIGHING time

GOD'S PRESENCE has always been a great comfort and support when life's difficulties have been stacked against me.

DURING MY PHARMACY student days I was always slower than everyone else but I was frequently commended on the superb quality of my dispensing, the preparation of mixtures, ointments, pills and lotions, and the accuracy of my analytical and bacteriological work. They repeatedly said I would never get enough done to pass the final examination, so when all the numbers were allocated to identify each student, they saved unlucky No. 13 for me, because they said it would not make any difference, as I was not going to pass anyway.

I APPRECIATED THEIR JOKE but what the Principal of the Establishment did not

Old chemist shop items

know was that 13 has always been very lucky for me and I passed first time with distinction. Even so, I have never been able to attach much importance to any number, although 28 has a life of its own as described earlier, but most important is the 7th day of rest, having worked for six.

THERE WAS A REASON for the apparent slowness in all my work. I was not just doing enough to get the job done and go home early, I was exploring and experimenting along the way. I was in fact gaining more from my alternative activities and observations than my fellow students, not in a big headed manner, but to me it was all very fascinating, thrilling scientific work, and this was my opportunity of a lifetime, a wonderful experience, not something that had to be endured to qualify, but an enjoyment.

Analysis

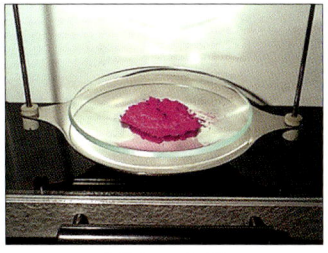

WEIGHING belief?

IT WAS DURING ONE of these early time consuming other activities, when I began to observe an unusual phenomenon. This only occurred occasionally and seemed to depend upon what I was thinking about at the time. Briefly: I was weighing out a small quantity of a chemical substance on a very sensitive enclosed scientific balance. I had completed the process and it was balanced at 2.624g.

2.624g. or is it?

I SUDDENLY THOUGHT the amount of powder looked very much larger than a similar sample I had weighed out earlier in the day. At the very moment of my thought process the balance pan, with the powder on it, began to move down and stayed down. The sample had apparently increased in weight by over 30mg. I walked away and asked a friend to check the weight for me and returned when he had finished.

"Yes," he said, "2.624g."

WHICH WAS the same as my original weight and, as I still thought it seemed to be a larger sample, I watched and pondered and again it increased in weight, but not by quite as much this time; my conviction must have diminished by a few milligrams. Is it possible (I thought) that belief can be quantified, even as a few milligrams?

THIS GAVE ME my first 'almost' scientific evidence, that you can affect the physical world by what you think or believe. It began to become apparent that no experiment performed by a thinking human being, scientist or otherwise, can take place devoid of interference by their mind.

THIS MAY BE WHY some scientists can repeat a positive experiment because they believe it will work, while others, who do not even think it is possible, usually get negative results, and of course these are the researchers who publish, the others are a little more wary of their reputations. But, for the sceptics, there is nothing to lose if they find a negative result, so they go into print.

IF I HAD EXPRESSED thoughts like these while I was still a student, I probably would not even have been given No. 13 as an Examination number.

Willing it to move

BELIEVER or sceptic?

THERE IS A WONDERFUL experiment, using a paper cylinder instead of a microbalance, in which you will try to make it rotate, just by thinking about it. Do this and be astonished, then you will know what the experience is like, for at this moment you only think you know the answer. During the cylinder experiment you will increase your ability to become more aware of our Creator's Presence.

WE ARE PROBABLY using the same brain cells during these moments of extending our thoughts outside the skull, as we would use to feel God's Presence. Do remember that you are performing these experiments on your abilities; you are the experiment, you are not just observing something happening in front of you; you are making it happen. Do not even think this is impossible; make it possible, 'WILL' it to rotate, because most minds cannot hold two opposing thoughts at the same time. BE POSITIVE!

HOW WILL YOU APPROACH THIS? AS A BELIEVER OR A SCEPTIC?

THE CYLINDER experiment

Influencing inanimate objects by thought. (Mind Contact)

SOME EXPERIMENTS have been carried out using dice, in which the 'power' of thought was employed to influence what figures would turn up when the dice were thrown, say a six or a two, or whatever was in the operator's mind at the time. Beware of people with a six on every side!!!

APART FROM THE DICE being rather a heavy object to influence, precognition and chance also enter into such experiments, so we would suggest the use of a rotating paper cylinder, pivoted on a needle point and balanced on a slender glass or plastic upturned bottle.

CONSTRUCT a paper cylinder as per the dimensions shown.

● Fig. 1. Cut a piece of fairly light note paper, about 8 inches long and 4 inches deep.

NOTE:
You may wish to paint vertical stripes on the outer surface to make its rotation more obvious. Use a dye or coloured ink for this and not a pigment containing metal compounds, which may interfere with the rotation. It is easier to do this when the paper is flat.

● Fig. 2. Shape the paper into a curve, in preparation for making the cylinder. See facing page.

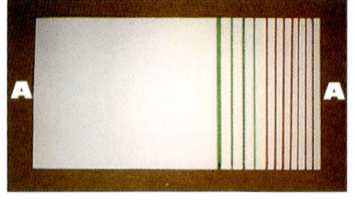

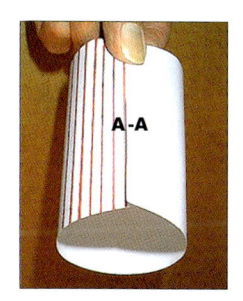

● Fig. 3. Form this into a cylinder by gumming the edges A - A together using about an eighth of an inch overlap.

● Fig. 4. Now measure across the top of the cylinder, the distance (D) the diameter, and cut a strip of postcard (C) half an inch longer than the measurement (D) and a quarter of an inch wide. Then fold down at right angles a quarter of an inch piece at each end of the strip (C).

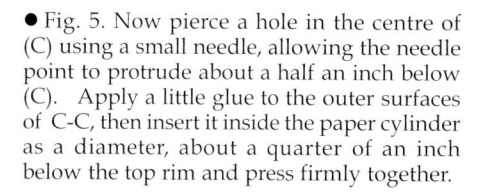

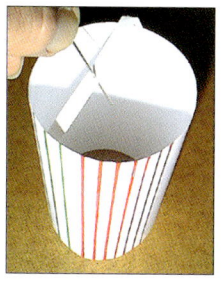

● Fig. 5. Now pierce a hole in the centre of (C) using a small needle, allowing the needle point to protrude about a half an inch below (C). Apply a little glue to the outer surfaces of C-C, then insert it inside the paper cylinder as a diameter, about a quarter of an inch below the top rim and press firmly together.

● Fig. 6. Place the prepared cylinder over a thin glass or plastic upturned container, with the needle point pivoted on top.

CHECK the cylinder, to make sure it rotates freely in either direction, so as not to touch the supporting container at all.

YOU ARE NOW READY FOR THE EXPERIMENT

SEATED AT A TABLE, set the cylinder in front of you, so it will rotate freely. Rest your elbows on the table for comfort, place your hands one on either side and about three inches from the cylinder.

THIS SHOULD BE performed in a draught free room, with the doors and windows closed, and you should take care not to lean over the cylinder and not to breathe on it.

NOW IN YOUR MIND
'WILL' the cylinder to rotate.

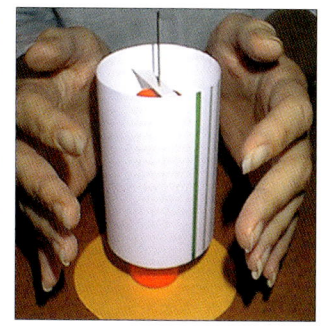

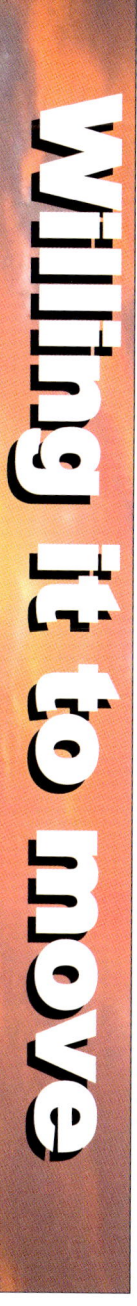

71

MIND

YOU WILL FIND the cylinder responds to your thoughts right from the beginning and an unusual sensation develops on the top of your head, which is not very easy to describe, as we are sure that the experience is not quite the same for everyone. You may feel it as a coolness, or as if your head extends a few inches beyond the top of your skull. It is a pleasant sensation, almost of elation or excitement, or as if you are with someone who is responding, like a two way conversation.

PERHAPS START by 'willing' the cylinder to rotate clockwise, then 'will' it to stop and restart, perhaps rotating in an anticlockwise direction this time. You should be alone during this procedure, to prevent any interference from another person's mind.

THE FACT THAT IT ESCAPES description does not really matter but it is important you are able to recognise it, as it feels to you, so you can analyse it, think about it, and reproduce it without always having to use the cylinder experiment.

THIS LAST POINT is very important, you must try to reproduce the sensation without using the cylinder. But first you must sense it, then continue to repeat the procedure until you can easily produce these feelings.

AT THESE MOMENTS there is an outflow of information or 'vibrational' energy of some kind from you, during which the mind may also have acquired incoming material or knowledge that previously it did not possess. This is the frame of mind in which you can experience God's Presence. In other words you are not locked into the physical world, as if nothing else exists. There is much more to this life than most of us are aware.

THERE IS ALWAYS the chance you may think you are fooling yourself, that you are really breathing on the cylinder, or there is a draught blowing, or someone else could say there is, or they may offer a plausible reason for the rotation, but do not let this bother you. Ask them to try it for themselves, then there will be some explaining to do!

ERECT A TRANSPARENT rigid plastic cover over the experiment, as an added protection for the cylinder; make elasticated openings for your arms to enter, or even a 'polythene' bag, with a wooden or wire frame to make it rigid. The walls of this bag must not be allowed to move, as it would cause air movement inside the cover. Place your arms and hands inside, keep them still and repeat the mental requests for the cylinder to rotate.

ROTATION INSIDE A CLOSED GLASS VESSEL

THE CYLINDER may be set up on the inside of the lid of an inverted wide mouthed glass jar, and then the jar screwed tightly but gently into the lid, without disturbing the pivoted cylinder. Make sure it is still able to rotate without touching the sides of the covering jar or the support pedestal. Do not have the jar too wide, so when your hands are placed by the cylinder, outside the jar, they are about three inches distant

CONTACT

from the cylinder as before. The height of the jar is not important. An empty 'fizzy' lemonade 2 litre plastic bottle could be used for simplicity; just cut off the top and turn it over. It is not as complicated as it reads and can soon be achieved with very little effort, but is well worth the time.

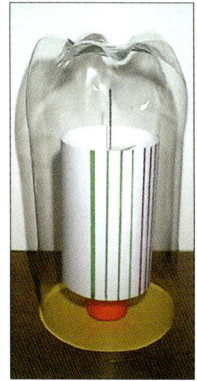

YOU WILL FIND the cylinder is still capable of being controlled by the mind but it requires a little longer to respond and does not always rotate quite as fast. We must point out that a very positive attitude is needed; there is no value in the experiment if you ask the cylinder to rotate while your mind is occupied by thoughts of it not being possible inside a glass jar. This is your Negative Gene rearing its ugly head. Remember, your mind cannot hold two opposing ideas at the same time. Either you are 'willing' it to rotate or you are not, because you cannot believe it; so be positive and you will never forget the experience.

PLEASE READ THE LAST PARAGRAPH AGAIN.
We must also repeat; although this is a scientific experiment, you are not just an observer of something which is taking place on its own, you are actually making it come about. Therefore you must not even entertain the thought 'I wonder if it will happen?' It is you who is making it happen.

Inverted container

NOW GET READY FOR THIS!!
ROTATION OF THE CYLINDER AT A DISTANCE

USING the original set up, with the uncovered pivoted cylinder on a table in a draught free room, sit some distance away from it, about three yards to start with, and then increase the distance when you have achieved good results. Sit in a comfortable chair, in a relaxed position, so you can concentrate on what you are doing, then 'will' the cylinder to rotate. At this distance you need have no fear of breathing on it. Perform the same sort of experiments as before; revolving clockwise or anticlockwise, then to stop, start and stop again. Amaze yourself! Repeat the procedure, perhaps after using the mind stimulating methods and/or meditating, which we write about later.

ONCE AGAIN try to analyse the sensations which occur on the top of your head and then attempt to create these feelings without using the cylinder.

WE FIND that it responds better at a distance when we have a light shining on us, rather than shining on the cylinder, providing it is not too bright, to impair our view of the experiment. You may also wish to improve on these ideas.

IT IS DURING these altered states of consciousness that spontaneous creative activity occurs in the brain and unusual sounds or sensations may become apparent; in the left ear in most males or in the right ear in females. Make notes of any other experiences.

DETECTION OF SUBSTANCES
by mind contact

THIS IS CLOSELY related to the ability to rotate a paper cylinder but in a different manner. Here the hand is acting as an extension of the brain, through the nervous system, to detect the presence of various substances hidden under a large piece of thick brown paper, or similar material.

HAVE AN ASSISTANT place small pieces of various metals, such as iron, copper, zinc, nickel, aluminium, and non-metals such as carbon, rock sulphur, glass, plastics and others, on a table and cover them over with brown paper or thick opaque white paper. It would be interesting for you to note any different sensations between the metals mentioned above, as some of them occur during the transition from the first group of 28 elements to the second group, as on pages No. 29 - 30.

Objects for detection, six inches apart to allow the hand to determine different sensations.

THIS PREPARATION should be completed in your absence. Now place your outstretched arm with the palm of your hand downwards, over the paper, about two inches above the surface, and move it from side to side, until the whole area has been traversed. Mark on the paper with a coloured soft felt pen, each time you feel a tingle, or any other sensation in your fingers or palm of the hand. Do not press on the paper when marking it, to prevent the sample from showing through, if it should be there, and do not use your 'detecting' hand for making the marks.

THIS EXPERIMENT may be repeated over and over again, using a different coloured pen on each occasion, and then the same procedure using the other hand. Make a note, as you go along, of which colour is the first, second, or third experiment, of left or right hand. Then, without disturbing anything, feel through the paper from the top surface and locate each sample, drawing round its outline, so that when you have finished, the coloured marks and the shapes of the samples will be visible on the upper surface of the paper.

Detecting hidden items

LIFTING UP THE paper carefully, make a note of what the material was of each sample and try to remember, or make notes of, any differences in the sensations when your hand was over the various specimens, to help with your experiments on future occasions.

THIS TECHNIQUE INCREASES the ability to become aware of extrasensory information and should be developed to benefit Creative Thinking and experiencing God's Presence.

DURING THIS PROCEDURE you should be examining the sensations occurring within the brain and in the hands. It is not important to be able to reproduce those experiences in the hands but it is important for you to develop their sensitivity, so they can be successfully directed during any healing work you may wish to pursue. For Healing others is something we should all be involved in, it is not just for a few, but is a natural gift we all have, although not used by many people, because the negative gene overwhelms the belief systems.

NATURAL HEALING WITH GOD'S PRESENCE SHOULD BE THE FIRST LINE OF THOUGHT, NOT THE LAST RESORT. YOU ONLY HAVE TO ASK FOR HIS HELP, EVEN IF MEDICINES AND CHEMICAL PREPARATIONS ARE ALSO BEING USED.

DIVINING or DOWSING

THIS PHENOMENON should be classified here under 'Mind Contact', as it really has very little to do with any property of hazel twigs or 'divining rods'. It is the mind that detects the water or the minerals under the ground and then transmits messages to the hands, in subtle ways of which we are not aware, and they subconsciously move and make the hazel twig twitch, dip downwards or flip upwards or, in the case of 'rods', makes them cross over each other or diverge.

THIS IS QUITE different from people saying, you moved them yourself. You did not; they were moved by a subconscious link between your mind and hands and you are only aware of the movement as it occurs.

Fig. 1.
THE SIMPLEST WAY of developing this extrasensory ability is by using thin metal 'rods'. These may be made by bending $1/8$th inch (3mm.) thick wire at right angles, with one limb about fourteen inches long and the other one about four inches long.

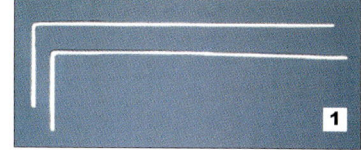

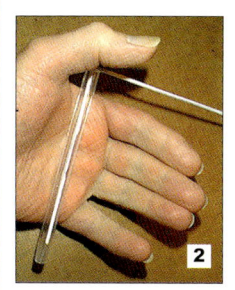

Fig. 2.
THE SHORT four inch limb could be inserted in a ball point pen holder with the ink tube and ball removed.

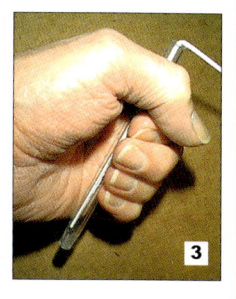

Fig. 3.
THIS WOULD allow for the free rotation of the 'rods' when grasped in the semi-clenched hand.

Fig. 4.
TWO OF THESE are used; one is held in each hand, with the elbows gently pressed into the waist, and the arms and hands slightly forward. Allow the 'rods' to rest lightly in the semi-clenched, but tension free hand, with the long limb of each 'rod' protruding forward and hanging downwards by just two or three degrees, so they do not go swinging round like the fingers of a demented clock.

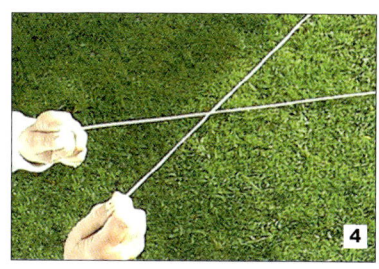

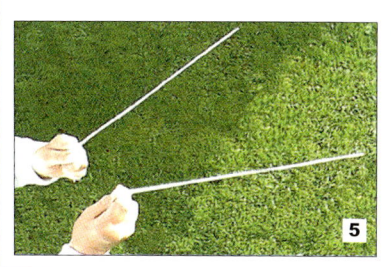

Fig. 5.
ASK SOMEONE TO bury metal objects in the soil or under the grass without your knowledge of their positions; then walk over the area, systematically covering the ground, and watch for the dowsing 'rods' to cross over or diverge, as in Fig. 4 and 5.

'I AM SEARCHING'

THERE IS NO POINT in being haphazard about this dowsing experiment. You should know what metal you are looking for, so you can walk about with the thought in your mind: 'I am searching for copper or iron or whatever was buried'.

YOU MAY ARRANGE for a container of water to be buried, but be reasonable and do not bury it in a marsh, get to know what you are capable of doing; choose dry ground but do not let anyone leave telltale marks, they should rake the whole area after covering the container. You will probably notice that the 'rods' move in a different manner to the occasion when the copper or iron was located, thereby, you are building up a pattern of movements produced by several different materials, which will be useful on future dowsings.

YOU COULD THEN walk over a patch of land, searching for water only, or iron only, and you would know exactly when it had been located. The main requirements for this experiment are belief that you can do it and a positive request to your mind; you are searching for a particular substance. Once you can do it, you know you can, so it always happens (like swimming or riding a bicycle). 'It is time to take off those water wings and side wheel stabilisers!' Simple, natural, it is only our negative thoughts preventing it. MANKIND has always had these abilities during our evolution but the less we use them, the more they degenerate.

REMEMBER IT HAS very little to do with what you are using for dowsing, even knitting needles, but do cast off first!! Any odd twig will suffice, providing it has a certain elasticity and tension or 'spring' to it and does not split too readily. The technique with the hazel or other twig is quite different and if you find this of great interest it is worth investigating.

ANOTHER EXPERIMENT, similar to this, is to use a simple pendulum, any 'bob' on the end of a thin thread of cotton or fibre. It is possible to locate a person or an object over a map by allowing the pendulum to swing or rotate. First, check how the device moves when using it to look for known people or objects. In other words discover how it swings for you, so there will be no doubt when actively searching. Then use larger scale maps, and eventually road maps or individual houses.

THE MIND is doing the work of receiving and interpreting extrasensory information, the 'rods' or twig are only a device to satisfy man's needs. He always feels he must have a dial or a meter or something moving to show him he has found what he is searching for, instead of relying on the abilities of his mind.

PEOPLE WOULD also be thinking he looked so silly, just aimlessly walking backwards and forwards over a large field, digging little holes and gazing into space every few minutes. It is much more dignified with an instrument. This is quite acceptable to his friends or colleagues, so he escapes the label 'nut case'.

IT CAN LOOK even more scientific if you carry a black box, or the really 'in' colour is a bright yellow one, with two wires emerging from it, one going to each hand, but with nothing inside the box!!

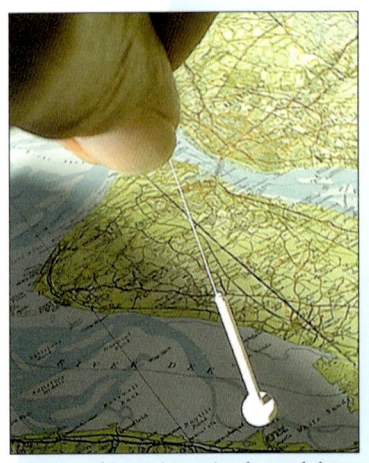

Map searching using a simple pendulum.

SCIENTIFIC AGE

WE CANNOT just ask you to listen to the little 'thoughts' inside your head, although eventually, you will be doing this subconsciously without realising it. They are, of course, not quite voices but very positive creative thoughts or sensations. You should therefore be more interested in your state of mind, when the 'rods' move or the twig twitches, and not concentrate on the device itself. You are exploring your inner abilities, of which you were probably unaware.

NOTE. Some people are more successful with arms outstretched, rather than having their elbows into the waist, not that it matters, as we have already mentioned, but it may be more comfortable. We are trying to develop the sensitivity of the mind.

WRITING ABOUT AWARENESS always brings to mind a simple test we can all do at any time when other people are nearby. Quite simply, stare at the back of someone's neck and 'will' them to turn around. Many respond and, if they are unknown to you, then you have to look away, but if they are friends or family they would make very good partners for a telepathy experiment. Ask them to try and make you turn around at some future time unknown to you.

THIS IS ALSO WORTHWHILE setting up as a proper experiment, to determine what sensations are experienced when another person stares at the back of your neck. Then extend it to just thinking about staring, without actually doing so. Much will be achieved and your abilities increased; you are making more contact with the inner soul, inhabiting your physical body, and God's Creative Presence becomes more real to you.

YOU ARE BEGINNING to know that we all belong to each other and are all part of one remarkable mind within His Creative Framework. Separated by being trapped in 'human forms' of physical material, animated to move things and move itself into places which were only thoughts, yearning to make contact, not only with other minds but with God Himself. We are programmed to find Him, He made it so. Then why have we avoided Him and taken such a long time to realise exactly what Jesus said? Why do we think that we can 'go it alone', when we cannot even move without Him? His patience is astonishing, His forgiveness overwhelming. MAKE IT SOON!

**IF WE BELIEVE THEN WE WILL SUCCEED,
IN PROPORTION TO THE STRENGTH OF OUR BELIEF.**

Jesus said: "All things are possible to him who believes."

CANCER PREVENTION WITH HERBS OF ANTIQUITY

● Pictured above: Hundreds of years ago extract of Stag's horn root was used for fevers of unknown origin. Although cancers were not recognised as such, Mulberry fruit was used as a treatment and cure in Jesus' time.

INTRODUCTION

BEFORE we become too involved with the following scientific details, it should be noted that all sixty of these beneficial herbs would be best used together in powder form for your research.

We have used the word research here because it would probably be frowned upon to say cure or even prevention. There is so much beneficial information coming to hand each month and there are more than sixty herbs which can be used.

GOD'S GARDEN

THERE MAY BE difficulty obtaining all of them but if you can acquire about twenty-eight or even less, then make a start, you can always add others later. We have included these paragraphs early in the book, should anyone need the wonderful help of the herbs, while we reach for God's Presence. They go together, as a perfect partnership of His glorious plant creations and His Creative Forces, for which we only have to ask and then allow His Influence. He is already within us all but we have to acknowledge His Presence to be rejuvenated and regenerated by the subtle substances from the flowers and plants of God's Garden. We should also ask Him to lay His Miraculous Forces upon us to perfect our immunity to all diseases.

I BECAME A PHARMACIST in the days when many of the medications were of plant and natural origin, and the decline in their use has saddened me, but Jesus knew the value of them all. It is of great interest to us, as it should be to everyone, that scientists are now able to show how God's Garden

Mulberry Leaf

Horsetail

Ginkgo biloba

Rosemary

These all contain remarkable anticancer and tissue restorative substances.

is indeed a masterpiece of superior engineering. He relegates the pressure vessels and toxic processes of the chemical industry to the dark ages. He does it all with photons and the frequencies of light, gentle warmth, water, insects, bees and breezes, along with His Creative Touch.

SPECIAL CONSIDERATIONS

SEVERAL DIFFERENT herbs containing similar active compounds have been chosen to be part of the formula to increase the presence of that activity, without overloading the body with unnecessary components, which would occur if we were using only a few herbs.

IF YOU ARE keen and able to grow or pick your own herbs in the wild, take care that you have the correct species and learn about the many special ways to pick and dry them at different times of the year. There are individual ways to grind and powder them taking care with temperature, moisture and storage conditions.

NO! THIS IS NOT A DAUNTING TASK. The thrill of prolonging many healthy lives and saving others makes it all worthwhile. We use these herbs to help many people and, to complement God's Purpose, we have accompanied them with Prayers and Laying on Hands. They can also be used as a supplemental treatment at the same time as surgery, chemotherapy and irradiation, which may be discussed with the medical advisers. The benefits are phenomenal.

Photo: Formby Times
Alan researching Resveratrol in the Mulberry fruit as an anticancer herb.

SO YOU CAN be helping God's work, at least part of the way, by giving the body what He may need to make the repairs and throw off cancer cells, then rejuvenate the whole being. He will do the rest; and all the things we cannot do.

Jesus said, in a fragment of the Dead Sea Scrolls, that the Mulberry produces wine. He would know of its miraculous properties for returning to health.

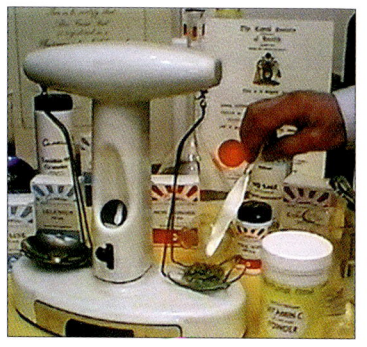

EVEN WHEN WE ASK Jesus for help and Healing, it should be within God's Creative Framework. We should not really be asking Him to do things for us that we should be doing for ourselves, such as the simple things like obtaining food and water, sleeping and everything else He has already programmed into us, as our responsibility. In the same way all car manufacturers specify that petrol, oil, water and maintenance are very necessary to keep the vehicle active.

OF COURSE we should not be asking for help either, if we continue to do things which we know are detrimental to health and may even have brought about the illness. But we may ask God for help to overcome our errors and unhealthy ways and help us to resist temptations; not expect Him to do it for us.

Herbal and vitamin preparations

THERE ARE MANY Herbal books available so, while collecting your materials together, read up about them all, then you will not only believe they are of benefit, but you will also know from all the available research that the beneficial effects are remarkable. So when you take them, it will be purposeful and not just hoping they are helpful; you will know they are.

FORMBY TIMES

Thursday, February 20, 1997

Mulberries may hold cancer cure

by Gareth Hollyman

A fruit tree immortalised in a children's nursery rhyme may hold the key to curing cancer, according to a Formby chemist.

The humble mulberry is thought to possess natural properties which strengthen the immune system.

But the world of science has largely ignored the implications for medicine and the theory remains unproven.

FACT FILE

● The Mulberry (Morus nigra) is a hardy, deciduous tree cultivated for its fruit and ornamental appearance.

● Mulberries are of Asiatic and North American origin, but have been grown in Britain since 1550.

● The common black variety can grow to 30ft and is much larger than the "bush" we associate with the fruit.

● The berries, resembling loganberries, ripen in late summer and have a pleasant, slightly acid flavour.

Now former Elson Road pharmacist Alan Bell is launching a one-man campaign to unearth the berry's secrets.

But there is just one hitch - he can't find enough mulberries for his research.

Said the 68-year-old: "I need to hear from local people or families who have eaten mulberries over a period of time or generations, or who even have a tree.

"I suspect these people may be cancer free," he added.

The orchard fruit, similar to the loganberry, is one of 70 plant species, including the grape and peanut, which contain beneficial natural compounds. So what's special about the mulberry?

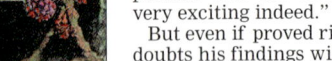

"Everyone eats peanuts and that makes the study groups too wide," explained Mr Bell.

"On the other hand if mulberry eaters' health shows similarities, maybe we can isolate the berry as a factor."

Now a health consultant, Alan Bell's research has spanned subjects as varied as faith healing and the use of vitamins, appearing as a TV pundit on both BBC and Granada.

He admits his theory is a long shot, but says he's not seeking funding, just peace of mind, saying:

"I've conducted a great deal of research into natural compounds and the mulberry is very exciting indeed."

But even if proved right, Alan doubts his findings will become commercially viable.

"Call me a cynic but the drug companies will only manufacture their own cure. Not one found naturally."

FUTURE FILE

● We are still seeking individuals or families who have eaten Mulberries regularly over generations, as we do need to know if those groups are free from cancer?
We expect this to be the case from our preliminary research.

HERBAL REGENERATION
for youth and health

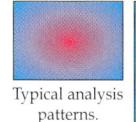

Typical analysis patterns.

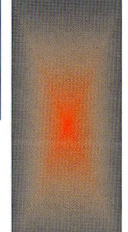

PURPOSE OF THE RESEARCH. Several years ago, before I had completed the formula, we lost a member of the family through cancer, but to avoid this happening again we take the sixty herbs each day before breakfast. We take them for three weeks at a time, then miss a week. The week without herbs gives the body a chance to make any necessary adjustments; this procedure is repeated every four weeks.

ANALYSIS
Modern scientific analytical methods are now so advanced it is possible to show that many of the herbal components listed here have cancer prevention and anticancer properties, even when the condition has already become established.

MANY HEALTH SHOPS and Herbalists should have several of these herbs, which are listed on pages 86, 87 and 88, or would be able to obtain them for you, even if a little persuasion may be needed.

EQUAL WEIGHTS of each of the sixty herbal powders would be ideal to mix together or, if weighing is not practicable, a near approximation would be an equal volume; a tablespoonful of each. Then the dose of the mixed powders would be ONE LEVEL 5ml. TEASPOONFUL.

Equal parts of each by weight or volume.

WHEN IN POWDER form they can be easily swallowed, mixed with water or fruit juice, after first sterilising the 5ml. spoonful of mixed herbs with two 5ml. spoonfuls of 45% or preferably 50% Vodka. Allow to stand for five minutes to complete the sterilisation; a little added Colloidal Silver would hasten this process.

IF ALCOHOLS HAVE to be avoided, then there is an infusion method of preparation, detailed later.

MANY PEOPLE HAVE COMMENTED on our youthful appearance. This was something we had not anticipated but it is scientifically correct, in that several of the herbs prevent cell damage from free radicals and oxidation. They aid circulation and replacement of damaged tissues, also cleansing the liver and kidneys, to improve the elimination of toxic pollutants. So we should look healthy. We also use purified water for cooking and drinking, with great benefit. There is more information about water purification in later paragraphs; as it is important.

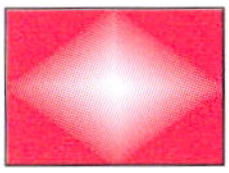

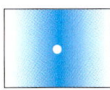

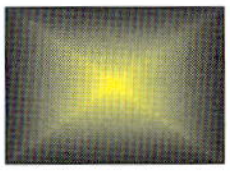

Years of research to perfect the formula.

TIME FOR A PAUSE TO THINK
IF THE NEED AROSE for one of us, it would only be a small step from prevention of cancer to a cure. We would increase the dose by three or four times and take several doses daily, until well again. And although this may seem old fashioned we would also apply a warm wet poultice of the same sixty or more herbal powders to any necessary accessible body surface, where help was required.

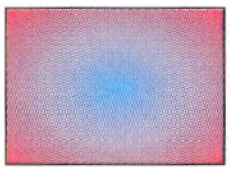

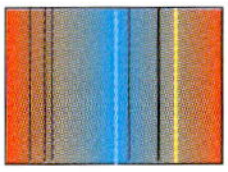

For us this would not be experimental research but positive action of known benefit, by taking and applying the herbs, and this is probably as much as we can legally say about what we really know to be true, without having a section of the Trade Descriptions Act thrown at us. This is, of course, why we frequently mention that all these herb details are for information only and not a diagnosis or prescription.

APART FROM OUR OWN research we have studied most of the scientific literature and obscure papers for all the hidden facts and information, in the same way we searched the Biblical Texts for all the sayings of Jesus, which present a wonderful truth when gathered together.

THIS WILL become more apparent in the paragraphs about His sayings and How To Feel God's Presence. Many of these herbs have been in use since His time and He would know more about them than we do today. There is also every good reason to seek Jesus' guidance concerning these matters, with prayer.

Ginkgo biloba leaf, used in disorders due to ageing, memory loss, ear problems, maintaining blood flow to the central nervous system.

YOUR RESEARCH

YOU DO NOT have to take our word for any of this information, it is all available in worldwide scientific literature and now on the Internet, but the knowledge is frequently fragmented and kept from us by vested interests. It is often hidden away and disguised in obscure publications, as most scientists need to publish their discovery in print, but some keep it as discreet as possible.

A compound in Fig leaves is beneficial for diabetics. The fruits have been used to relieve pain, inflammation and to treat tumours. Figs were used in Biblical Times.

THERE ARE STILL people and Governments who think that too much knowledge for the 'masses' is a danger; but we do need to know as much as possible about everything, because some strange mass experiments have been carried out on all of us in the past, without our knowledge at the time. This may sound rather curious but you will find it to be true, without us having to mention any recent scares.

THERE IS SOMETHING we can all do about it and this is to take our Health back into our own hands. It is not complicated; the knowledge is available; do not leave everything for someone else to tell you what to do, or to do it for you, as many would have an ulterior motive, usually money.

Ginger

THE FUTURE

WE FIRMLY BELIEVE all knowledge concerning our health, happiness and well-being should be freely available and not kept so someone can make a fortune from it. It is with this thought in mind that we write about our work with Colloidal Silver and also the Sixty herbal formula. We could make a large fortune ourselves from either of these and many more of our discoveries and formulations but money has no true value, unless it is used wisely to benefit mankind and our wonderful planet, so

Here are just three herbs with anticancer activity; we all know these but how many use them?

Garlic

Turmeric

we prefer to share with you what we have found, and the greatest of all these is the Reality of God's Presence and how He has made Himself known to us, by bringing alive Jesus' sayings.

THERE ARE MANY other items of vital importance which we touch upon during our journey of Discovery Of God's Presence. This Is The Ultimate Hidden Joy Of Life.

The Herbal Paradox

LARGE CHEMICAL COMPANIES can make a fortune by isolating a single chemical compound from a well known herb and modifying the molecule to make it their own, but frequently it has been shown that the total herb has more activity than the isolated compound. They could not, of course, ever recover their research costs by selling natural herbs, and on many occasions they have not been able to discover why the natural complete herb is more active, so they do not proceed any further and the value of the research is often lost.

THE FACTS YOU NEED

WE HAVE LISTED overleaf, many of these remarkable beneficially active anticancer compounds occurring in the formula, so everyone can share the knowledge and the benefits. Their activity is enhanced by the presence of the whole herb component.

You will also find some of these compounds in other plant species, as our list is not exhaustive.

IN THE BEGINNING

IF YOU want to start from the beginning, to seek out what we have already brought together, we encourage you to do this, and you could discover even more amazing facts but it may take twenty-five years. It probably took us a lot longer, if you think of the time required by Heather and myself to acquire all the scientific knowledge and understanding. Also years of study for the qualifications.

THE EVIDENCE

THERE ARE MANY well documented newspaper and magazine reports, and in the more official medical sources, of people overcoming cancer by using these herbs alone and some use them along with vitamins and minerals.

THEY ARE often taken at the same time as orthodox medical treatments, such as chemotherapy, surgery and irradiation, giving beneficial effects, protecting the many normal cells from damage and rejuvenating the immune system, along with several of the body's organs.

BENEFIT MANKIND

THESE ARE the facts, these are the herbs, the decision is yours. So you may use them in your own way, at your own discretion, to the benefit of mankind and pass on all this freely given knowledge to those in need of help.

IF ANYONE should try to discourage your work or tell you otherwise, then perform your own research to either agree with them or refute them, but get yourself well first if you are in need of help.

WRITE AND let us know of your findings, so that we may continue to learn; for each day brings new knowledge, new wisdom, and we get a little closer to God. Get yourself well, not to prove someone wrong or to prove anything to anyone, but only for the positive satisfaction of good health, so you can then help others to experience our Creator's Presence.

Morning glory - dawn of a new day

Yarrow flowers
Yarrow leaves
Whole plant
Small flowered Willowherb
Small flowered Willowherb

ACTION IS NECESSARY

IT IS OF NO VALUE to mankind to simply write about these herbs in scientific journals and papers. Someone has to put them all together, ready to be taken on a daily basis for prevention, as they have greater benefits together than a single herb or compound in isolation. Cancer prevention and cure is a complex process involving many metabolic systems. We did not want to put it quite so bluntly but now it is up to you.

THE FUTURE LOOKS GOOD

THE PROBLEMS OF OBTAINING and blending the herbs are easily overcome and are well worthwhile and, if expense is a difficulty or having to buy 500g. instead of what you need, some people have grouped together to acquire what they wanted and sometimes we have helped. Many of my friends and colleagues want to know why I have not yet retired ? Now that is easy to answer. There are so many important things always around the corner and I seem to be involved in so much fresh research, what would I retire from first? So I think we will still be busy with something special to about one hundred and twenty. But we will not have worked alone all that time, for Our Creator has made contact with us and guides our every thought, and brings us back if we have wandered off the track. This is the joyful journey we are trying to share with you.

NATURAL REMISSION

WHEN PEOPLE we know have returned to good health, by using herbs and vitamins alone, along with the Hand Of God, they are often 'passed off' by orthodox medical practitioners as:

"Oh! just another natural remission."

THE WORD 'natural' has a beautiful ring to it and should not be used in a derogatory manner. It is natural because you are giving the body what it requires to eliminate foreign materials, then repair and rejuvenate the tissues, and all with a lot of help from Above, Around and Within; from GOD HIMSELF.

NATURE'S PHARMACY

THESE ARE SOME of the most remarkable substances which occur in the natural herbs listed on pages 86, 87, 88, and are all in the formula. We start with one that most people know: Bioflavonoids, then there are the Isoflavonoids, Genistein, Biochanin A, Diosmin, Pratensin, Daidzein, Apigenin, Formononetin, Genkwanin, Glabrin, Glabrol, Glabridin, and many more. All wonderful names; each one created for a purpose.

HERE IS ANOTHER group of fascinating compounds, a complete book could be written about these: Beta-sitosterol, other Phytosterols, and Beta-carotene.

THE SHAPES of each molecule are just as beautiful as many of the words: Anthocyanins, Polyphenols - including the Catechins and Proanthocyanidins. Their activities in our bodies are miraculous but it is unlikely that man could even make one of them.

A FEW THAT ARE MORE FAMILIAR: Vitamin C (one of the fruit acids - Ascorbic), Vitamin E, both occur as antioxidants; there are traces of Vitamin A and K and many well known minerals such as Calcium, Potassium, Zinc and Selenium. Even the much maligned Germanium has been shown by scientists to be present in a few of these beneficial herbs such as Brazilian Suma, and may well add to their anticancer activity. Germanium has been shown to be present in The Water At Lourdes.

SOME OF US will remember the original Crystal Sets (Wireless). At that time we had to gently touch a small beautiful crystal of Germanium with a very fine wire, known as a cat's whisker, to hear the B.B.C. or 2L.O. in very heavy Ericsson earphones. They now make mobile microwave telephones. If you wobbled the table or breathed on it you lost the signal and had to start again; with a lot of 'sshush - sshushing.'

EVEN THE SETS with lead sulphide crystals, Galena, were often a remarkable and new experience. Now, when we take our garden cuttings to the local rubbish tip, we see televisions, only a few years old, dumped because they have been replaced with up-to-date technology. These did not exist when we were twisting little bits of wire together as children but I still have my lovely Germanium crystal.

Galena crystal

PLANT MATERIALS contain an astonishing number of organic acids of infinite value to the body and of simple or great complexity, such as the amino acids, the building blocks of life itself, like Lysine, Arginine, Glutamine and many more. There are fruit, seed and root acids, Ursolic, Ellagic, Folic, Gamolenic, Glycyrrhetinic acid, Citric, Malic, Butyric, Silicic, Gallic, Rosmarinic, Guaiaretic acids. These are a few of them, which all have great benefit for a healthy life.

THERE ARE MANY STRANGE WORDS to follow, such as Sanguinarine, Berberine, Hydrastine, Polyacetylenes, High Molecular Weight Polysaccharides. They all have a function in the prevention of cancer but to describe the activity of each would cover too many pages; that is if you are still reading these paragraphs!

WE WOULD END up writing a book about herbs, which would further delay stating the Formula, for this is what is necessary. All these special compounds along with many more are in the herbs we use. Neither must we delay discussions about the very special sayings of Jesus.

Raspberry leaf, Passion leaf and Herb Robert

THE WORD LIGNANS will be a part of everyday vocabulary in the years to come, such as Arctigenin, Enedione-lignans, Furanolignans, Flavonlignans and many more similar compounds.

THERE ARE dozens of unique Volatile Oils and Lectins, also beneficial to health as are Resveratrol and related molecules contained in the skin of Red Grapes and Mulberry fruit.

YOU WILL COME ACROSS most of these names during your own research and you will be astonished that each single word, no matter how small, has a wonderful story to tell.

SOME PLANTS are torn up by their roots and thrown away as weeds and yet each one is a chemical factory able to produce remarkable compounds of great benefit and usefulness to mankind, but we have no way of making them ourselves.

MIRACULOUS Molecules

THEY ARE ALL HERE, over sixty of God's Herbal Remedies; living silent chemical 'plants' each one producing a multitude of miraculous molecules, capable of restoring or perfecting the physical and spiritual balance of human life. Some of them are only parts of the plant but each one contributes a very special harmony, so unlike the discordant notes of many man-made marvels, which often disturb rejuvenation.

THE MULBERRY FRUIT and leaf, Mistletoe leaf, Burdock root, Black Walnut hull, Green leaf Tea and many more. You may notice several 'Old Wives' Tales' coming to life, when you study the 'Formula' and find them to be scientifically true. Do not be put off by anyone who doubts; check each one for yourself, in the most up to date literature you can find.

THE FORMULA

TO AVOID ERRORS the binomial system, using a pair of Latin or Latinised words, has been adopted here, as they are understood by most languages.

ROOTS AND RHIZOMES (In The Formula)

Allium sativum	(Garlic, clove of the bulb)
Alpina officinarum	(Galangal)
Arctium lappa	(Burdock root)
Astragalus membranaceus	(Milk Vetch), roots
Curcuma longa	(Turmeric)
Eleutherococcus senticosus	(Siberian Ginseng)
Echinacea angustifolia	(Coneflower root)
Echinacea pallida	(Coneflower root)
Echinacea purpurea	(Coneflower root)
Glycyrrhiza glabra	(Liquorice)
Hydrastis canadensis	(Golden Seal)
Panax ginseng	(Ginseng)
Pfaffia paniculata	(Suma, Brazilian Ginseng)
Rheum officinale	(Rhubarb)
Sanguinaria canadensis	(Bloodroot)
Taraxacum officinale	(Dandelion)
Urtica dioica	(Nettle)
Zingiber officinale	(Ginger)

FLOWERS (In the Formula)

Calendula officinalis	(Marigold)
Eugenia caryophyllata	(Cloves, flower buds) or
Syzgium aromaticum	(Cloves, flower buds)
Sambucus nigra	(Elder)
Trifolium pratense	(Red Clover flowering tops)

BERRIES, FRUITS AND SEEDS (In the Formula)

Carduus marianus	(Milk Thistle)	powder or grind in a coffee mill
	(Silybum seeds)	
Juniperus communis	(Juniper berries)	powder or grind in a coffee mill
Juglans nigra	(Black Walnut)	use the green unripe rind, i.e. outer pericarp of the shell,
Juglans regia	(English Walnut)	use both fresh or as a tincture
Linum usitatissimum	(Linseed seeds)	powder or grind in a coffee mill
Morus nigra	(Black Mulberry fruit)	may be juiced, dried gently, below 100 °C. powdered in coffee mill, or eat fresh cooked fruit
Trigonella foenum-graecum	(Fenugreek seeds)	grind in a coffee mill
Schisandra chinensis	(Schisandra as dried fruits)	grind first in a coffee mill
Serenoa serrulata	(Saw Palmeto)	grind these also
Sesamum indicum	(Sesame seeds)	need grinding in the coffee mill
Zanthoxyllum clava-herculis	(Southern Prickly Ash)	berries may be available as powder, otherwise, back to the grind stone

HERBS AND LEAVES (In the Formula)

Achillea millefolium	(Yarrow)	whole plant
Anemone pulsatilla	(P. vulgaris, Pasque Flower)	whole flowering plant
Artemisia annua	(Sweet Wormwood)	herb
Artemisia absinthium	(Wormwood)	tops, stem and leaves
Artemisia vulgaris	(Mugwort, Chinese Moxa)	leaves mainly
Camellia sinensis	(Unfermented Green Tea)	leaf
Carbenia benedicta	(Blessed Thistle)	whole plant
Cassia angustifolia	(Alexandrian Senna)	leaves
Epilobium parviflorum	(Small flowered Willowherb)	whole plant
Euphorbia hirta	(Asthma Weed)	whole plant
Galium aparine	(Cleavers, Goosegrass)	whole plant and seeds
Ginkgo biloba	(Maidenhair tree)	leaves
Glechoma hederacea	(Ground Ivy or Alehoof)	whole plant
Juglans nigra	(Black Walnut)	leaves
Juglans regia	(English Walnut)	leaves
Medicago sativa	(Alfalfa)	whole plant, leaves, not seeds unless sprouted
Morus nigra	(Black Mulberry)	leaves
Rosemarinus officinalis	(Rosemary)	leaves, flowering tops
Salvia officinalis	(Sage)	leaves
Urtica dioica	(Nettle)	leaves, whole plant
Viscum album	(Mistletoe)	leaves and stems only, NO fruits
Viola odorata	(Sweet Violet)	leaves and flowers

BARKS, WOODS, GUMS AND RESINS (In the Formula)

Astragalus tragacantha	(Tragacanth)	Gum
Berberis vulgaris	(Common Barberry)	Bark
Commiphora molmol	(Myrrh)	Gum-resin
Guaiacum offininale	(Lignum Vitae)	Resin
Picraenia excelsa	(Quassia, Bitter Ash)	Wood
Tabebuia impetiginosa	(Pau d'arco Tea)	Wood/inner bark
Uncaria tomentosa	(Cat's Claw)	Bark
Zanthoxyllum clava-herculis	(Southern Prickly Ash)	Bark

TO SIMPLIFY THE DOSAGE

IF YOU ARE ABLE to obtain about sixty of these, even by buying along with friends, then that is wonderful, if not do try and aim for at least the magic twenty-eight. It may not sound very scientific but it lies comfortably with so many of the natural requirements and cycles of human life and evolution, as we touched upon during the paragraphs concerning silver, the minerals and elements. Choose some from each of the five herbal groups but do add more as soon as possible.

HOW TO PREPARE THE HERBAL MIXTURE AND INFUSION

THIS METHOD may be used if you do not wish to take the alcohol sterilised powders or if you have not been able to obtain them all in powder form.

WEIGH out into a bowl equal amounts (say 10 or 20 grams) of each of the dried Herbal components, whether leaf, flower, root or other. Mix together thoroughly. You may not be able to obtain them all as powders but use them very finely chopped or diminished in a coffee mill, so they can all be mixed together without any lumps protruding from the surface. In this way the weight of each is well dispersed and not contained in only one dose. Some of the herbs are very difficult to powder, so this infusion method is quite useful for those that can only be chopped into very small pieces.

Herbs added to boiling water.

IF A BALANCE IS NOT AVAILABLE for weighing, then measure equal amounts as above into a bowl using a dessertspoonful or tablespoonful of each and mix as before.

NOW BRING ONE LITRE OF PURIFIED WATER TO THE BOIL in a large Teflon coated or Pyrex glass pan, but not an aluminium or copper one and preferably not stainless steel, although this would suffice in an emergency. ADD TWO LEVEL TABLESPOONFULS of the mixed herbs and simmer very gently for TWO minutes, while covered with the lid. Then allow to cool with the lid still in place.

Simmer for 2 minutes with lid on.

WHEN COLD, pour it all into a well washed, sterilised, one litre plastic bottle (including the herbs), screw the cap on well and store in the refrigerator over night. Next day, shake the bottle, allow any large particles to settle for a minute, then strain into another clean container through a sterile sieve with holes that are not too fine; this is just to remove fibres and any <u>gross</u> particles; the strained liquid will still have most of the fine suspended material and will not be clear. This is as it should be, see page 89.

Allow to cool with lid still in place.

Decant cold herbs into 1 litre bottle.

Store in refrigerator overnight. Next day shake, settle for 1 min., strain into another 1 litre bottle and return to fridge.

Enjoy! Here's to a healthy future.

AS A CANCER PREVENTION we would take 100ml. or about three and a half fluid ounces, once each day, before a meal or between meals. If the taste is not palatable, it may be diluted with more water or mixed with fruit juice. Store in a refrigerator for not more than nine days at about 4°C., not frozen. We would then make another batch so we can take the infusion for three weeks, then miss a week and start again. This gives the body a chance to adjust itself to what it needs. We would also add two 5ml. spoonfuls of the 30ppm. Colloidal Silver to the one litre bottle to keep it perfectly fresh during the nine days. Always shake before pouring out the dose.

AS A CANCER CURE, we would take 100ml. several times daily, depending on our needs, until well again, but we would definitely aim for the total sixty herbs to prepare this infusion.

POSITIVE HEALTH
Additional materials for cancer control

THE BENEFICIAL EFFECTS of the following are also of great interest and have been shown to have anticancer properties, especially when used along with the above herbal formula.

VITAMIN C

One gram (1000mg.) taken with each meal is a superb antioxidant, free radical scavenger, and helps the liver to detoxify aflatoxins and mycotoxins from damaged fruits, nuts and other foods. Vitamin C also helps to keep iron in a chemical form that can better compete with any excess copper burden, from pipes and mains water treatment processes. Its total value to human health can only be touched on here. Eminent scientists, Ewan Cameron and Linus Pauling, nearly twenty years ago indicated in their research papers that vitamin C extends the life of cancer patients, with an enhanced sense of well-being. So just think what can be achieved with the Herbs, Colloidal Silver and the 'Zapper', described later. Not forgetting God's Presence, whose value is beyond everything else.

EVEN NOW, just talking about vitamin C in some medical circles is a 'charged topic', as many do not agree about its therapeutic benefits. We shake our heads in disbelief and wonder if we have progressed at all. Where are we now, twenty years later? Thankfully the choice is yours.

SO WHAT CHANCE have we of waiting for a herbal formula, when great minds cannot even agree on something as obvious as vitamin C? We do have a superb chance of doing it for ourselves; our Creator did not fashion all the wonderful plants for us to simply look at. Each one has a purpose and each one of us has the chance To Take Our Health Back Into Our Own Hands, just as it was in bygone years. 'Ye Olde Herbs', but now there is a vast difference. Science has contributed so much that we know what remarkable properties these little plants possess.

JOIN WITH OUR CREATOR and eat your way back to health, and just hope that there is no intervention, E.E.C. or otherwise, to limit or restrict the supply of these LITTLE CHEMICAL FACTORIES CALLED 'HERBS'. THEY ARE MIRACULOUS.

THESE EXTRA NOTES are not in order of importance; they are all of equal value and should already be part of every day life.

BIOFLAVONOIDS
Writing about vitamin C always brings to mind the Bioflavonoids. They work well together in doses of 500mg. twice daily with vitamin C at meal times.

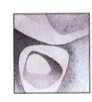

ZINC
Zinc is essential and yet many people are deficient of this mineral. It aids the body to repair damaged tissues and even individual cells; it displaces high copper content of foods and water supplies, i.e. from copper pipes. This deficiency of zinc in the population is made even worse by the general excess of copper.

LYCOPENE
A valuable carotinoid compound occurs in bright red tomatoes which should be eaten frequently, even the tinned plum variety. These are always a good colour and contain high proportions of lycopene.

Plum tomato

BETA-CAROTENE
We would take 10,000mcg. (i.e. 10mg.) daily with a meal. From this, the body can form all the vitamin A it needs, without excess.

GRAPES
Do not peel them. Red grapes are particularly useful, with or without seeds. They must be washed well, not just in a little water but in warm soapy water, with a soft bottle brush. Make a good lather in a bowl, swishing them about with the brush. This removes most of the chemical spray residues, moulds and fly contamination. After washing, rinse well several times in clean water. Eat the skins with the grapes, about 4 to 8oz. (120 to 240g.) throughout the day, each day, always depending on your needs. Organic or your own home grown grapes, without any chemical treatment, would be best but even these need washing as above.

Grape washing

MULBERRY FRUIT
May be available in some country areas. Eating 30 to 50grams daily would be a good regime. This could be more convenient than trying to include them in the herbal formula, as they remain sticky and are difficult to dry. They can readily be included in the herbal drink preparation (juiced) and could make it a better flavour if sufficient are used. These, along with Grape skin, contain a valuable anticancer compound (Resveratrol).

Mulberry fruit

APPLES - PEARS - PLUMS AND OTHERS

Always peel these, unless you grow them yourself organically without sprays of any kind and even then they should be washed well. All commercially grown fruit should always be washed before peeling and rinsed thoroughly afterwards, to avoid the unnecessary transfer of bacterial and chemical contamination to the peeled fruit. The crops that are grown organically without any treatment may be poor in appearance and size but they will be of superb value to a creative mind developing its sensitivity to God's Presence.

Fruits of the garden

HOME GROWN VEGETABLES

Similarly, under natural conditions, these are more beneficial and should be free from all insecticides, weedkillers, aphid sprays, slug baits and moss controls. Calomel was used for club root control in cabbage but ideally fresh ground should be used each year, with at least a three foot separation from last year's crop position.

Cauliflower and broccoli

CABBAGE - CAULIFLOWER - BROCCOLI - SPROUTS

Include a large helping of at least one of these each day, cooked or steamed in very little water, and only occasionally uncooked.

VITAMIN E

We take 100iu. twice daily with meals and one at night. This is an antioxidant that performs well in the fatty tissues of the body and also prevents oxidation during digestion.

SELENIUM

100mcg. twice daily with meals, is beneficial against cancer and together with vitamins A and E, protects and prolongs cell life. Once daily is sufficient as a food supplement.

LECITHIN

Is easily taken as granules sprinkled on breakfast cereal, porridge or in soups - one 5ml. spoonful once or twice daily would be an adequate dose.

CITRUS FRUITS

Orange, Lemon, Lime, Grapefruit and Tangerine, as below; at least two helpings of any one of these is necessary every day or 300ml. to 400ml. of the fresh juice of your choice.

STORAGE AND PREPARATION

◆ STORE FOODS IN a refrigerator, not above 4°C., and FROZEN FOODS at minus 18°C. or below.

◆ TOAST ALL SLICED BREAD to a light golden brown on both sides, preferably wholemeal, to destroy any bacteria, moulds or yeasts introduced during slicing.

◆ REMEMBER TO COVER all foods appropriately when storing or leaving unattended.

Frozen foods should be stored at minus 18°C or below.

Fridge not above 4°C.

NEGATIVE EFFECTS

These Induce or Perpetuate Cancers and should be avoided.

◆ Benzpyrene in cigarette and tobacco smoke, and also from burning organic matter in bonfires; avoid all burnt foods.

◆ AVOID: Parsnips, Celery and Parsley, as they all contain compounds, which increase our sensitivity to ultraviolet light.

◆ AVOID: solvents such as Benzene, Acetone, Isopropyl alcohol (some Bourbon Whisky contains Isopropyl alcohol but there is none in Scottish Whisky). Also avoid Toluene, Xylene, Trichlorethylene and Methanol (Wood alcohol). You cannot eat them, so do not BREATHE them. Simple but very sound advice.

◆ AVOID: all damaged or mouldy fruits, nuts and other foods and vegetables, as many of the moulds, particularly in apples, release toxins, some of which are Cancer producing. Extra vitamin C helps to protect against these.

◆ AVOID: the use of Aluminium and Copper as pans and cookware and also avoid their contact with all foods, not just acid ones, as Aluminium dissolves in alkaline solutions too. We also avoid the use of Aluminium foil in direct contact with all foods.

◆ AVOID: food Colourings and Flavourings; these often contain Isopropyl alcohol as a solvent and many of the colours and flavours are also detrimental to health.

◆ AVOID: Asbestos, even in hairdryers and washing machine belts (check with manufacturers).

◆ AVOID: all Radioactive materials, as some watches and clocks still contain these in their fluorescent figures and fingers. Yellow and yellow/greenish fluorescent glassware and jewellery stones usually contain radioactive Uranium. Avoid contact with camping gas mantles containing radioactive Thorium, even the dust of an old one. There was a radioactive scare on a beach in the north of the Isle of Man some years ago; the local residents had been blaming materials washed or blown over from the Sellafield plant, but on analysis the problem was found to be camping gas mantle dust from a beach party.

Uranium pendant

MOST SMOKE alarms require renewing after five years; many contain a small amount of radioactive material; check with the local authority for methods of safe disposal.

Uranium glass

HIDDEN dangers - To watch out for!

THIS WATCH, with radioactive fingers and figures, was placed face downwards on the top of a sealed packet of photographic bromide printing paper. Later it was opened in the 'dark room' and the first few sheets of paper were developed. The Radium radiations had passed through the thick outer paper wrapping, through all the instruction sheets and also an opaque black polythene bag. It produced a strong image on the first piece of printing paper, less of an image on the second piece and so on through the pack, which was now of course useless for printing photographs.

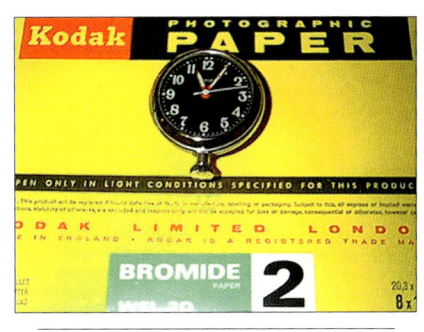

Radiation passes through many layers of material; paper, plastic, thin metals and skin.

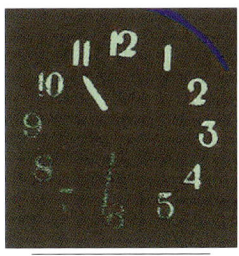

Radium induced light emissions from a pocket watch.

◆ IN 'THE OLD DAYS' people had these watches in their waistcoat pockets or fixed to the dashboard of the family car. They were always fluorescent, even on the darkest night, but the workers who made the watches became dreadfully ill, so it is not surprising that people are wary about radioactivity. It is best to avoid such items.

Showing the ability of radiation to penetrate materials.

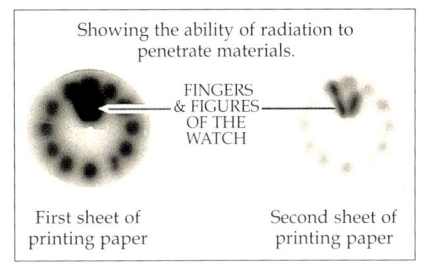

FINGERS & FIGURES OF THE WATCH

First sheet of printing paper

Second sheet of printing paper

NEGATIVE EFFECTS continued:

◆ AVOID using heated fats and oils more than once. Use only cold pressed oils, preferably Olive Oil stored in a cold place in airtight containers. Never use any fat or oil that has even a hint of rancidity.

◆ AVOID any bottled water or food item that contains Nitrates or Nitrites over one or two parts per million (1 or 2 ppm.). Avoid them completely if you can.

◆ AVOID inhaling all household chemicals and sprays, including personal ones, hair sprays, deodorants and others, even if they are so called ozone friendly, as they nearly all contain detrimental solvents and propellants, salts of Aluminium and Zirconium, and some with resins, silicones and preservatives.

◆ COFFEE has not been confirmed as being carcinogenic, although it is a burnt bean, but tea is safer. In fact China Green Tea taken without milk is actually beneficial and is added to the herbal formula. Dark brown fermented teas usually require milk to prevent damage to intestinal linings.

AVOID: Burnt and undercooked foods. We continue to be amazed, by the fact that scientists have spent the past sixty years perfecting the modern cooking stoves to prevent burning our foods, only to find the barbecue burns nearly everything on the outside, producing detrimental benzpyrene and other carcinogens, but often leaves the interior of the food undercooked, full of live bacteria and other organisms, i.e. parasites, which are discussed later.

APART FROM undercooking, you can never tell if your guests have arrived because only half of them are visible through the thick choking fatty smoke and, if it does blow away into next door's garden, you have all the fire alarms screeching down to the end of the road. Oh! happy summer days and the delight of a breath of fresh air, and, when the wind changes around, the chap on the other side retaliates with his bonfire suitably dampened down to produce the most smoke. So now you cannot even see the few guests who did arrive but there are at least two left; you can hear them coughing. Sorry about that, I've just had to shut the window!! No! We do not have a barbecue. Would you have guessed?

JESUS told us that we should commune with The Angel of Air:

"Who spreads the perfume,
Of sweet smelling fields,
Of spring grass after rain,
Of the opening buds of the
Rose of Sharon."

Jesus is speaking of the virtue, benefits and pleasure of breathing air cleansed by rain and perfumed by God's Creations.

THE ROSE OF SHARON is usually said to be Hypericum calycinum, with a beautiful perfume, but a related species, St. John's Wort, is almost odourless (Hypericum perforatum). Jesus would also know of the remarkable healing properties of several Hypericum species.

GENETICALLY MODIFIED FOODS

We should all be very cautious about eating G.M. foods, until more safety research has taken place. Growing crops of these in open countryside fields should be abandoned, as the effects on natural evolution could be devastating.

SOME of the G.M. plants are created by transferring genetic material from animals to plants, which does not occur in nature. Even a human gene has been used in some experiments. It is quite immoral for scientists to say that they are safe - just because everything has already evolved during millions of years by mutation of genetic material; we do not know they are safe and there are certainly no natural plant foods containing mutant animal or human genes.

MANY PLANT materials are already toxic, so we do not eat them, but it has taken thousands of years for us to know this and gaining the knowledge has caused suffering and illness. No one can tell us what possible toxic compounds will be formed by the introduction of a new gene and it is quite improper to 'wait and see' when we are talking about human life, health and well-being.

WE MUST INSIST on more research; there is no going back, once it is performed and released into nature, it cannot be undone. It is wrong to say we could produce more food for the starving nations by using this technology; it is wars, droughts and man's greed that bring about these starving situations or makes them worse, and the weapons of mass destruction which they use, even in the impoverished countries are supplied by the well nourished nations.

WE NEED to feel our Creator's Presence in all our work and in making each decision, none should be made in isolation. The scientists should think again; they are experimenting with our lives and future, while destroying GOD'S work by interfering with His basic genetic codes.

JESUS said: *"Holy Wisdom, The Understanding that unfolds continuously, as a Holy Scroll, yet does not come through learning. All Wisdom cometh from The Heavenly Father."*

DNA double helix

The DNA, the double Helix, could be a Holy scroll of The Heavenly Father that unfolds continuously. Scientists' gift of understanding has only come through study and learning. Now they need the Wisdom of The Heavenly Father before they over-reach the boundaries. Their work is wonderful, life would not be the same without them, but they need restraint. They have lost the art of pausing to contemplate the future outcome of all their actions. (Einstein would have had thoughts on this).

JESUS said:
*"He who is without wisdom,
his words are empty, and his deeds harmful."*

We should all Pray for the scientists and ask God to make contact, to change their ways, to pause and think that just because something can be done, DOES NOT IMPART A GIVEN RIGHT TO DO IT.

Why a helix for the DNA?
The sign of our Creator *"A Movement and a Rest"*
His rotations are ever present.

BUT ONCE AGAIN, we can Take Our Health Back Into Our Own Hands and avoid these materials, if they are thrust upon us, or even grow our own, as most vegetables have beautiful leaves and flowers and may be interspersed with herbs and other beneficial plants. In the hope that we may be able to maintain and protect God's original species. In the future we may have to grow God's own creations in sealed glasshouses, to avoid contamination from man made G.M. mutants, whereas it should be the mutants which are contained in sealed environments.

A GENTLEMAN CAME to see us for help and, as he stepped into the Healing Garden he said: "I can see you're not much of a gardener".

I DID NOT REPLY, for he had missed all the beauty of everything that was growing and the peace, tranquillity and wonder of God's Presence. He had already trodden on a group of four leaf clovers, unaware he had brushed against a wonderful bush of Rosemary Herb, kicked the Mulberry with a clumsy movement and not even noticed the yellow leaves of Autumn on a

Ginkgo biloba tree. There was much more he had also missed but he responded well to God's Healing, by experiencing His Touch, and returned to his home as a changed being. If we spent our days growing thousands of brightly coloured flowers, we would not have the time to help so many people. It would have only taken him a moment longer to see the beauty of the herbs, a Mulberry fruit, a Ginkgo leaf and many others.

Autumn Ginkgo leaf

Rosemary plant

NOW BEFORE WE DRIFT AWAY from herbs and plants and things, there is an item of concern.

BRACKEN

This is another situation which has crept upon us and we can all do something about it, although strangely it is not widely known, but concerns one particular plant - Bracken.

IT HAS NOT been created by man, in some odd experiment, but has a unique survival ability of its own, having been on earth for about 200 million years, and is now continuing to spread rapidly across The British Isles. IT IS TOXIC and has been linked to cancer formation.

ALL SKIN CONTACT with it must be avoided and the dust like spores in August and September must not be inhaled or swallowed. Pull it up, cut it

Bracken grows as a single stalk and spreads rapidly under the ground.

down and burn it but wear protective waterproof gloves, not cotton or material types, and if your clothing is contaminated with the Bracken juice, they should be well washed before wearing again. Protect your breathing. One day science may find it contains something useful but not yet; probably because we have not investigated all its toxic and other compounds.

IF YOU USE a garden strimmer on large areas, remember to cover as much of your exposed skin as possible; tie plastic bags round the lower legs to prevent the bracken juice from soaking the trousers or skin. DO NOT inhale any spray mist produced by the strimmer and even use a hose pipe afterwards to douse the whole area with water, washing the juice and spores into the ground. A garden flame device is most useful, if the area is safe to use one.

Ferns produce fronds from a small base circle and spread quite slowly.

BE SURE you can identify the difference between garden ferns and bracken, they are not the same. FERNS produce their fronds from a small 'circle', two or three inches in diameter if viewed from above, or all from one small area if viewed from the side.

BRACKEN tends to come up through the ground as a single stalk and gradually unrolls this stem as it becomes taller and vertical, whereas a fern frond lolls outwards from the centre circle, like the feathers on a shuttlecock. Also note; the bracken fronds reach out sideways almost horizontally from the vertical stem, depending on the angle of sunshine, and the roots (or rhizomes) spread under the soil to come up close by or at a distance, so covering a large area. A fern, however, tends to be on its own or just with one or two others and stays where it is.

Close up of fern centre

SOME GOOD NEWS . . .

Cranberry Fruit (Vaccinium oxycoccus) should also be in the herbal formula, but these are now easy to buy in tablet form, saving the trouble of drying and preparing. The cranberry fruit is one of the most beneficial herbs to be taken for urinary and bladder problems, in males and females, particularly for infections, and could be part of the daily diet along with vitamin C. Do not forget the Colloidal Silver for any infections, it may be taken or applied.

SMALL FLOWERED WILLOW HERB

Epilobium parviflorum, which is in the herbal formula, is of great value for the male of our species in its beneficial effects on prostate problems. It may be used quite separately, apart from being in the sixty herbal formula, if the necessity arises.

HERB ROBERT

(Geranium robertianum) The whole plant is used as an astringent mildly diuretic herb, that checks bleeding and mucus discharge and promotes healing. It is used for gastro-intestinal infections, peptic ulcer, herpes, inflamed gums and throat and may be applied to skin eruptions and wounds. It also has potential as a treatment of cancer.

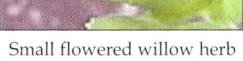

Small flowered willow herb

HAWTHORN

Crataegus oxyacantha improves the peripheral circulation, regulates heart rate, blood pressure and coronary blood flow. It is usually used by qualified practitioners and is remarkable, because it restores high or low blood pressure to normal. It improves the circulation of blood in the head, enhancing memory and is similar to Ginkgo biloba in this last respect.

TINCTURE OF ARNICA

IS NOT for oral use, but has been applied to bruises for as long as living memory. There is also a cream containing about 10% of the tincture, which is of great value for deep painful muscle damage when the bruise does not show on the skin surface. It should be massaged in gently several times daily. We are not talking of an homeopathic remedy here, the cream should contain about 10% of tincture. Colloidal Silver may be added to the application, at the time of massage, to help the damaged tissues to regenerate more rapidly.

Herb Robert

Hawthorne

UNIQUE VIBRATIONS

EVEN IF WE WERE ABLE to manufacture these complex vegetable chemicals, we would consume vast supplies of energy resources to heat and pressurise, bubble and boil, distill and freeze, and so on; and yet the plants, leaves, stalks, fruits and roots perform these functions, using only sunlight, enzymes, salts, air and the magic of water, but we hardly ever see it happening.

"Mother Earth"
"Heavenly Father."
*"I speak to you,
through the dew of the morning.
Be still, know I am God."*
(From the Vision of Enoch; God Speaks to Man.)

IT IS ALL SO QUIET

SO PEACEFUL, GREEN and beautiful and, with God's control pollution free, no huge smoking chimneys, just perfumed petalled living sculptures, nodding in the breezes, closing up at night and greeting each new dawn with added strength, every one giving pleasure to those with time to stand still and stare, even for a moment.

HE HAS HIS MIND on the pulse of Life and must wish that we would only use what He has already Created, rather than thinking that we can do better. He has a gene for everything and each one should remain where it belongs. Why should we transpose even one, when we do not yet know what we already have or the purpose of each gene? If we had more wisdom to accompany our knowledge, we would be content to move along with Him, as part of the framework in which He placed us.

IT IS A WONDERFUL WORLD we live in and, if you have time to read some more of these fascinating names, just think that He Created each one with a purpose, for nothing exists which did not first occur in His Mind. We are surrounded by them and every molecule has a unique vibration of its own, creating a perfect harmony in the place where it belongs, each one with its companion molecules, always working together.

COMPANION MOLECULES

IF YOU ARE really interested in these, there are many more worth investigating: Echinacin, Echinacein, Saturated safe Pyrrolizidines, Trigonelline, Fenugreekine, Allicin and sulphur related Esters, Lecithins, Mucilaginous fibres, Lycopene, Leutein, Ginkgolide cage molecules, Ginkgo-flavonoids, Eleutherosides-including Lignan structural types, Ginsenosides, and Panax-polysaccharides, Guaiacin, Isoguaiacin, Cnicin terpinoid, Quassin, Aloe-emodin, Emodin, Chrysophanol, Carnosol, Lapachol, Silymarin (flavonlignans), Beta-pachyman, Pachymic acid, and Juglone.

CANCER PREVENTION ACTIVITIES

THERE IS CONTINUOUS RESEARCH taking place concerning the doses of these beneficial compounds in terms of cancer prevention. This relates to some areas of the world population, which have very low numbers of cancer cases of all kinds and the daily amounts of these materials, such as lignans and isoflavonoids, occurring naturally in most of their diets.

THERE ARE no absolute doses determined at the present time but, as all scientific research is an ongoing process, you may wish to follow them in the years to come. They are an essential part of everyday diet.

Conifer flowers.
The barks of some trees are miraculous.

HERBS HOW THEY WORK

SOME RESEARCH has shown that many different cancers and tumours are caused by the intestinal parasite Fasciolopsis buskii and its offsprings circulating in the blood vessels to the liver and other organs. Here they facilitate the production of ortho-phospho-tyrosine, a cell growth stimulant, to enable its own survival.

THIS ALSO MAKES human cells multiply in excess, without possessing the proper function of the organ to which the cells originally belonged, leading to cancers. This is slightly over simplified but gives an idea of one process, described by Dr. Hulda Clark.

SEVERAL OF THE HERBS ELIMINATE these parasites and offsprings, allowing the tissues to return to normal function, while some of the other herbs inhibit the enzyme that makes the ortho-phospho-tyrosine, thereby diminishing the production of cancer cells, without harming the immune system of the body.

THESE HERBS are, of course, active in all the tissues of the body and within the solid materials passing along inside the gut.

THE FREQUENCY GENERATOR, described on pages 101 - 103, does not always destroy all the parasites trapped in the foods on their journey through the body, or those embedded in solid organs. There are many other parasites which also infest humans and are similarly destroyed by the herbs alone, or along with the frequency generator.

NORMALLY THIS PARASITE Fasciolopsis buskii would pass through the human digestive tract without causing too much damage and complete the next stages of its life cycle externally to us, in the pond snails, then re-infest us at a later date in water and food like wild watercress, which has not been properly washed.

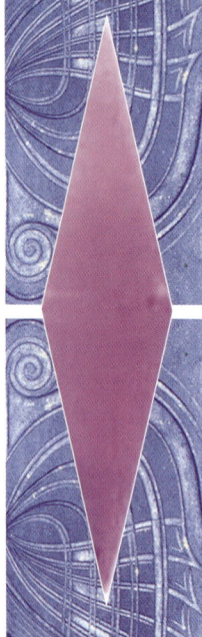

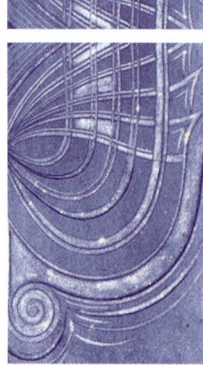

TOXIC MODERN LIFESTYLE

WITH THE excessive use of Isopropyl alcohol in foods, flavourings, colourings, cosmetics, cleaning agents, polishes and many other items, the parasite can now complete its whole life cycle in the human body, where it facilitates the production of ortho-phospho-tyrosine, to our detriment, by allowing the formation of cancers and tumours.

SOME OF THE HERBS kill the parasites and offsprings, boost the immune system and also destroy invading bacteria and viruses, which may have already lowered the body's defences. Many of the herbs help tissues like the liver to regenerate, as this organ has to cope with so much toxic material, and the kidneys are cleansed by others, to aid the excretion of this toxic burden. Colloidal Silver would also be of great value here in destroying bacteria, viruses, fungi, yeasts and the single cell offsprings of the parasites, then helping any damaged normal tissues to regenerate.

SOME HERBS DESTROY OTHER PARASITES, yeasts and fungi, some limit the damage caused by aflatoxins, patulin and other mycotoxins, which often occur in imperfect or rotten fruits and plants, while other herbs help the body to eliminate toxic metals. It is worth mentioning that vitamin C overcomes the destructive effects of aflatoxins and should be taken with each meal, hence the need for fruits several times daily and a vitamin C supplement, not just to prevent cancer but to maintain good health.

WHEN THE PARASITES have gone, Dr. H. Clark has shown that the cancer ceases to grow.

SOME HERBS DESTROY CANCER CELLS and prevent new ones from forming or progressing, some stimulate the body to produce Tumour Necrosis Factor which destroys tumours that have already formed.

THE FORMULA does not contain any materials of animal origin and there are no soya, yeast or peanut products. The formula should not be used during pregnancy or breast feeding, or by epileptics or children without medical advice or approval, or by those with cardiovascular problems. In the same way that any other dietary supplement should be taken; with discretion, as for instance, in avoiding excess salt, sugar, fats and alcohol.

IF YOU ARE in immediate need, use the lists on pages 86, 87, 88 and order the herbs as soon as possible from your Herbalist or Health shop. We are obliged to remind you from time to time: these facts and details are for information only and are not a diagnosis or prescription for any illness or health condition.

KEEP IN MIND, all the time, that Jesus gave us clear ways to experience God's Presence, to Feel The Kingdom of God.

As you know already, all these paragraphs and details are leading towards the moment of truth, when He will reveal Himself to you in His own way, as He has revealed Himself to us (page 117 onwards).

THE FREQUENCY GENERATOR

AS CHILDREN we had grown up experimenting with hand rotating dynamos, sparking coils operated by batteries and other devices; we had blown little holes in pieces of paper with a 'harmless' spark of high voltage but negligible current; we had seen electric sparks travel through flames and hot fumes. These ideas had stimulated further research in later life concerning purification of water and electrical methods for producing Colloidal Silver.

MANY STRANGE ELECTRICAL methods of treating human illness have been used over the past seventy years and most have been abandoned; and some others should be.

A FEW YEARS AGO we came across a report by Dr. Hulda Clark Ph.D., N.D. concerning a positive offset frequency generator which seemed to be unlike any other device previously in use. It is not an electrical method of treating illness, as were the others which have been abandoned, but a device to destroy the many parasites infesting the human body. This produces a frequency of about 30 kilohertz, at very low voltage and low current, using only a small battery. Dr. Clark states that, providing her Copyright is acknowledged, the circuit diagram may be reproduced.

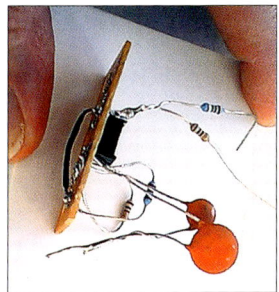

IT IS OF SIGNIFICANT IMPORTANCE and is detailed here. We are very pleased we came upon it and feel that everyone should know. We have already freely given details of our Colloidal Silver production for home use and the sixty remarkable anticancer herbs, so we are pleased to add Dr. Clark's circuit diagram, also freely given by herself.

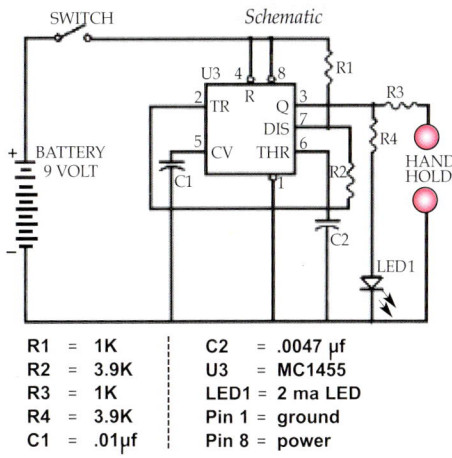

A simple circuit - no larger than a couple of fingers and fits in a little box with an On/Off switch, LED light, red and black sockets for the hand hold wires and a battery. It only required an afternoon to make.

THIS POSITIVE offset circuit makes all the difference, as the design shows. It is not necessary to understand it but is very easy to make, or have someone expert in electronics to build one for you. We have made a few for ourselves, so they cannot be too difficult!

R1 = 1K
R2 = 3.9K
R3 = 1K
R4 = 3.9K
C1 = .01µf

C2 = .0047 µf
U3 = MC1455
LED1 = 2 ma LED
Pin 1 = ground
Pin 8 = power

101

DURING OUR OWN RESEARCH, in those early teenage years, we missed this vital offset modification and also, unfortunately, we did not have the fascinating modern electronic components and microchips we have today.

SOME HELPFUL NOTES
All the joins are best soldered using the minimum heat and fresh three core flux solder, with a quick application, to keep all the components cool during assembly, and do not insert the microchip into its socket until all the joins are completed and cold.

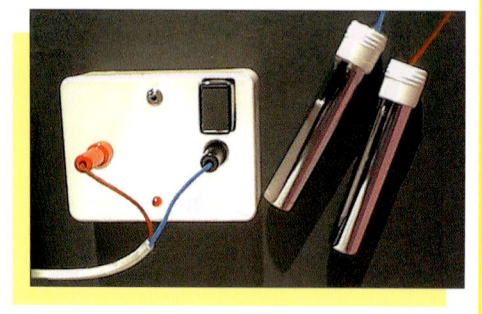

Zapper - one we made earlier!

FIRST OF ALL it can be shown experimentally that this frequency generator will destroy internal and external parasites, bacteria, viruses, yeasts, mites and some fungi. The limitations in part seem to be in applying the frequency to all body tissues. This is an area of our continued research, as there are a few tissues in which the parasites are not easily destroyed, so antiparasitic herbs should also be used along with the generator. These herbs are included in the anticancer formula, to help us all to return to complete health without any harmful organisms setting up home in our organs or on the surface.

WE HAVE MADE several different shaped electrodes, in place of the cylindrical hand held ones, for our own research work; you may wish to experiment with this idea.

THE CYLINDRICAL ELECTRODES or hand holds are made quite simply from three quarter inch copper plumbing pipe, but a pipe of larger diameter is more comfortable to hold in the hands and chromium plated ones would be superior, as less copper would enter the skin. This material may be more difficult to purchase but try a DIY store; if not, make the best use of what you can obtain. These are connected as shown in the circuit diagram. The hand holds should be wrapped around individually with a wet tissue, prior to using. Tap water, which contains some minerals to help conductivity, is suitable for this purpose with an added pinch of salt.

REMEMBER, the activity is from the positive offset frequency; do not use a stronger battery.

THE DEVICE is used by switching on and holding the electrodes for seven minutes, then switch off and spend the next twenty-five minutes doing something else. Now switch on again and use for another seven minutes. Take another break of twenty-five minutes and repeat the procedure; do not forget to switch on.

IT IS PARTICULARLY interesting that nothing is felt in the hands. A few people may have a faint tingling but in a case where there is no real feeling you do need to make sure, you switch on each time, so the indicator light is bright red and, of course switch off, to maintain the battery strength. Hold an electrode in each hand keeping the tissues wet during the three seven minute sessions.

THESE THREE sessions are all you require. The first seven minutes kills the parasites, the second seven minutes kills the bacteria and viruses liberated from those parasites on their demise and the third seven minutes kills the viruses released from the dead bacteria. It must be stressed that these three sessions are adhered to, so the body is not swamped with a bacterial and viral burden from the destroyed parasites.

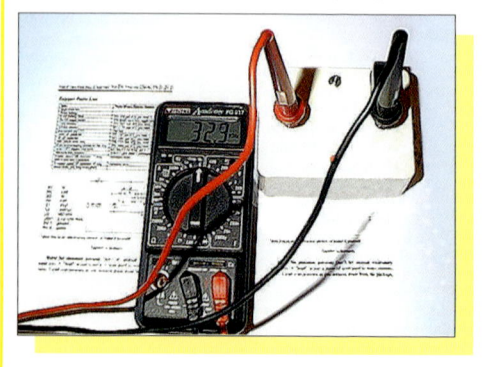

Testing the zapper frequency, about 30 kHz.
Many TV repairers would do this for you.

DO NOT USE THIS DEVICE if pregnant or if wearing a pacemaker, as no research has been performed concerning these. Otherwise you may repeat the procedure each day until you are well again.

Dr. Hulda Clark has named this equipment a 'ZAPPER' but in some countries people have made other devices with the same name, which have other functions, so it should be referred to as a POSITIVE OFFSET FREQUENCY GENERATOR AT 30kilohertz. It is obvious why she calls it a 'Zapper', with a name this long.

IF THIS IS THE FIRST time you have used the frequency generator, try to have a restful day on the one following, while your body eliminates the toxins from any parasites you may have had and the toxic materials from the destroyed bacteria and viruses, not forgetting any moulds, fungi, yeasts and mites, which have also been eliminated.

FAST FORWARD ... Regeneration

IT WOULD BE VERY BENEFICIAL to have two or three doses of Colloidal Silver daily, over the next few days, to help rapid healing of tissues damaged by parasitic infestations leaving your body.

IT IS VERY INTERESTING to us that Silver in Colloidal form is not ionised like a salt dissolved in water but it does carry an electrical charge and helps the tissues to regenerate. Regeneration of bone tissue has been shown to occur by Dr. Robert O. Becker in America using pure silver wires inserted into either side of broken bones, which have not healed and are also surrounded by infected soft tissues of long standing, when no other orthodox treatment had helped.

EXTREMELY LOW voltage and current was applied to these silver wires and the broken bones healed rapidly by producing new bone tissue in the gap between the break. The infected surrounding soft tissue was also regenerated and slowly returned to good health over a period of time. We do not know if this effect was due to the silver charged 'ions' produced by the passage of a very low current or if a localised silver colloid was formed by association with organic molecules of the body, but apparently the benefits were not the same using other metals as electrodes. The presence of Silver is essential.

IF HE USED VOLTAGES ABOVE 0.9, bubbles of gas were generated by electrolysis within the human cells, near the wires which he inserted, and the cells died. So it is essential that any voltage applied to a human MUST BE BELOW THIS LEVEL, if the duration of contact is prolonged.

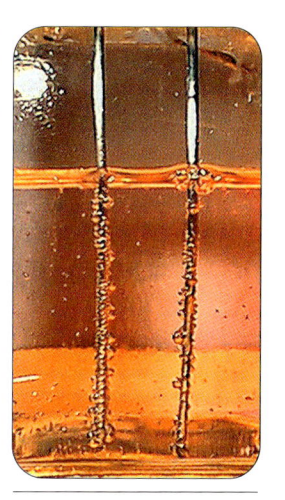

Cell damage arises if a voltage above 0.9 is used, due to bubble formation.

WE HAVE EXPERIMENTED using external pure silver contacts and Colloidal Silver on arthritic limbs and swellings with very good results but more scientific research is needed before this can be discussed in detail.

WE OFTEN EXPRESS the thought that the closer you become to God or being a Christian, the more difficult it gets. Scientific research is very similar; the nearer you are to a solution to a problem, the more questions are presented. This is not a matter of the soul but the expenses incurred to complete the work. Many brilliant thoughts and ideas have to be lost because of lack of funds. We have to be careful, as we fund all our own research work.

REMARKABLE REVELATIONS

DURING our many years of scientific research we have stumbled upon several unique phenomena, which, to Heather's and my surprise, are identical to those described by Jesus in the Biblical Texts.

THESE PHENOMENA BRING JESUS DIRECTLY INTO TODAY'S WORLD, NOT IN TERMS OF THE GLOOM AND DOOM OF MODERN DAY PROPHETS AND SCIENTISTS, BUT AS AN ABSOLUTE CONFIRMATION OF OUR CREATOR'S PRESENCE, NOW.

ALL IS WELL WITH THE WORLD, we are not rapidly zooming towards the end.

Jesus said to His Disciples:
"Have you then discovered the beginning, so that you inquire about the end?"
"For where the beginning is, there shall be the end."

HE INDICATES here that where one sequence has ended, there is another one beginning. This is in keeping with His remarks about the 'circle', where no one is first, no one is last, but we are all behind one another and in front; so there is always something to follow.

THE FUTURE IS GOOD but we can choose to go against God's Natural Presence or we could all go along with Him and feel great happiness as our lives change. We hope to be able to pass on our findings and help you to experience our Creator's Presence, now in today's world.

MOST OF MY FRIENDS and colleagues seem to think of me as a scientist, although I started my professional career as a Pharmaceutical Chemist. I sold my Chemist shop and Dispensary to devote the future to independent scientific research into all the conditions that influence mankind's health and well-being. Some of these are quite unusual but have a profound effect on an individual's health, happiness and abilities.

MY RESEARCH COVERED telepathy, dowsing, ghosts, poltergeists, divine healing, faith healing, laying on hands, the use of vitamins, minerals, and amino acids to bring people back to good health and then to maintain their health. Also the use of herbs to alleviate and prevent illness and disease. All these are not drugs but the natural building blocks of life. Many are really foods but are often missing in our diets.

WE WANT TO COME back later to Divine Healing because this is where our most important research findings occurred and are truly remarkable.

on the edge of discovery

TO TOUCH ON TELEPATHY FIRST. It seems to become possible to extend the sensitivity of the mind and to use areas of the brain which are lying dormant, because our five normal senses serve us all so well; everything is very loud and bright, all things are perfumed or flavour enhanced. It comes as quite a surprise that information can also reach us in subtle ways. We describe an experiment in which you can check this for yourself.

IN DOWSING, as described earlier, you do begin to feel there is a sensitivity beyond the confines of the skull and you can detect water, metals, minerals and missing people, by using a pendulum over a map or with hazel twigs and dowsing 'rods', over a field or larger area. You begin to realise we are much more than walking compounds of physical material. We can think and have experiences, beyond those which are obvious, and receive information in subtle ways.

GHOSTS AND POLTERGEISTS are so often disruptive to a happy life, they are nearly always damaging to health and people frequently need special help to overcome or understand their problems. These disruptive forces may interfere with your sensitivity to feel our Creator's Presence but His help is always here for you and He will indicate the way forward. Prepare to be surprised but do not become involved with them, remain an outside observer.

IT SEEMS from our research that poltergeists come about by someone's inadvertent or deliberate transgressions of God's natural Laws. Ghosts on the other hand seem to be a memory attached to a location, to which some people have a sensitivity or awareness and their mind may in some way replay an impinged recording of an event from the past or maybe they can just step back in time, within their mind, when in a certain location and see what took place.

IF THIS IS the case then these same people may be able to take a step forward because everything that determines the next moment of our existence has already happened. What follows is the effect or outcome of causes that have already taken place and only God's Influence can change this.

There may be a condition of our mind, in which we have in some way absorbed enough of the causes of the immediate past, to experience a moment of their effects or, in other words a glimpse into the future.

TEMPLE of the Soul

THE PURIFICATION of the physical body together with proper nutrition are so important we must spend a little time on them now, because when we reach the research work on Divine Healing and the relationship with Jesus' sayings, you may not wish to turn back to study these basic requirements.

THE BODY IS THE TEMPLE OF THE SOUL

THROW OUT, and flush out, everything that may interfere with its environment. Also clear the mind and memory of immoral or improper thoughts. If you have to cut God out of your mind to think or do something; DON'T do it. If you still have difficulty, ask for His help not to do it.

THE PHYSICAL PURIFICATION of the body refers to the removal of toxic materials, due to the presence of pollution, having accumulated over many years, from everything we eat, drink, breathe and touch.

THERE ARE NO true toxin eliminating diets; the only way is using and drinking Purified Water to remove them from the whole body and also to prevent it from absorbing dozens more; we have already referred to Jesus' comments about water, for He knows more of its secrets than we do.

SOME MINERALS and organic compounds will help in releasing toxic metals from the body's tissues, and are well worth a little research. Then purified water will remove them, but many tap waters, if already grossly contaminated will not. Alpha lipoic acid is used for this.

OVER TWENTY YEARS ago, having realised the high levels of pollution after intensive analysis of many water samples from all over Britain and a few other countries, I began to make distilled water to use for all drinking purposes and cooking for our family. The improvement in our health and well-being was remarkable, we even felt younger.

Jesus said:
"All the waters the Creator hath made, are Holy."

I DESIGNED AND BUILT a fairly large water purification unit, which would produce many gallons each day, without the expensive use of electricity for distillation, only for electrical pumps and for ultraviolet light generation. The main process we use here is Reverse Osmosis, which many people know about, and some of these devices operate on ordinary mains water pressure, in domestic under the sink units.

WE NEEDED so much water, I also installed a pumping system with larger R/O membranes. This enabled us to supply our families and friends, nursing homes, doctors, allergy and dialysis patients and many others. Unfortunately the supply is only available for a small area in the North West, as transport costs make it impossible to be otherwise. Our son Paul developed and operates this business under his PURA-LIFE label, while we service the scientific requirements.

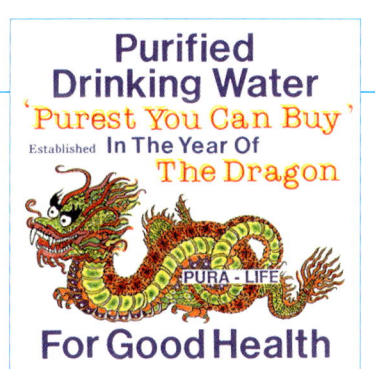

Purified Drinking Water
'Purest You Can Buy'
Established In The Year Of **The Dragon**

For Good Health

THE PROCESS IS quite complicated and involves using several filtration systems before the water even reaches the R/O devices. Ultraviolet light is used for water storage and sterilisation of bottles but there are many more smaller, simpler, domestic systems available which are now very efficient. They have to be properly maintained, so do not let anyone tell you otherwise, and should be capable of sterilisation at least every two months, including the R/O membrane, its housing (container) and all the filters. Some filters may have to be washed before sterilising or should be replaced.

CARBON GRANULE FILTERS should only be used prior to the R/O system, as they often harbour bacteria which breed there, as the granules absorb materials, and in so doing bring them together to form new compounds, many of which become nutrients for the contaminating organisms.

WE have written in another paragraph about the wonders of water bringing chemicals together which would not have come near each other, but the carbon brings them closer and in much greater concentrations.

IT IS NECESSARY to study the details of all these devices very well indeed, because they are quite expensive and are not free from maintenance. This does not mean just replacing a couple of filters. There are several other systems but those using reverse osmosis are superior in most aspects.

WE DO not feel we should take up too much space on this, although it is a study in itself, but just wish to make the knowledge available that there is a way forward. Because most of the media, including television, always give the gloom and doom but seldom tell us what to do about it in a positive way.

MOST PEOPLE THINK ALL the bottled waters are purified and there are many wonderful names but they are not purified, just well promoted and advertised. They may be filtered free of particles and most living organisms, but several are no different from tap water; some are even worse, containing 20 parts per million (20ppm.) or more of nitrates and other harmful substances. Some have deceptively 'posh' names and hide in artistic bottles!

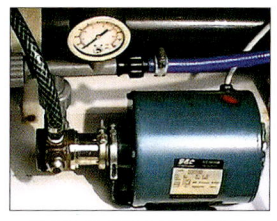

Pressure pumps and filters

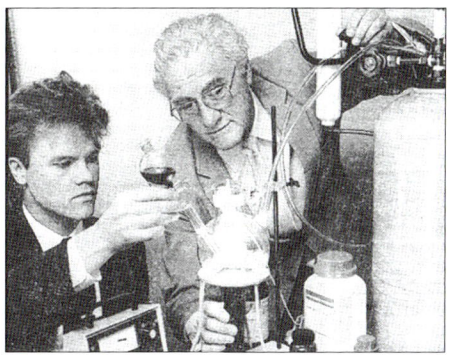

Reverse Osmosis membranes

PURE SCIENCE: Paul and Alan completing a water analysis for an investigation by the Daily Post.

National Television — SEPTEMBER 10, 1990

AS SEEN BY FIVE MILLION VIEWERS

Pura~Life

Purified Drinking Water

Recommended & Used By
Doctors & Chemists
Homeopaths
Health Consultants
and Allergy Specialists

Not Just Another
Bottled Water
This Is
Purified To Perfection

The Purest You Can Buy

DEMONSTRATED ON THE

Garden Party programme by:

Springwater Mineral Water
Tap Water
PURA~LIFE Purified Drinking Water

Alan Fraser Bell Ph.C., M.P.S., M.R.S.H.
SCIENTIFIC CONSULTANT
To PURA~LIFE
DEMONSTRATION
All Tapwater, Springwater & Mineral Waters contain colourless Chemical Pollutants.

Electrolysis makes these visible as colours and sediments.

PURA~LIFE WATER STAYS CLEAR

Drinking Water of Superb Quality
The Purest You Can Buy

LABORATORY NOTE: This experiment makes an interesting demonstration for Television, but at the Pura~Life Laboratory they test for individual contaminants, such as: Nitrates - Lead - Arsenic - Aluminium - Radioactivity Bacteria and dozens more, as listed on the Bottle label. These are all removed by special procedures.

PURA ~ LIFE WATER
helps the body to eliminate its own toxic waste and avoids absorbing hundreds of other poisons

USES
For Tea, Coffee, Beverages, Fruit Juices, Mixers, Cooking, Jams, Baking, Steam Irons and Car Batteries. For Complexion & Hair Rinses. For Long Cool Drinks by itself and making PURE CLEAR ICE CUBES.

PURA~LIFE
For Good Health

To Prepare Chemical Free Baby Foods; boil first in stainless steel, polypropylene, Teflon or Pyrex, or in a CLEAN kettle. NOT aluminium, copper or enamel.

DAILY POST

Friday, September 18, 1987 — Price 20p

PURA~LIFE

Water: Fresher than a mountain spring . . .

By LARRY NEILD

BOTTLED water is big business in supermarkets as more people opt for mountain-fresh spring waters.

But a Merseyside man has just launched the world's purest drinking water which has already got customers raising their glasses to its success. The amazing thing is this new product starts life as ordinary everyday tap water. A series of processes convert it into something special.

"It is as pure as the day the earth was created" said scientist Alan Fraser Bell, the brains behind the scheme. "A lot of science and technology has been used. My life's work is in that water."

A series of impressive tests show just what we are letting ourselves in for when we consume not only tap water, but many of the bottled varieties.

"With the nitrates, minerals and various salts in some of the bottled water you would be better off drinking tap water" revealed Mr Bell, who lives in Formby.

Distilled

For years he and his family have consumed treated water - firstly distilled and now his own purified version. And he says there are many reasons why pure water is important to maintain good health. It can even help get rid of long standing ailments.

Totally clean water helps to flush toxins out of the body, but most water these days is so contaminated it adds more unwanted chemicals to the system.

And more than that . . . Mr Bell holds a Geiger counter close to a filter. The needle moves, and the counter starts to make a familiar noise. The tap water which passed through the filter had contained radioactivity.

Electrodes are placed in the tap water - which most of us drink and regard as reasonably clean. Within two minutes the electrical activity has turned the water into a glass of green slimy liquid, caused says Mr Bell, because the water contains so much rubbish.

Similar tests with his own apparatus have a totally different result. The Geiger counter remains silent, the water exposed to the electrodes remains crystal clear.

Mr Bell's son Paul, has launched the family's special product onto the market. Pura~Life has found its way onto the shelves of health shops throughout Merseyside and the North West.

Paul is well known on the club circuit as solo singer Paul Sebastian. But he has also spent many years in marketing and sales.

Added Mr Bell senior: "A lot of people now buy spring water because they are not satisfied with tap water. They tend to think it is purer, but it is not. Most contain materials that should not be there - toxic metals, nitrates, etc. What we have done is take a water and remove the lot. There is nothing in the world that approaches our water for purity. This process can be used on any water anywhere."

Paul hopes, if the product takes off he will establish a bigger production plant. The water goes through four processes, the major one being reverse osmosis, which even gets rid of any radioactive contaminants.

Allergic

Said Paul: "One of my customers on Merseyside was so allergic to tap water she was on the brink of putting her home up for sale. Now she drinks our water and everything is fine."

What about that plentiful and cheap stuff that pours from our taps?

Said Mr Bell snr: "The state of tap water is pretty grim. You cannot blame the water authority. They do an amazing, almost impossible job, making it as clean as it is. But with contaminated rivers and streams you cannot have totally pure tap water."

Good health - water purified to perfection
Paul and Alan with before and after samples.

109

THE MIRACLE of water

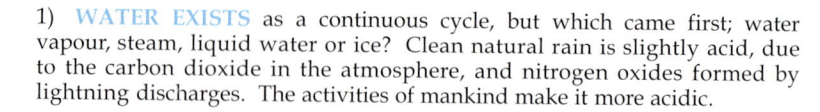

1) WATER EXISTS as a continuous cycle, but which came first; water vapour, steam, liquid water or ice? Clean natural rain is slightly acid, due to the carbon dioxide in the atmosphere, and nitrogen oxides formed by lightning discharges. The activities of mankind make it more acidic.

2) ALTHOUGH we think of the human body as being fairly solid, with 206 bones in an adult (a few more in a child), we contain about 70% water. More than half the atoms in the body are hydrogen and these atoms are composed of one proton and one electron, one positive charge and one negative. If they were not being kept apart by mysterious forces, they would disappear! What Forces?

3) PURE STEAM condenses into Purified water (distillation) and has its greatest density at $4°C$. Rather strangely, it expands when you warm it up from $4°C$. and also expands as you cool it down from $4°C$. to zero degrees. Then it stays liquid for a short time, as it loses its hidden heat and turns into ice, which is lighter than water and always floats. Only one eighth of a floating iceberg is above the surface of the sea.

4) PURIFIED or Distilled water barely conducts electricity at all; it is the salts, which are nearly always present in all water samples, that conduct the current.

5) THE SAME elements in sea water, such as Calcium, Magnesium, Sodium and so on, are almost in the same proportions in the fluids of the human body!

6) SALT MELTS ICE because it lowers the freezing point of water, so salty water only becomes solid at a much lower temperature; the more salt it contains the lower its freezing point. So the seas always need a very low temperature to freeze over.

7) THERE are a few strange bacteria which induce very cold water to form ice crystals. Every snow crystal has a different shape but all have six points.

8) TREES GROW more wood in wet years than they do in dry ones, so for hundreds of years in the past we can know what the weather was like.

9) LIFE ON EARTH, as we know it, would not exist without water. It is essential for all life forms. WATER covers about 71% of the earth's surface and the oceans have a volume of approximately 1,320 million cubic metres. It is a fact but has very little meaning to us.

10) THE GRAVITATIONAL pull of the moon creates the ocean tides and, to a smaller extent, the sun contributes to the movement, as the waters are free to move over the surface of the sea-beds. During a solar eclipse, as the moon passes in front of the sun, they are both pulling in the same direction and the tides are higher. Incidentally there have been 228 solar eclipses in the 20th century. When the moon is on the opposite side of the earth to the sun they pull in opposite directions, so the tides are smaller. Then our earth may cast a complete shadow over the moon.

H₂O

DURING A LUNAR ECLIPSE the moon glows with a rosy copper colour, due to the sunlight being deflected as it passes through the earth's atmosphere. And again incidentally, there have been 147 eclipses of the moon by the earth in the 20th century. What will our New Millennium bring?

11) THE SUN must always be behind you to see a rainbow and must be lower than 42°. The sunlight is reflected and refracted by the raindrops to produce the bow.

12) IF HYDROGEN AND OXYGEN are combined together by using a catalyst in a pair of electrodes, electricity is produced directly and water is the by-product, H_2O. In other words, the energy produced by the two gases combining is electricity instead of a flash of light and a loud bang.

13) WATER CARRIES AWAY most of the toxic waste of the human body and helps to regulate a fairly constant temperature by evaporation of moisture from the surface of the skin and every exhaled breath. The same water we have today has already cooled down the Dinosaurs, because Our Creator has designed and perfected methods of purifying and recycling every drop since the beginning of time.

14) WATER IS OFTEN hidden in beautiful crystals, such as copper sulphate, which everyone knows; each molecule of copper sulphate has 5 molecules of water concealed in the crystals. When heated to 250°C. the water vapourises leaving a residue of greyish/white powder, still copper sulphate but anhydrous.

15) A SOAP BUBBLE only forms because the pressure of air inside balances the surface tension of the film of water, which tends to make the surface shrink. The thickness of this liquid layer depends on the soap or detergent molecules and is the same for bubbles of different sizes.

16) WATER WAS FOUND IN A METEORITE thought to date back to the birth of the solar system, five billion years ago. Could this have contained genetic material from another world?

17) THE SURFACE TENSION of water is so strong that a steel needle of greater density can be floated on its surface. Many insects make use of this without getting their feet wet!

18) THE MOVING RIPPLES etched on the sand by the oceans and seas of the world are curiously related to the ripples sculpting the planet's vast deserts. These patterns are so similar and yet no tides of moving water wash these textured sands. Does the wind carry the same message as the waves? Water transfers subtle memories to and from everything it touches.

Copper sulphate

LIFE supplemental

WE MUST MAKE some brief comments on the foods we eat to build and maintain the body, so it can be an adequate Temple for the soul and spirit material to continue in residence, in a state of activity rather than being dormant or overcome by toxins and devious thoughts.

DIET (just a few notes). We must all avoid being overweight. Yes! you have heard it all before, so we do not intend to develop this subject, as there is adequate information available in almost all magazines, ('Oh! deep joy'). Most people are aware that foods fall into three main categories; fats, carbohydrates and proteins.

BEING SLIGHTLY UNDERWEIGHT IS not so important, providing you are receiving the additional factors, such as vitamins, minerals, fruits, vegetables and herbs.

WE JUST WISH to indicate the relevance all these have to a Creative Thinking Mind and the ability to be aware of God's Presence. We know He will take over if an eating problem reaches a critical state, as He does during unconsciousness, of which we have already spoken, when He will carry you.

HE HAS PROGRAMMED US TO LOOK AFTER OURSELVES, so we should be doing it properly, as He has provided all these wonderful plants, foods and pure water for our progress and happiness through life.

THE IMPORTANT DETAILS

THE QUALITY, the type of food, the presence or absence of the necessary vitamins and minerals are all important.

Briefly, the dietary proportions should be about: 25% Protein, 43% Carbohydrate and about 15% or less Fat, about 1% each of combined Phosphorus, Potassium, Magnesium, Calcium and Chlorine and 0.5% combined Sodium.

THE DIET must of course contain Iron, and Iodine, in even smaller amounts, and all the vitamins: A, B1, B2, B6, B12 and the other compounds in the B complex, such as Biotin, Choline, Inositol, Lipoic acid, Nicotinic acid, Folic Acid and Pantothenic acid.

ALSO VITAMINS C, D, E and K, plus the trace elements Zinc, Copper, Manganese, Selenium, Molybdenum and Fluorine.

TRACES OF OTHERS, like Chromium, Tin and Vanadium, probably occur in most prepared foods and the Cobalt comes from foods containing vitamin B12, although this often needs to be supplemented.

Vitamins + minerals

SELENIUM is nearly always in need of supplementation, as all British crops are deficient because there is none in many soils, and even imported grains and other foods are similarly becoming depleted in selenium.

ALL THE VITAMINS AND MINERALS may be added to the diet in supplement form, except the Fluorine, as there is an adequate amount in cups of tea or as a fluoride toothpaste. Be careful, particularly with young children, that the toothpaste is not swallowed and only used in small amounts, not spread along the whole length of the brush, as shown in many adverts. It should always be thoroughly rinsed away, several times, with plenty of fresh water.

IF THIS ALL SEEMS complicated, the simple way to cope is to take a top brand Multi-Vitamin and Mineral supplement containing all those mentioned above (do check, they are all in it) for six days, then miss a day to give the body a chance to adjust its needs, if necessary.

NONE CONTAIN enough vitamin C for our present day requirements; extra should be taken separately. We use at least 2g. daily and this may easily be increased or decreased, if food passes through too quickly. This would be the most natural way, along with extra fruits and vegetables, to avoid constipation and prevent a build up of toxic materials in the body, so drugs need not be used for this purpose.

AN INTERESTING NOTE

AS THE BODY does not seem to store vitamin C in the tissues, once you have established the dose that suits you, it is best not to miss a day, as we do with the other vitamins.

VITAMIN C helps in the absorption of Iron, and Iron prevents the absorption of Lead. It is fascinating how the body can look after itself, if only life was as it should be. Similarly Zinc prevents the absorption of Cadmium, another toxic metal like Lead. This is why Iron and Zinc are almost essential as supplements.

WE HAVE ONLY touched on some of the wonders here but they are all well worth following up in your own research; there is so much more.

FOR COMPLETE DETAILS, there is a wealth of information in the literature, which should be consulted, with reference to a weight/height relationship chart, then a decision should be reached as to whether you are under or overweight, or of natural proportions.

HEALTH check

WE HAVE emphasised in these past few paragraphs the necessity for proper foods and the use of vitamin-mineral supplements during all your creative work, in preparation for experiencing God's Presence and receiving His gifts.

WE MUST avoid converting our text into another vitamin book. There is a vast amount of information available and it is all worth studying.

WEIGH YOURSELF each week, this is the simplest guide; if you are still overweight, eat less food, particularly reduce the intake of carbohydrates and fats, such as biscuits, cakes, pastries, sweets, chocolates, cereals, bread, starches, sugars, potatoes and of course crisps.

LIBERAL applications of cream, salt, butter and salad dressings, should be avoided.

MAKE A DELIBERATE attempt to increase your intake of all the fresh fruit and cooked green vegetables, to supply fibrous materials, and the many other remarkable components in God's Garden. Then drink more purified water.

BE SURE you eat most of the root vegetables also, and occasionally uncooked, but well washed with the outer surface removed.

ALL THE EDIBLE BERRIES, although small and often troublesome to pick and prepare, are some of God's most remarkable creations: Raspberry, Blackberry, Strawberry, Mulberry, Bilberry, Cranberry and others should be part of one meal each day. They all have near miraculous properties and are so often neglected in the diet.

IF YOU PICK them yourself, always avoid those near a roadway, as they are contaminated with lead from petrol fumes and other toxic materials. Although lead is no longer permitted from the year 2000, it will remain in the roadside soil for a long time.

SOME ARE IMMORTALISED in children's nursery rhymes, and there are very good reasons for this. To teach the children.

"Round and Round
The Mulberry Bush."

DO YOU remember it?
Think about it!
It is all to do with health.

"This is the way we live our lives."
"On a cold and frosty morning."

THE MULBERRY is not really a bush, but a very handsome tree, with deep red/purple fruits and wonderful golden yellow autumn leaves, but it takes a long time to become a tree, hence people think of it as a bush.

THERE ARE MANY trees in this country that are two or three hundred years old; they have a long life, as we should have, but they do not begin to blossom until about eleven years old and are not in full bloom until their twenties. Is there a moral here somewhere?

THE MULBERRY FRUITS, as many people know, contain the miraculous compound Resveratrol, which has special anticancer properties, and in past centuries, many people were overcome with this condition without knowing what it was.

BUT SOME of them knew how to treat it, with the benefits of Mulberry and whole Grapes, Sheep's Sorrel herb and many others, to make them well again.

THERE ARE WILD PONIES living on the Moors in Britain who have such tough mouths and tongues that they are able to eat Brambles, which are of course Blackberries, but not just the fruits as we do (after getting torn to shreds picking them). They eat the stems, shoots, twigs, flowers, the whole plant; quite remarkable!

AND HERE is an astonishing thought. These lovely friendly creatures have been living in the wild, without any help from man, for hundreds of years, in perfect health. Now that says something about Blackberries!!

HOME GROWN fruits and vegetables are wonderful for health but the soil must not be contaminated with old paint scrapings, distemper and rolls of wallpaper, carrying coloured toxic compounds of cadmium, arsenic, lead and mercury.

THIS OFTEN occurs when unknown items are burnt on a garden bonfire. It is better to dispose of these safely.

IF YOU GROW your crops in the soil, then only burn garden rubbish or, better still, convert it all into useful compost.

OVER generous application of nitrate to any green leafy crops such as lettuce should be avoided, as it passes into the leaf structures and interferes with the creative processes of the body and brain when eaten.

NITRITES are often produced from nitrates by the activity of bacteria and could lead to the formation of nitrosamines in the gut, which are cancer producing in susceptible people.

VITAMIN C is of great value here to prevent this action and is even more valuable if taken with a meal which may contain a winter grown shop lettuce or one forced through the summer.

IN FACT we take vitamin C with every meal, which is as God intended it to be, if we were still plucking berries from the bushes as we wandered through the countryside.

PLEASE NOTICE how we have avoided the saying, 'swinging through the trees'!! There is no evidence of mankind evolving from apes. We were created and placed here as a separate species.

HEALTH check

OTHER INTERESTING NOTES: Milk containing about 2% fat is probably the best way for the body to absorb and use Calcium for bone structures. For strong bones we also require an equal amount of Magnesium, a few mcgs. of vitamin D, Phosphorus, Silicon as Silica and only very small traces of Fluorine.

THE QUANTITY of animal fats ingested should be kept as low as possible and some replaced by cold pressed Olive Oil, not those oils which have been hardened using hydrogen and a nickel catalyst, often shown as (trans) fats on food labels.

MANY FISH contain a few toxic compounds from polluted rivers and artificial fish farming but those from the deep sea are still less polluted and are a valuable source of protein, as it is very difficult for many people to be truly vegetarian. The body can deteriorate through lack of all the necessary amino acids.

SEPARATED wheat germ contains many essential amino acids and can be easily added to soups and cereals.

SPACE: Every living thing, plant or animal, requires space of its own in which to move, grow and develop. When humans are restricted in this way, they become frustrated, irritable and aggressive and their chance of creative achievement is minimal.

THEREFORE, if possible, make a room available for yourself at home or even a portion or corner of a room; an area were you can work and hopefully practise and develop, undisturbed for at least some part of each day.

BREATHE IN AS DEEPLY as possible while counting up to five, hold your breath for a further count of five, then exhale slowly to a count of seven. While you are inhaling, feel that you are taking in goodness and strength; while exhaling, know you are disposing of toxic waste.

THIS IS not just for reading, it really should be acted upon, particularly if a fresh breeze is blowing in from the sea.

CONSUMPTION of all meats should be very small and some replaced by vegetable sources of protein, as farming methods have changed so much over the years; they frequently contain the metabolites of antibiotics and other chemicals.

WE ALL know they contribute to the emergence of antibiotic resistant strains of bacteria, and these are very difficult to overcome in human disease.

IF NUTS ARE ADDED to or are part of the diet, to replace animal proteins, care should be taken to eat only the completely wholesome kernels, as many moulds and particularly dry dust like spores are disastrous for creative development.

AFTER inhalation of even a small amount of dust (spores) from so called 'puff balls' and similar growths among grass and wooded areas, creativity has been disturbed for many weeks. This word creativity of course encompasses sensitivity to and awareness of all the minute sources of information, other than those which reach us via the five usual physical senses.

FRESH AIR: Try to ensure that you live and work in well ventilated or air conditioned rooms, where the air is drawn in from outside, washed and filtered, not where the same air is recycled.

IDEALLY the incoming air should be washed with a renewable supply of purified water, not tap water which contains chlorine and other volatile compounds, as these would then be transferred to the washed air.

AVOID THE SMOKE soot and fumes of coal, coke and oil burners and the exhaust gases of petrol and diesel vehicles. Do not inhale the smoke of garden bonfires and other refuse; avoid cigarette, cigar or pipe smoking.

IF YOU CANNOT give up the habit, then do it very slowly; make a note of how many you use today, then smoke one less each day for the next two weeks, and another one less for the following two weeks. Continue with this regime until you have reduced to about four a day; stay on those for a while, then stop altogether.

WE ARE CONTINUING our research into COLLOIDAL SILVER which could well control all these mutant resistant strains, easily and cheaply with the little home generator, we have described, and we are hoping to take this work into AIDS and other areas.

TO CONTROL outbreaks of diseases, which arise in the squalid and primitive conditions in which many people of the world find themselves, during oppressions, wars, poverty and natural disasters.

THE GREATEST SINGLE STEP

arising from Creativity is, of course, to actually Feel God's Presence. Not just to believe He is with you but to actually know He is and to be able to tell someone else how to find Him and feel His Presence.

A NEGATIVE AIR IONISER is always a great asset in improving all indoor situations. It is also especially beneficial for a perfect night's sleep so you awake feeling refreshed.

IF YOU LIVE and work in a dusty, smoke laden, oppressive atmosphere, then try to have a period away by the sea or high in the hills and practise several deep breathing exercises.

GOD TOUCHED YOU

IF YOU have become involved in the Experiments we have described so far and you are checking your life for moments when God touched you, as we have been trying to indicate, you will be very thrilled with your progress. This is your beginning, your way forward...

The following pages reveal how our own path changed direction in a most remarkable way.

For us, what was previously a deep belief in God, is now beyond belief; it's knowing.

We know Our Creator exists, we have seen His works, experienced His Presence, we know we are not alone. All God's creations totally eclipse those of mankind.

Moon Eclipse
21. 1. 2000
In The Healing Garden.

THE MOST REMARKABLE EXPERIENCE OF A LIFETIME

How We Discovered God's Presence

DURING OUR research work into Faith Healing and Divine Healing, God's Creative Presence began to emerge and this has nothing to do with the spirit world.

WE SAW MANY MIRACLES take place; people would begin to walk, see, hear, talk again, spines would straighten, arthritic limbs would move again without pain, cancers and tumours disperse, heart conditions improve and many more benefits, just by placing our hands on someone's head and asking God for help, asking Jesus to be with us.

IT IS ALL SO UNBELIEVABLY simple but very difficult to explain scientifically. I know, from my own medical and pharmaceutical knowledge, that these miracles are just not possible within the scientific framework of life but they happened with us every day.

WE SEEMED TO BECOME HEALERS, although this was not something we had sought to do; it was as if it were thrust upon us. It was all so simple and natural. The use of drugs and surgical techniques seemed to be the strange ones, although very necessary in many cases.

SOME REMARKABLE EXPERIENCES occurred as Our Creator began to make His Presence known and felt. We write about these and tell how thousands of people now know God is with us all. We Are Not Alone. Jesus, and The Holy Spirit are here also. We were all born into a hostile world, but not abandoned, and left to get on with it. The world has been even more hostile than it is today, with the extinction of many species, and yet mankind has survived; we are still in a process of evolution, of guidance and creation.

FOR US, what was previously a deep belief in God, is now beyond belief; it is knowing. We know Our Creator exists, we have seen His works, experienced His Presence, we know we are not alone. We use the word He, as mentioned earlier, as a way of writing about a remarkable Creative Presence with perfect intellect, knowledge and wisdom.

IT IS NOT ONLY THE HEALINGS that amaze us. So many unusual flowers have grown in the garden where people have walked, who have been made well again.

The Resurrection Sculpture.
Now Jesus can be with us all today without the limitations of a physical body.

S INCE OUR DISCOVERY OF GOD'S PRESENCE we often think of a saying of Jesus, which did not come to light, until later:

"W ith The Angels of The Heavenly Father, will you learn to see the unseen, and to hear that which cannot be heard."

SUBTLE changes

A FOXGLOVE PLANT with one large beautiful compound flower at the top of the stalk and the usual ones hanging downwards, just below it.

BEFORE EASTER there were Honesty flowers with a white cross at their centres as mentioned earlier.

ALL THOSE that opened after Easter Sunday were entirely the normal purple, and on the same plant.

MANY FOUR LEAF CLOVERS have grown in the grass where miracles have taken place.

FUCHSIAS
With no purple centres at all, only the red segments around the outside, and some have three or five of these instead of four.

SYCAMORE AND HOLLY seedlings, with three cotyledons instead of the usual two, and these grow into trees that are different.

IN THE LITTLE HEALING ROOM in the garden there is the imprint of a spine left in the polish on the back of a chair, after asking Jesus to heal someone's vertebrae.

WE HAVE TRIED to apply the same scientific principles to understand these happenings as we would use in our medical analytical research, but nothing becomes clear and we always end up with one of Jesus sayings in our minds.

"My Heavenly Father is in all things, and He will manifest Himself."

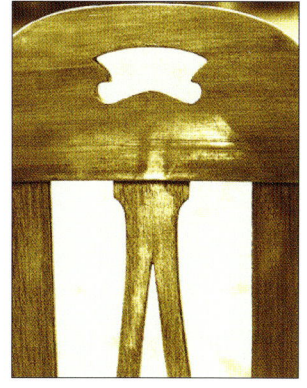

HE IS always making Himself known in subtle ways

We can see them, hear them, touch them or ignore them and explain them away if we can but it would be our great loss and a mistake to do so.

THIS IS ALL TOO MUCH to expect everyone to believe but, before we reach the end of the book, you will not have to believe, you will be able to FEEL GOD'S PRESENCE for yourself.

YOU WILL pass from a state of doubt, directly into one of knowing, without even going through a deep intellectual process. For this is not something arising from knowledge and study, it comes spontaneously from God, from Jesus and The Holy Spirit; for want of a better word you have 'allowed' it to happen to you, without erecting any barriers to prevent it.

HE WILL HAVE MADE CONTACT WITH YOU

No effort is required, no knowledge, no intellect, no cleverness, no skills but only a heartfelt need to be at one with Him, and not questioning 'will it happen?'

HE IS HERE FOR EVERYONE

SEVERAL FRIENDS HAVE experienced brief moments of what we describe as The Healing Wavelength in later paragraphs, when they were reading through these notes, before they were in print. Some have seen pinpoints of light in the side margins.

LET US SHARE WITH YOU our first wonderful experience of Jesus' Presence, as He made Himself known to us.

OUR DAUGHTER HEATHER had become afflicted with a serious spinal condition, for which several operations were to be arranged for fusion of the vertebrae, with metal inserts, springs and screws. She did not feel that she could go through all this and my wife and I did not think so either. So we were written off by the medical profession, as erring stupid parents. We were desolate; utter despair was upon us.

WE WERE ON OUR OWN - OR WERE WE?

ON THE FOLLOWING SUNDAY morning, my daughter and I stood facing each other in the lounge at home; we held hands outstretched in front of us and asked Jesus for help. It was all so very simple; no long prayers, we were desperate, we needed help and placed ourselves entirely in His Care. We needed Him to carry us into the future, through this troubled time.

IN the space

IN THE SPACE BETWEEN OUR hands, two beautifully radiant, mauve coloured cones began to form, with their bases joined together in the middle, as an elongated diamond shape, with a point at the top and bottom. It was not made of material or matter of any kind but of LIGHT.

It seemed to rotate and as it spun it passed into Heather's body; she could feel her spine being manipulated, being stretched, and she grew nearly nine inches in the following months.

SINCE THAT DAY WE HAVE OFTEN THOUGHT of a saying of Jesus, which did not come to light, until sometime later:

"With The Angels of The Heavenly Father, will you learn to see the unseen, and to hear that which cannot be heard."

SEE the unseen

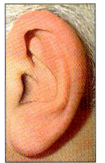

WE HAD SEEN THE UNSEEN; a beautiful mauve diamond shape, and here is the mystery of that which cannot be heard, for after the mauve shape had gone, we simply said: "Thank you".

A MOMENT LATER a high pitched squeak occurred in my left ear and Heather heard it in her right ear, so we thought it was coming from one side of us, as we were still facing each other.

WE MOVED AROUND but the squeak remained in the same ear, my left, Heather's right, and it moved with us. It was not an external sound at all but one we were hearing within the ear, and what was most fascinating, so astonishing, it was only in one ear, in both of us, but they were opposite ears.

HEAR that which cannot be heard

WE PONDERED ON THIS sound in the following days and, every time we asked Jesus for continued help, it was there, a squeak in only one ear, and since then it has always become apparent in my left ear, and always in Heather's right.

IF WE WERE WITH SOMEONE IN PAIN or in trouble, the high pitched squeak or chord would occur the moment we shook hands or touched them, even if we had not asked or prayed for help, and they got better. So we began to call it The Healing Wavelength, rather than the squeak, as it seemed very irreverent to do so, and people began to talk of our flowers and sculptures as "The Healing Garden".

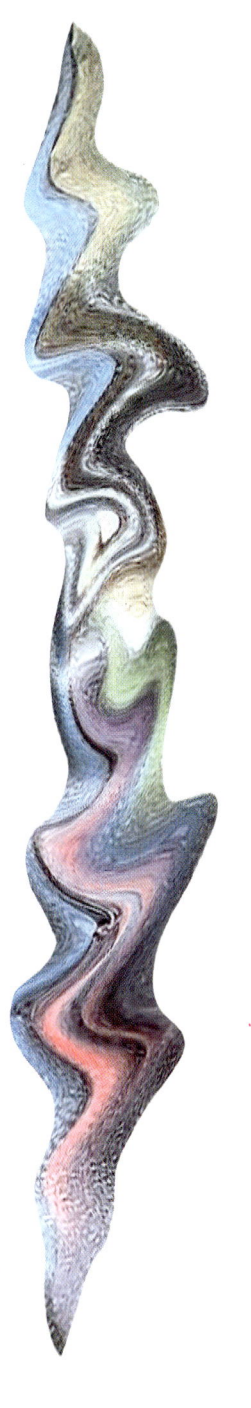

Hear The Miracle

A FEW WEEKS LATER, while we were working, I began to feel we had missed something significant.

I SUDDENLY THOUGHT, is The Healing Wavelength actually a real communication from Jesus Himself; is He speaking to us?

INSTANTLY it was there in my left ear, just as it is now as I write about it. I was overjoyed, amazed and I do not remember completing the analysis.

I MUST have remained in this state for a long time; hours had passed by; all my chemical tests were cold, some of their colours had changed and I seemed to be quite alone.

I was absolutely still, both arms were resting on the bench, my elbows were sore, I had not even moved but the beautiful chord had gone.

THIS APPARENT change or speeding up of time is really strange; for on some occasions we have been with a person in need of help or Healing, placed our hands on their head and, with a little silent prayer asking Jesus for help, an hour or more has passed by but it only seemed like minutes.

THIS IS experienced by everyone present and reminds us of a very beautiful passage we came upon many years after this first occasion.

Sparks Flew Upwards From Jesus' Hair

FROM THE GOSPEL OF PEACE BY THE DISCIPLE JOHN:
Translated by Edmond Szekely & Purcell Weaver.

After speaking to the multitude: "Jesus rose, but all else remained sitting, for every man felt the power of His words.

Sparks flew upwards from His hair, and He stood among them in the moonlight, as though He hovered in the air.

And no man moved, neither was the voice of any heard. And no one knew how long a time had passed, for time stood still.........

And for a long while yet the company sat still.... as though they listened to some wondrous music."

THIS PASSAGE IS SUPERB, especially to us, as we did not come across it until after our own experiences of the Time Phenomenon, the choirs, music and The Healing Wavelength.

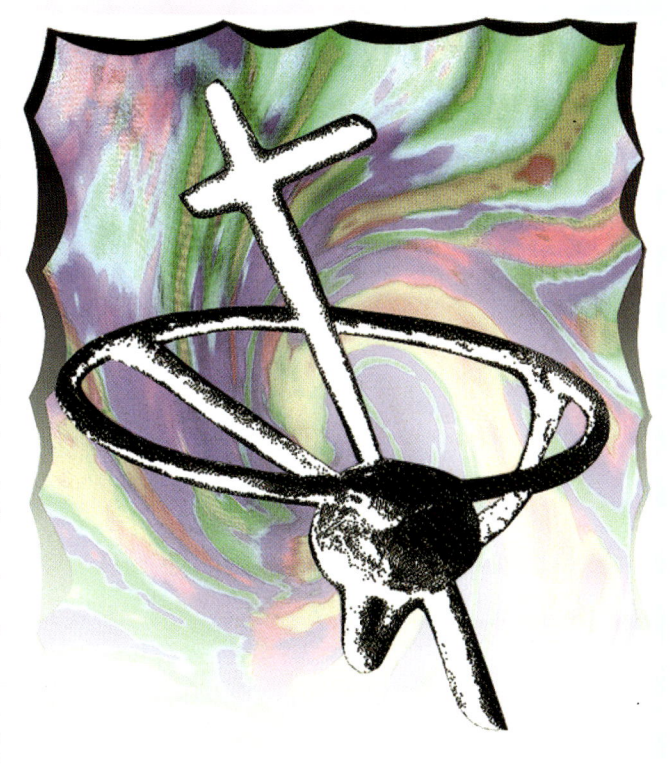

I TRIED AGAIN to think about Jesus speaking to us but this time, not just wondering if the chord was a communication from Him, but actually asking a definite question. I spoke the words out loud:

"Jesus, is The Healing Wavelength from you?"

IT SWELLED UP very loudly in my left ear and from that moment I knew we were not alone. Our lives had a whole new meaning, a new purpose, a fresh start, for Jesus had answered my question.

IT IS FROM HIM, HE REALLY IS WITH US ALL.

INSTANT REVELATION

WE CONTINUED with our Healing research work, each time saying: "Jesus may we receive you", not necessarily out loud, but just in the mind, and instantly the Wavelength was with us, always in one EAR, and Jesus' Miracles continued.

YEARS LATER Heather was watching a television programme about Jesus' travels near the sea of Galilee. Across the bottom of the screen appeared the printed words:

JESUS said: *"You Hear With One Ear."*

THIS WAS AN INSTANT REVELATION for her but had little meaning to most people watching, even some theologians thought that Jesus meant you were only half listening to what He was saying, as you were only listening with one EAR.

IS THIS BIOLOGICALLY possible, to listen with one EAR, or were they describing something they could not understand, with another obscurity?

WE KNOW FROM OUR WONDERFUL experiences Jesus was telling us how we can hear His Presence today, as the high pitched chord in only one EAR. We will always feel elated and happy for having found Him. Although He was not lost, mankind had ignored Him and many have heard Him but not known what it was.

EVEN MEDICAL diagnosis has been unsure in many patients, as some have been told they have 'Meniere's or Tinnitus', but we know from our own research, this is not always correct. Several of the patients have been experiencing Jesus' Presence.

THE SENSE of hearing stays with us during the transition from this world to the next. A continuing link from the physical to the spiritual, the last of the senses to fade.

Jesus said: *"You Hear With One Ear."*

OUR LIFE AS A FAMILY HAS CHANGED FOREVER

IF YOU WERE TO SEEK A REASON for Jesus coming to Earth as a living person, it would be to show us THE WAY; to show us how we could find The Kingdom of God, to feel God's Presence. All His actions, and everything He said, were for that one purpose, to show us . . .THE WAY.

THESE PHENOMENA BRING
JESUS
directly into today's world

AS THE WEEKS PASSED we began to notice even more unusual sensations. If we asked Jesus for help and placed our hands an inch or two above someone's head or over a limb where healing was needed, a warm breeze would blow gently between us and little pinpoints of light would hover over a place where healing was in progress.

SOMETIMES A TICKLING sensation occurred on the forehead or cheeks and you would move to wipe it away but it would still be there, like a cobweb, and yet there was nothing there to be wiped away.

OCCASIONALLY AN INVOLUNTARY muscle movement would happen in an arm or leg, just one single twitch, for no apparent reason; even when the limb was relaxed and not in an uncomfortable position.

DURING THE FOLLOWING MONTHS we decided to search The Biblical Texts and others, to seek out all the unusual sayings of Jesus, to see if He had quietly told us of any more phenomena, that would indicate His ways of communicating with us in the centuries which were to follow His Ministry, up to this present day.

WE WERE SURPRISED TO FIND so many descriptive sayings scattered in between the lovely stories, quite easy to miss and very difficult to understand, unless of course you have already experienced the phenomena, as you will; then you will suddenly know what He was talking about. We have helped hundreds of people to feel them, to see and hear them and to know they are not alone. He has touched their lives.

HAND to hand

HE WANTED HIS MESSAGES TO BE PASSED ON, from one person to another, from hand to hand and not just as cold dry words in a book or manuscript, which could so easily be lost or destroyed as many old writings were. We are sure this is why Jesus never wrote anything down Himself, although He was perfectly able to do so, for He had the same completeness as The Father. He knew He would always have instant access to our souls and no external writings would have the same impact as a direct communication, even today. He is waiting for you, to accept His Message. Yes! it is unbelievable, it is Miraculous. If only we would listen to the voice within; Jesus said: *"The words of God are written in His works."* (You and I)

OCCASIONALLY HE WROTE IN THE SAND but these messages were either blown or washed away. All His sayings are there in The Biblical Texts and Scriptures but His words have a very special meaning if they can be experienced. So having found them, we are compelled to pass them on, usually by contact and conversations between ourselves and others, hand to hand.

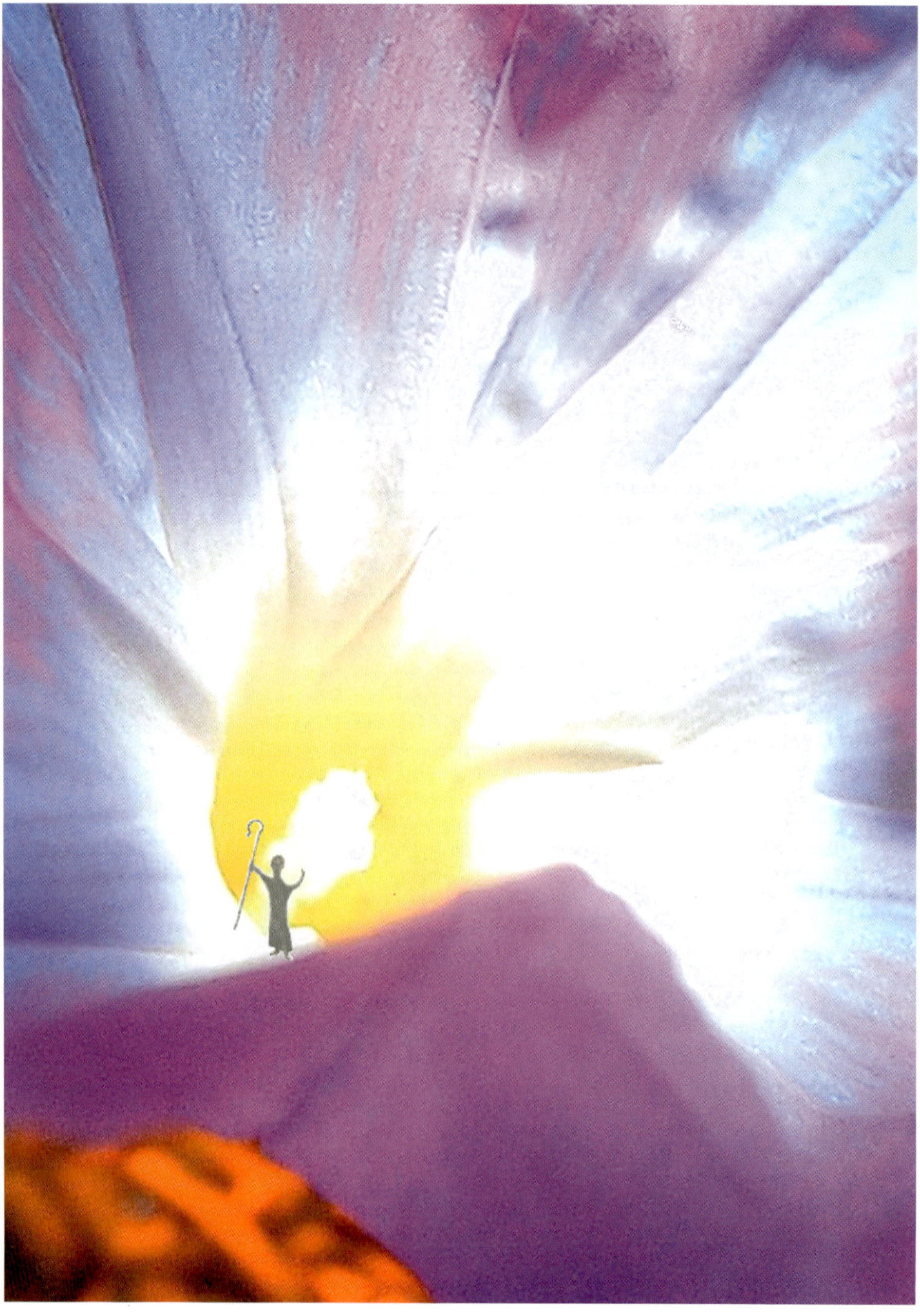

AND WHEN THE SUN ROSE OVER THE EARTH'S RIM

They saw Jesus coming towards them from the mountain, with the brightness
of the rising sun about His head.

And He raised His hand and smiled upon them, saying:

"Peace be with you."

And He lifted His face to the rising sun and the radiance of its rays filled His eyes
as He spoke - of the Communions with
The Heavenly Father and The Earthly Mother.

JESUS also said that His Father would manifest Himself
but His Image is concealed by His Light.

In other words, we would never see The Father
but we would see His Light.

*Top Extract taken from the
'Gospel of the Essenes',
The Communions.*

*Lower Extract taken from the
'Gospel According To Thomas'.*

Left: A genuine photograph inside a Morning Glory flower with superimposed silhouette.

Right: A new beginning, white crocuses herald the spring.

JESUS' SAYINGS

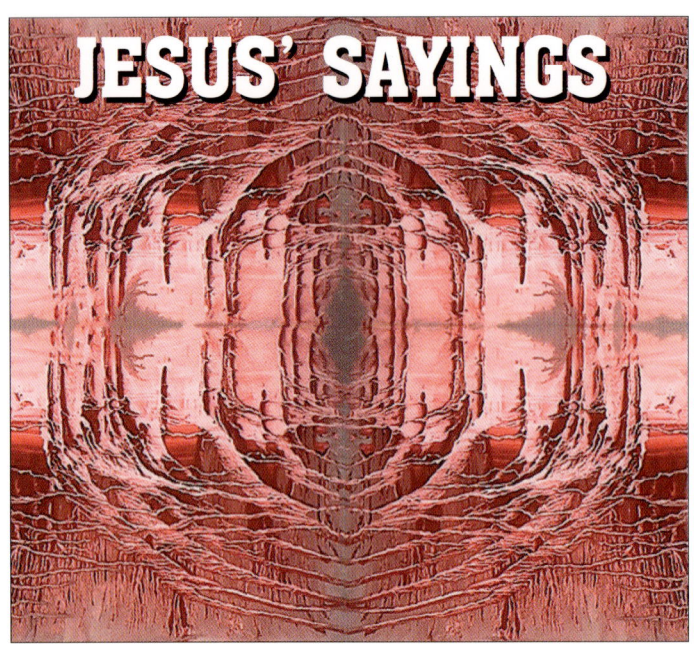

JESUS said:

"All living things are nearer to God than the Scripture, which is without life."

(They are only written words.)

"God wrote not the laws in the pages of books, but in your heart and in your spirit."

IS JESUS indicating here that we have individual hearts but are all of one Spirit? And we all belong to one another, having within us a central Temple, sharing a few special vibrations of God's Presence.

2000 Year Time Tunnel from the past . . .

"The words of God are written in His works", said Jesus.

(His works of course are you and I and all His Creations.)

SURELY JESUS is explaining here why He never wrote anything down in words, for the writings are in our hearts and in our spirit. We only have to find God's Presence within and ask Him to influence our life.

THERE IS A WAY, so simple we are astonished we had not realised it sooner, so His Message and the experience of His Presence can be spread more rapidly in today's world, and again it occurs in one of His sayings and depends upon it. You may realise this yourself as we write about His words.

THE SCULPTURE IN THE HEALING GARDEN represents the Resurrection, the return to life of Jesus. I created this work during a prayerful meditation on His Presence for He is more active in Spirit form, in today's world, than He was as a real live person 2000 years ago, because mankind did not give Him a chance. He knew that was the way it had to be, for He was restricted in the people He could reach, even though He travelled far and wide.

NOW HE is with everyone, all the time, so we have a second chance to meet Him, no matter where we are.

The Resurrection Sculpture. Set amongst the honeysuckle. Jesus spoke of the perfumed flowers.

REACH OUT, DON'T LET HIM PASS BY - In a few pages you will know how simple this can be.

We must now write about one of
JESUS' MOST EXCITING SAYINGS

THEN YOU WILL KNOW what to expect; and in this one He speaks of the ways in which we will feel His Presence, as a true live communication from Him, The Father and The Holy Spirit.

> Jesus said: "I will give you . . .
> What the eye has not seen, what the ear has not heard,
> What hand has not touched,
> And what has not arisen in the heart of man."

HERE JESUS IS TELLING US how He will contact us and make Himself known to future generations.
This is His Special Invitation To Feel God's Presence.
HE SAYS:
"I will give you what the eye has not seen."

HE IS SPEAKING of the mauve shapes that appear between people, like the diamond shape in our experience and the pinpoints of light hovering over an area of Healing, when you have asked for His help.

THESE HAVE HAPPENED to many of us but without realising what they are and have been ignored, forgotten, or explained away.

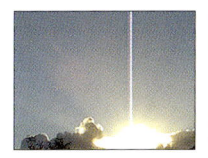

JESUS also said that His Father would manifest Himself (show Himself) but His Image is concealed by His Light. In other words, we would never see The Father but we would see His Light. HE IS in the pinpoints of light that accompany a healing, and in the mauve shapes, but we do not see Him because as Jesus said:
"God's Image is concealed by His Light."

JESUS SAYS in this passage:
"I will give you."
This has a future feel to it, an ongoing for all time, even now in this present day, not just for His Disciples 2000 years ago but for all His disciples through the years since then. Now, you.

THEN HE SAID:
"I will give you what the ear has not heard."
This is the beautiful high pitched chord (The Healing Wavelength) you hear in only one ear, when you ask to be allowed to receive Him; and He has already said:
"You hear with one ear."

"I Will Give You ..."

Across the Sea of Galilee

HE FOLLOWS THIS WITH:
"I will give you what hand has not touched."

THIS IS THE WARM BREEZE blowing between two people in His Presence, when you extend your hand towards another person.

HE IS MAKING Himself known to us in His own way, as He said He would, and not by standing in front of us as a man with a beard, as some people still expect.

Kirlian hand image

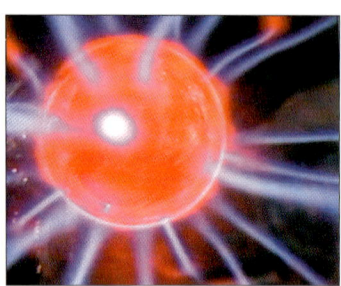

IN ANOTHER PASSAGE HIS WORDS ARE:
"Whoever is near to me, is near to the fire."
Has this also to do with the warm breeze?

HE CONTINUED:
"What thou shalt hear in thine ear and in the other ear,
(maybe referring to male and female hearing in opposite ears)
that preach from your house tops; for no one lights a lamp and puts it under a bushel, nor does he put it in a hidden place."

I KNOW WE HAVE WRITTEN about this earlier, when my wife and I heard the Heavenly Music and Choir. Here He is telling us that, having found God, having experienced His Presence as a physical reality, we must make our findings known, we must pass this knowledge on to everyone and not hide it or keep it to ourselves. We are compelled to write this book.

IN ALL THESE SAYINGS HE has described perfectly all the phenomena we have been experiencing over the years but the phrase starting the next page took a long time and many prayers to understand, but we felt we must do so, for it would have a special meaning.

JESUS SAID:
"I will give you . . .
..what has not arisen in the heart of man."

WE WERE BAFFLED; then suddenly realised what takes place here. When you have experienced some or all of these beautiful phenomena, a change has occurred in your heart, in your whole being.

IT IS NOT JUST A HOPE or belief any more. You actually know you are not alone. We do have a Creator. HE IS REAL. We have met the intellect and wisdom, who brought us into life.

GOD, JESUS and THE HOLY SPIRIT have answered and touched you in many ways, it is a re-awakening, a rebirth; you have made peace between the Soul, the Spirit and the Body.

THE TEMPLE IS COMPLETE

For as Jesus said:

"God wrote not the laws in the pages of books, but in your heart and in your Spirit."

ALL THROUGH THE MINISTRY of Jesus He spoke frequently of the ear;
"Whoever has ears to hear - let him hear."

HE WAS not just telling people to listen to Him then, 2000 years ago, but we should always be listening for Him, especially today. When we hear His Wavelength in only one ear, then we will know who it is.

THOSE WORDS are small and few but very important. For 'then we will know who it is'.

THE BEAUTIFUL CHORD in only one ear is a direct communication from God, Jesus and The Holy Spirit. This is a unique way of contacting us and there must be a very good reason for us to be able to help so many people to hear it. Perhaps to be ready for a Spectacular Overshadowing.

The Disciples said to Jesus: "Show us the place where thou art?"

Jesus replied: *"Whoever has ears, let him hear."*

WAS HE TELLING THEM 'the place' was in the ear? He had already said that when His Father had a thought to send Him to Earth, He entered into Mary by the ear and He came forth by the ear. So He was not just telling them to listen to His words.

JESUS' BIRTH OCCURRED UNSEEN
Because of the brilliance of The Light of The Heavenly Father.

His Spiritual birth involved the EAR,
in some miraculous manner, unknown to us.

WE HAVE MENTIONED THIS previously and it is not surprising that, when we ask for His help or He realises we need Him, we should experience a beautiful chord in only one ear or even music and choirs singing, along with brilliant pinpoints of light. And now we know who it is.

Jesus said:

"He who loves me, will be loved by my Father, and I shall love him, and shall manifest myself to him."

HERE JESUS actually says He will make Himself known to us, which He has done. He manifests Himself to all of us but many have ignored Him by not knowing what it was they heard or experienced. Some people have even thought they have some form of illness and medical diagnosis tries to confirm this, unsuccessfully, but what they are experiencing is not a condition of an ailing physical body but a wonderful communication from Jesus directly to their Soul.

HE TOLD HIS DISCIPLES that, where He was going, they could not now follow. He knew it was His time to be Crucified and said:

"I will pray The Father (ask God) *to send another Counsellor to be with you all forever."*

Then He breathed on them and they were filled with The Holy Spirit.

WE HAVE WRITTEN already that, along with those in need of help, we feel a tickling, blowing sensation on our foreheads and cheeks, like a cobweb, with movement, like a breeze, which will not wipe away. Here Jesus is breathing on us and we have been allowed to experience the touch of The Holy Spirit, another Counsellor, for whose presence Jesus had prayed to The Father.

HE SAID TO HIS DISCIPLES:

"If they ask you: 'What is the sign of your Heavenly Father in you?' say to them: 'It is a Movement and a Rest'."

A very strange remark, until you think about it - a movement and a rest.

WITHOUT OUR CREATOR'S PRESENCE, we would not move at all, we would be quite still. Everything mankind has achieved is only because we can move things and ourselves. We can press a button, as in modern times, or not press a button. We can move a hand, a foot, a body, or leave it where it is. We can pull or lift something, we can do work against gravity like this or against some other force.

MADE Himself known

BIOLOGICALLY WE KNOW how the brain sends impulses of an electrical nature along the nerves to make a muscle move but do we know what initiates the impulse in the brain; a conscious thought perhaps?

WE DO NOT KNOW where our consciousness exists but our Creator does and He has direct access to it and can make a muscle give a single twitch, when you have asked Him to be with you. He has made Himself known, if we would only be more aware of ourselves and the gentle subtleties in our surroundings, instead of being overwhelmed by the intensity of modern living.

THE TWITCH WAS a movement you did not initiate yourself, it happened to you. It was just a little message, a reminder; you would not move at all without Him.

Impulses from the brain

IF YOU WERE TO ASK GOD TO DECLARE His Presence to you, it is unlikely He would do so; it is best to ask to be allowed to receive or hear Him, then wait for His reply. You may hear The Healing Wavelength, feel a cobweb on your face, a muscle may move on its own or you may become quite warm. You may have to wait; He will contact you in His own time and in His own way, when He is ready. You must prepare yourself to meet Him by purifying body and soul, as best you can; not just as a casual desire but as a heartfelt need to know Him.

HE KNOWS our imperfections and difficulties in this preparation, for He allowed us to be like this in the first place, so we could learn from our experiences on earth, but His forgiveness is boundless if we are genuine in our quest for knowledge of His Wisdom.

NOT A TEST . . .

NEVER DO THIS as a test to check if He will communicate with you but only when you believe or know that He will. It is you, who will have to make yourself ready for this superb event, to be worthy of His contact.

YOU MUST NEVER PUT GOD OR JESUS to the test in any way at all, it is not this kind of scientific research; it is your own abilities you are testing. Can you purify your body and mind, can you prepare the body as a Temple to receive Him? Can you be sure you are ready to be with Him for His purpose, and not to gain some advantage over others, but to be a servant of mankind as Jesus taught us, by washing the feet of His Disciples?

Gently touched by His web of consciousness.

GOD, JESUS AND THE HOLY SPIRIT will be with you always, if you allow it to happen. By this we mean, do not crowd your mind with doubt or even intense desire. Be peaceful, meditate and perhaps listen for The Healing Wavelength, in the right ear if you are a female or in the left if a male, as this is the order of things. Repeat the Cylinder and other experiments to increase your sensitivity, if necessary. There are more experiments and details to follow which will help you hear His Wavelength.

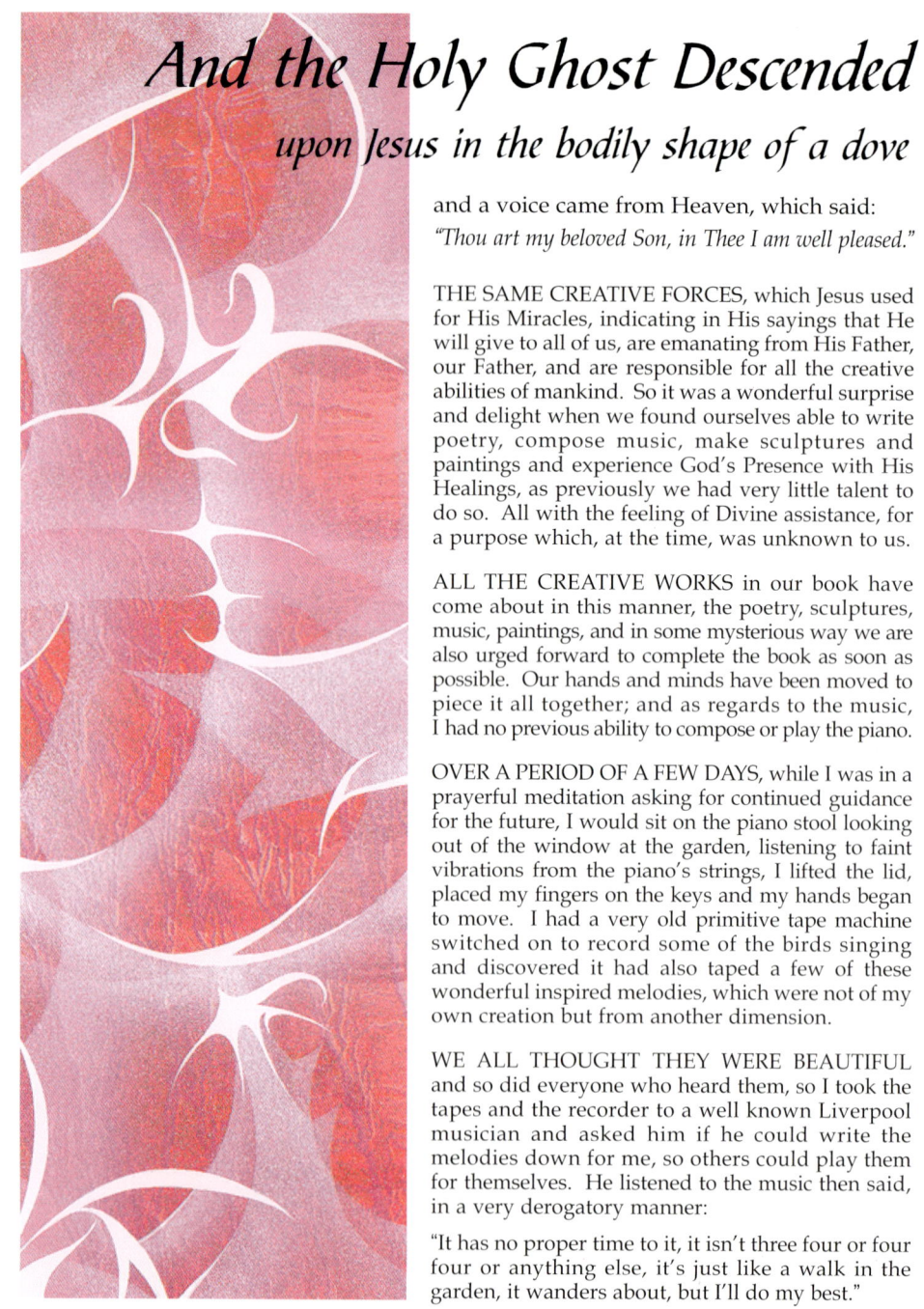

And the Holy Ghost Descended
upon Jesus in the bodily shape of a dove

and a voice came from Heaven, which said:
"Thou art my beloved Son, in Thee I am well pleased."

THE SAME CREATIVE FORCES, which Jesus used for His Miracles, indicating in His sayings that He will give to all of us, are emanating from His Father, our Father, and are responsible for all the creative abilities of mankind. So it was a wonderful surprise and delight when we found ourselves able to write poetry, compose music, make sculptures and paintings and experience God's Presence with His Healings, as previously we had very little talent to do so. All with the feeling of Divine assistance, for a purpose which, at the time, was unknown to us.

ALL THE CREATIVE WORKS in our book have come about in this manner, the poetry, sculptures, music, paintings, and in some mysterious way we are also urged forward to complete the book as soon as possible. Our hands and minds have been moved to piece it all together; and as regards to the music, I had no previous ability to compose or play the piano.

OVER A PERIOD OF A FEW DAYS, while I was in a prayerful meditation asking for continued guidance for the future, I would sit on the piano stool looking out of the window at the garden, listening to faint vibrations from the piano's strings, I lifted the lid, placed my fingers on the keys and my hands began to move. I had a very old primitive tape machine switched on to record some of the birds singing and discovered it had also taped a few of these wonderful inspired melodies, which were not of my own creation but from another dimension.

WE ALL THOUGHT THEY WERE BEAUTIFUL and so did everyone who heard them, so I took the tapes and the recorder to a well known Liverpool musician and asked him if he could write the melodies down for me, so others could play them for themselves. He listened to the music then said, in a very derogatory manner:

"It has no proper time to it, it isn't three four or four four or anything else, it's just like a walk in the garden, it wanders about, but I'll do my best."

Healing Music

LITTLE DID HE KNOW, his remark was absolutely perfect, the music is in fact a walk in The Healing Garden.

I took these two pages of his transcriptions, and many more, to another musician to hear how it sounded being played by someone else.

Regrettably, it did not have the same ethereal mystery of the original, so I played the tape recording for him.
"You could never write that down," he said, "It's not part of this world."

The Healing Music
ANDANTE
(1)
Cantando. Legato.
m. f.
P P
Ped.
m. f.
8va
m. f.
Ped.
8va
P
Ped.
8va
m. f.
Poco. vivace
Ped.
8va
P
Cresc
P
Ped.
8va
Dim.
P
Ped.

The Healing Music
8va
(11)
m. f.
P
m. f.
Ped.
Ped.
8va
P
m. f.
P
Ped.
8va
Poco. vivace
m. f.
P
Ped.
Ped.
Ped.
Ped.
8va
Cresc
Ped.
Ped.
8va
f
Dim.
Ped.
Ped.
8va
P
m. f.

Spring crocus, one of His inspiring Creations.

CAVERN sounds

OVER MANY YEARS I have also composed and recorded many hours of very unusual music, not on the piano keyboard like The Healing Record but inside the piano with the lid raised. It is played as if it were a harp along with percussion sounds, using fingers and palms on the frame and timbers to create the drum beats and rhythms of nature.

SEVERAL of these pieces are deeply moving and a remarkable experience; the stereophonic sounds gently vibrate the body along with a fascinating audible enjoyment. Out of this world but in a different way, and slightly reminiscent of the beautiful 'stereo' sounds we heard above us at various times of our life.

■ Composing on the strings

Dozens of listeners telephoned and wrote to Mr. Bell, giving details of the benefits they experienced from hearing The Healing Music record on Radio City.

■ THUMPONIUM

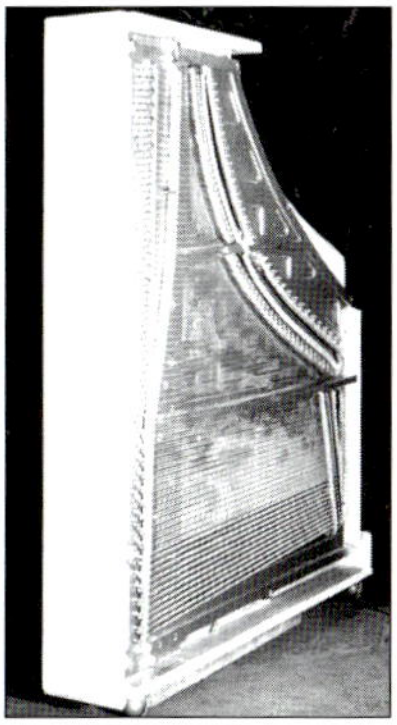

I CREATED an instrument from an old piano which someone was about to throw away, as the electric guitar had arrived on the scene. I spent many hours sawing the woodwork to liberate the solid iron frame and strings and named it The Thumponium, because of the method of playing on it, by percussion and plucking. The music is beautiful and I made a lovely sculpture from the woodwork, which I cut out all in one piece, and called it Octavia, for obvious reasons.

AT THE CAVERN IN MATHEW STREET, some recordings made on this instrument were played for Bob Wooler and his colleagues in the early 1960's. They were intrigued by the quality, emotions, exuberance and rhythms of the music and listened to many of them.

■ OCTAVIA

BUT, AS BOB so rightly pointed out: "You can't dance to it and that's what all the youngsters want to do."

SO VERY few teenagers of the era have even heard it, and most of them are nearly 60 now, but we understand some modern venues have an area called a 'chillout room,' where the exhausted dancers go to be revitalised. This is where the music should be experienced, although it has been used in some Cinema films and Television mysteries adding many special effects.

I NEARLY HAD the chance to play it at The Philharmonic Hall in Liverpool at a Charity Concert. There it was standing, almost filling the passage way at the Leece's Street side entrance of The Hall. I was told their insurance policy would not cover such an unconventional instrument on the stage.
"IT'S ONLY the inside of a piano," I replied.
"Yes, but where are it's legs."
So I showed them a photograph of my Octavia sculpture. I played it in the passage way, while they were rehearsing something else on stage. Fortunately the door was shut. Willie Rushton, also on the Programme, wished me luck.

Record

IN 1979 we had some vinyl discs pressed by a record company from my original quarter inch tapes and this music has helped to heal people all over the world. We know the music does not produce the healings, but it enables people to feel God's Presence, wherever they live.

SOME DISCS have been played over and over, to destruction; what a shame digital technology had not arrived at the time. But we still have the original tapes; so one day we may do it all again.

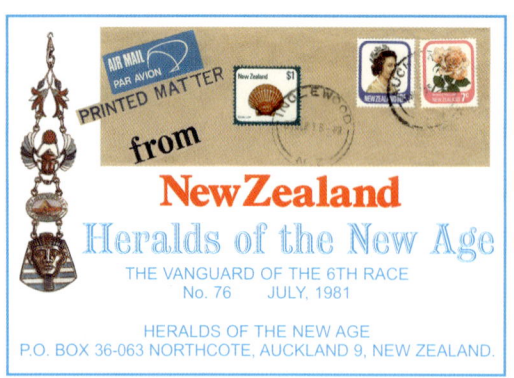

New Zealand publication detailed the Healing Music Record.

IF YOU ARE A PIANIST, say a little silent prayer to receive the same Creative Presence, to bring these primitive melodies to life, in your own way. Not as a test to check if it is there, but make it so. They are not just notes, they induce vibrations touching upon God's Frequencies and, in a certain state of mind, these will be identical to the original recording, because your soul will have made contact with Him. So it should be very special, when you think of how He had to cope with my primitive lack of piano expertise. Allow God to superimpose His Presence upon your playing and do not let yourself be restricted by these written manuscripts. The experience will be with you forever. You may be able to complete the whole work yourself, without seeing any more of our pages. We are sure it is possible! And it may even be the same.

OUR HEALING WORK was only a step along the way, although we did feel it was our ultimate purpose in life, but it began to evolve.

IT SOON BECAME APPARENT that our future had to be devoted to helping as many people as possible to actually feel The Presence of God and Jesus, in a practical way as a reality, in the same way we have, and not just hoping and wondering if He is really here. The following newspaper extracts indicate how our work developed and our path was guided as He reached out ahead of us.

Letters received from across the World

REVEILLE!

BRITAIN'S BRIGHTER WEEKLY
Oct. 8, 1976
No. 1903
9p

Strange power of the man with 'magic' hands

by JUDY WADE

CHEMIST Alan Bell is the man with "magic" hands.

He plays the piano to concert standard and his compositions are strangely like those of Beethoven. He carves beautiful sculptures out of stone with something of the skill of a Rodin.

And when he touches someone who is ill, they feel better. Yet Mr. Bell, of Andrews Lane, Formby, Lancs, has never been taught how to compose music, never had formal art lessons and is not a physician or a surgeon. In fact, his talents only express themselves when in a self-induced trance.

Can't explain it

And even then, Mr. Bell cannot explain his strange powers or how he is able to use them. Mr. Bell became involved in healing largely because of the number of people he saw in his chemist's shop in Formby. He said:

"The same people came in week after week saying 'The doctor's going to try this or that now.'

"I had always been interested in healing and decided to try to help some of them.

"I'd sit them down and work on them. Often they would leave without their prescriptions.

"My reputation began to spread and I closed the dispensary to devote myself to healing. I would never go back now."

Mr. Bell added: "Every day brings so much joy, so much celebration.

"When you see someone carried in crippled with pain and then see him or her almost skip down the garden path after a healing session, you cannot imagine any other way of life."

One of Mr. Bell's first patients was his daughter Heather. She, too, has become a healer and works with her father.

She said: "I just feel as if my hands are being guided over the person.

CHEMIST TURNS TO HEALING

"I feel the guidance comes from God."

Such joy

Mr. Bell said that some patients have reported feeling a heat generated by his hands, and that he and his patients have experienced a feeling of floating during healing. He has a similar "floating" sensation when he puts himself into a trance to play piano music.

He says: "I feel sufficiently aware to watch myself playing and to hear my music.

"It is like being a spectator at a concert but I am aware it is me.

"Can you imagine the joy of hearing music like a Beethoven piano Sonata and realise it is coming from you?"

141

BRITAIN'S TOP SELLING WEEKLY FOR WOMEN 15p JULY 7th 1979

WOMAN'S OWN

A GUIDE TO BRITAIN'S PSYCHIC WORLD

WOMAN'S OWN PSYCHIC DIRECTORY

Healers

Once upon a time the word psychic conjured up visions of little ladies with big earrings sitting in seaside tents. Now the psychic scene has taken a more serious turn and offers a complete range of services from spiritual healing to advice on happiness.

FAITH HEALING

ALAN AND HEATHER BELL, a father and daughter team, work by laying on hands and "linking with God." They and many of their patients say they hear "a beautiful musical chord" during healing, which they call "The Healing Wavelength."

Alan and Heather have worked together and separately to treat all ailments since Alan gave up his chemist shop to devote all his time to healing. He helped Heather overcome double curvature of her spine. One of Heather's patients was a young boy with a heart condition who, after treatment, started to lead a healthy, active life for the first time.

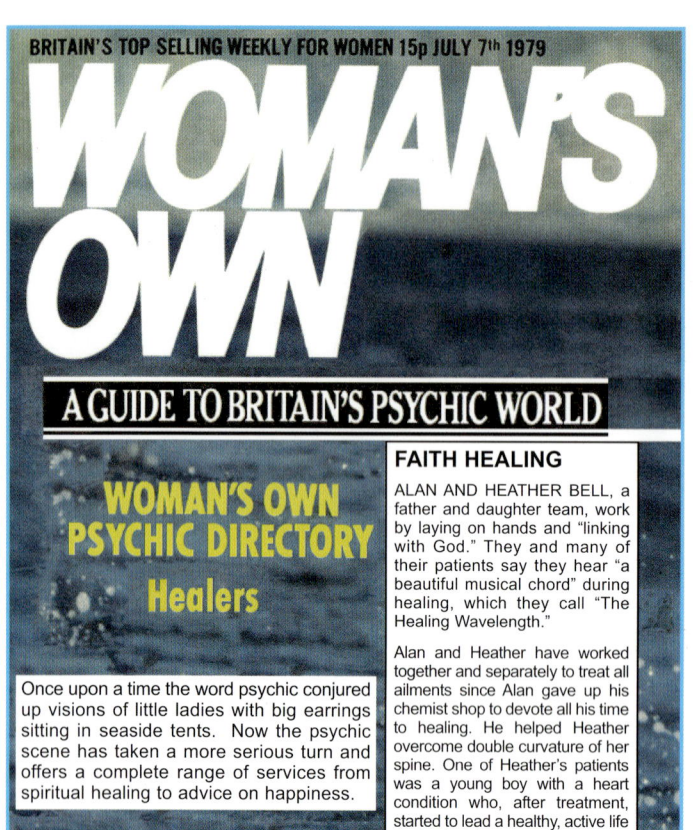

LONG lost ability

EVERYONE can make a fresh start, by bringing new hope, a new peace and understanding, which can spread across the earth. Not the end of the world, as so many have prophesied, but a step forward, a second chance.

THESE ARE NOT JUST lofty ideas, big headed thoughts, they are so very close to happening.

MAY WE REMIND YOU OF JESUS' SAYING:

"Have you then discovered the beginning, so that you inquire about the end?"

In other words, where one order ceases, another is already in place.

ALL DENOMINATIONS

WE DO NOT NEED A NEW RELIGION but only the renewal of a long lost ability to communicate with our Creator, so all religious denominations could become one, and all rituals, procedures and methods of worship would have less significance and would not be necessary. Because a direct personal practical felt relationship with God would overshadow all of us. Then each one would have an individual 'Direct Line' and we would all belong to each other. This is really the way it is now, BUT THE 'LINE' IS UNUSED or OUT OF ORDER. Mankind has gone against it and departed on his own little ways.

WHAT EVENTS WILL BRING US ALL TOGETHER?

OUR CREATOR HAS MADE CONTACT with us and it would be wonderful if everyone would acknowledge this and allow His Presence to be experienced.

THE WORLD WOULD REGENERATE, wars would cease. Peace, Tranquillity and Happiness would be upon us. Then God would be even more creative than He has been already and mankind could move on to unimaginable wonders, with Him rather than against Him. With nature, not against it. Each one of us with each other; no religious disharmony; one people; ONE GOD.

SUNDAY PEOPLE April 11. 1976

COME INTO THE GARDEN AND BE HEALED

PHARMACIST Alan Bell used to dispense relief to the sick and ailing from his chemist's shop.

Now he does it from his garden. His Garden of Healing, that is. And all without a prescription. Instead of dishing out drugs on doctors' orders, Alan Fraser Bell, Ph.C., M.P.S., M.R.S.H., now helps the sick by using the mysterious healing wavelengths.

He claims it enables him to bring relief to sufferers where ordinary medicines can't.

And he has an impressive list of case histories to back it up.

They include:

● The lecturer's wife who, within weeks of visiting the Healing Garden, was cured of the severe migraine she had suffered since her teens.

● Her daughter whose thyroid trouble disappeared after just two visits to Mr. Bell.

Mr Bell the chemist now works wonders

By ALWYN THOMAS

● A nursing sister and wife of a surgeon, who had lived with the agony of migraine for 21 years - until one visit to Mr. Bell ended it.

Her surgeon husband's reactions?

"He took it calmly and said if it worked it couldn't be bad and has sent several of his patients to Mr. Bell for help," she said.

The highly qualified Mr. Bell of Formby, Lancs, discovered his uncanny healing wavelength by accident.

After years of studying creative thinking - a kind of - mind over matter theory.

He claims the discovery enabled him to cure scores of sufferers.

The first was his daughter Heather, who was crippled by a double curvature of the spine.

HELP

Mr. Bell treated her and now she stands erect and well.

Mr. Bell's reputation as a healer spread fast.

"It became embarrassing," he said. "I'd sit them on a stool at the back of the shop, lay my hands on their heads and tune into the healing wavelength."

They'd go out leaving their walking sticks, crutches and prescriptions behind."

Later he sold his chemist's shop and opened the Garden of Healing at his home. There he heals by appointment.

He says: "I am convinced we have stumbled on something which is a fundamental part of nature ignored by mankind for too long."

Queueing to be healed

A week later: April 18, 1976 SUNDAY PEOPLE

THE SICK and crippled are queueing in hundreds for faith healing sessions in chemist Alan Bell's healing garden.

This week he's been deluged with inquiries from Sunday People readers, following last week's article on his work

Mr. Bell and his daughter Heather use a mysterious "healing wavelength" to cure the afflicted who come to their garden in Andrews Lane, Formby, Lancs.

"The phone has been red-hot ever since the article appeared," he said. "We have appointments stretching for weeks and weeks ahead."

SUNDAY PEOPLE: Cured ... By A Top Of The Pops Disc

CHEMIST Alan Bell whose mystical "healing wavelength" offered instant cures to thousands, has put his powers on record. Sales of the disc- recorded in his "healing garden" to the background of a dawn chorus of bird song- are booming.

One of Alan's most devoted followers is 25 year-old Kathleen Halliday, of Boston Spa, West Yorkshire. She has been deaf since birth but claims that without her hearing aid she can make out the sound of the piano on one side of his record.

"I can feel his presence even when I am alone," she said. "I still can't hear perfectly without my hearing aid, but before I saw him things were even worse." March 1980.

AT THE TIME the Sunday People newspaper were deeply involved with Investigative Journalism, exposing all types of fraud and malpractice. Heather and I were sure they had arrived in the Healing Garden with this in mind but they were very surprised to be able to interview real patients who had experienced genuine miracles.

In fact Alwyn Thomas who wrote the above Sunday People articles said, "It made a very pleasant surprise and an enjoyable experience to write these lovely stories." He wished us well for the future.

All smiles in the Healing Garden ... Former chemist Alan Bell and his daughter Heather.

A comment from Heather and myself. We now know that the Healing Wavelength is not a mysterious phenomenon that we use but is a direct communication from Jesus, Our Creator, and The Holy Spirit in response to a prayer or a desperate heartfelt plea for help from anyone.

AMERICA
NATIONAL
ENQUIRER

30¢

July 6, 1976   02-261   **LARGEST CIRCULATION OF ANY PAPER IN AMERICA**

Mysterious, High-Pitched Chord Is Heard as . . .

Incredible Healer Lays His Hands on the Sick And Crippled—And They Are Cured in Minutes

Doctors Confirm . . . That He Has Miraculous Powers

BY DAVID KLEIN

People who were sick or crippled for years say they were healed within minutes when British pharmacist Alan Fraser Bell laid hands on them - and doctors attest to the fact that they're cured.

A strange phenomenon accompanies the healings - a mysterious, high pitched musical chord that seems to come from nowhere.

Bell, who calls the mystical sound "the healing wavelength", treats the ailing in the garden of his home at Formby, in Lancashire, England.

PHARMACIST Alan Fraser Bell sold store to treat sick full-time.

A surgeon in Formby, Dr. P. M. Mace, told The ENQUIRER:

"Mr. Bell definitely cured my wife Pamela of her migraine - and there's no medical cure for it. She suffered badly for 21 years, with attacks so severe they'd cause vomiting and confine her to bed.

"Yet, after one 15 minute session with Mr. Bell, she was cured, and in the 18 months since has never had an attack.

"I've sent four of my patients to him. They had degenerative arthritis and there was nothing more I could do for them.

"All have experienced total recoveries since they saw him."

Bell, who sold his thriving drugstore in order to treat the sick full-time, said he discovered the healing wavelength 7 years ago.

His daughter Heather suffered from double curvature of the spine, and surgeons told Bell she had to undergo an operation or become a cripple.

Heather recalled: "Dad and I held hands and then asked God for help. Then I heard this high-pitched sound - a harmony of three notes - and felt as though my spine were being gently manipulated."

A local woman doctor told The ENQUIRER:

"X rays, photos and medical statements showed that she had a very serious double curvature, causing her to wear braces and harnesses. "She is now able to get around normally."

The same doctor, who asked that her name be withheld, said:

"Mr. Bell also cured my husband, who had suffered from a fusion of the vertebrae for over 30 years. He was bent over and in pain, but now stands erect and has no pain."

"I've seen Mr. Bell practicing and I've actually heard the musical chord myself."

Her husband, a 50-year old dental surgeon, added: "My condition was

STRAIGHT and slender as the daffodils she holds, Heather Bell.

the result of an auto accident. Orthodox medicine gave me little help. But Mr. Bell just put his hands on my head, then on the places that were affected, and now I'm so much better I can even play tennis!"

Mrs. Audrey Owen, a theatrical manager, is another who said she was cured of migraine by Bell. Her physician, Dr. Anthony Youll of Formby, affirmed:

"She had regular and severe attacks for many years, but she has not had one in the 16 months since seeing Mr. Bell. I find that remarkable."

144

AMERICA'S January 18, 1983
FASTEST GROWING WEEKLY

NATIONAL EXAMINER

In this issue: Father and daughter are psychic healers .... page 22

ROAMS THE WORLD FOR THE MOST ASTONISHING STORIES

Amazing healing power of father & daughter

A DENTIST who has been one of Mr. Bell's patients at his healing practice in Formby, England. said: "I was a complete skeptic. And in some ways I still am."
"I don't pretend to know how all this works. I just know it does."

"I have heard the tape recordings of Mr. Bell's compositions. I have seen his sculptures. I've seen too much evidence to dismiss it."

Desperate

The dentist added: "I went to Mr. Bell as a complete unbeliever. Medicine could do nothing for me. I was desperate enough to try anything."

"When I got home from my first session, my wife said, 'your're taller.' I said, 'that's the silliest thing you've ever said.' Then suddenly I realized I could see over the top of the wardrobe. I was two inches taller. I couldn't argue with that."

The dentist had known since childhood that he has a progressive arthritis of the spine. He was badly stooped and could only sleep in one position.

He was desperate. Then he heard of Mr. Bell.

The dentist now says: "I haven't been back to a doctor. But I am utterly convinced I am improved. My posture is better."

I cannot ignore the dramatic evidence of growing two inches.

"I don't know how Mr. Bell does it. But when you are in pain you are just grateful when it stops. You don't care how it happens. It certainly cannot be written off as faith healing, because I didn't believe."

Bell has also treated the mentally ill as part of his healing work. "I find that, for example, depressive illness, responds well to my treatment," he said. Bell, became involved with healing largely because of the people he saw daily in his own pharmacy before he sold it to devote himself, full-time to the healing he and his daughter Heather now do from their home.

"As my reputation spread, customers would say, 'Can't you do anything for me?' I'd sit them down and work on them. Often they would leave without having their prescriptions made up."

"But I didn't feel that was the right place to be doing it. And I felt I could do better for them by healing the ones medicine couldn't help, than by dispensing conventional medicine to them."

HEALING GARDEN

One of Mr. Bell's first patients was his daughter. Heather, now a tall attractive girl, dreamed of being a model until she was eleven. Then she discovered that her spine was curved.

One shoulder was becoming higher than the other. Her shoulder blades protruded.

She said: "I was about 13 when Dad started. Now I look quite normal."

Now Heather has joined her father as a healer.

Heather says:
"When I am healing I just feel as if my hands are being guided over the person being treated. I feel the guidance comes from somewhere - and I believe that it is from God."

"My wife is the baseline we all go back to. She keeps our feet on the ground," said Mr. Bell.

— JUDY BYRNE

FATHER & DAUGHTER, Alan Bell and Heather operate a successful healing practice from their home.

145

Exchange Flags

Television

Wednesday, 24 November 1982

2.00
Exchange Flags
ROGER BLYTH
OENONE WILLIAMS

Roger Blyth and Oenone Williams with Bob Greaves bring live issues, live comments and lively people together in an after lunchtime show that happens 'live' in Liverpool.

RESEARCH: Phil Griffin,
Mark Gorton,
Margaret Coen,
Stephen Boulton.

DESIGNER: Roy Graham.
EDITOR: Rod Caird.
DIRECTOR: Mike Lloyd.
PRODUCER: Robin Kent.

Presented by Gordon Burns with Natalie Anglesey

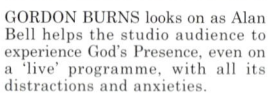

GORDON BURNS looks on as Alan Bell helps the studio audience to experience God's Presence, even on a 'live' programme, with all its distractions and anxieties.

This can also be shown scientifically by producing extended flares, around the fingers, in the Kirlian photographs he is holding.

Kirlian hand image

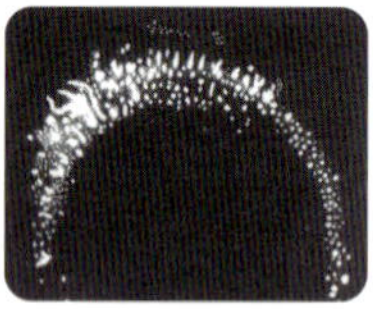

Normal Aura around a finger

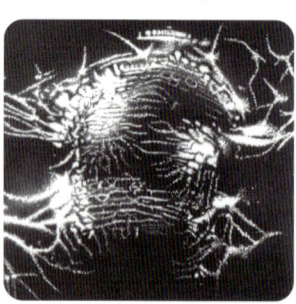

Aura during Healing

After many years of research Alan has produced Kirlian photographs of his own aura while healing the sick. The aura is more pronounced during healing and extends further in all directions.

Alan poses the question: "Could this be another sign of our Creator's Presence, following a prayerful intercession?" The research continues!

Alan Fraser Bell is an International Healer and Creativity Psychologist, and in this latter capacity has helped many people to reach their full potential and purpose in life.

As a healer he has helped almost every known illness, along with his daughter Heather, by linking with God, as Jesus told us in His remarkable teachings.

146

Letters From Home And Abroad
MIRACLES CAN BE PUT IN WRITING

THE FOLLOWING ARE EXCERPTS FROM THE MANY WONDERFUL LETTERS WE RECEIVE
They have been typed to make them easier to read, but the text has not been altered in any way.

My left eye that was blind, I'm happy to say I can see things that are close to me now. Week by week it seems to get stronger.

After all, look what has happened already with the Healing Wavelength - no earthly Agent could work the Miracles that have happened to me in this last year and now.

In fact the eventual circumstances leading up to the sale were so unusual that we strongly felt that your powers must have been at work.

Thank you so much for the record it seemed to bring great beauty and peace to my night's sleep.

I am delighted to tell you that I have not had another attack of those flashing lights before my eyes. Also the bladder trouble is getting more normal.

One night when my father was really ill again - - my mother rang you. While you were on the 'phone' all of a sudden my mind went blank and I felt as though I was floating, or in heaven, I went into the kitchen and cried, it wasn't until then that I really began to understand The Healing Wavelength.

My eye is still improving, I can now see the full screen on the TV. I can see over the road and cars as they pass.

My grateful thanks for all your prayers - God certainly listens to you, may His good works, through you, be seen to be done.

to thank you for the wonderful way in which you have helped my father and now you are helping my mother. My father could hardly walk or struggle out to the car, driven to Formby, when they arrived home I expected my father to come into the room exhausted, but to my amazement he was a different person.

Received your record, truly beautiful, time seems to stand still when you are listening to it.

quite a number of people have remarked about me being straighter and how I seem to be walking better, I can breathe better and take longer breaths.

My skin problem is so much better now and is showing a wonderful improvement. Also I find your healing record is very relaxing and helps to put my mind at peace. I am very grateful to you both.

When I was listening to side one today, of the Healing Music, I could hear you playing the piano and the Birds singing without my Hearing Aid, for the first time. It is wonderful and beautiful.

HE touches you

IT WOULD BE LOVELY TO PLACE OUR HANDS over yours to help you to feel the warm breeze blowing gently between us, and maybe a tingling sensation in your fingertips, and we would ask Jesus to allow you to hear the beautiful chord in only one ear. But we know, by the time you reach the end of the book, you will achieve this for yourself and everyone with you, and the days ahead will be glorious.

THE HEALINGS WE HAVE WRITTEN ABOUT are not our work, we do nothing really, other than arrange the situation for them to take place; they are all God's Miracles and we are together in His Presence. He Touches Us. The warm breeze is not something we do for you, when you are here with us, it is not something we are giving to you, we are not even a channel. It is, that together we are sharing the Presence of God, Jesus and The Holy Spirit, often with a silent prayer, and even unbelievers respond, returning to good health. For it only requires one person to believe and ask for His help, but many people surround themselves with artificial mental barriers and, with self-righteous intellect, push Him into obscurity.

"Within a man of light, there is light .. and he lights the world."

YOU CAN ALSO HELP everyone you meet because you will know you are not alone, it is no longer just a belief, it is real, it radiates from you, people feel it, you live it. It is a natural part of each and every one of us, which needs rejuvenation, renewal and the emergence of the soul to overcome the physical boundaries and limitations you have placed upon your mind.

IT IS VERY IMPORTANT to realise that your communications with God and Jesus and your ability to experience their Presence does not depend on a tutor or a charismatic personality or a cult leader. Your relationship is yours, it is you and He together, you do not need anyone between you or to act on your behalf, only JESUS.

ALL THROUGH THE BIBLICAL TEXTS Jesus constantly refers to the ear and to the left hand and the right hand and to light.

He said: *"Within a man of light, there is light, and he lights the whole world."*

When you have experienced His Presence it would radiate from you, not as a visible light, but you would have a special relationship with everyone, like a radiation you can feel, such as heat, which cannot be seen but you know it is there. It has a comforting effect; it is a joy to be near you.

JESUS SAID TO HIS DISCIPLES,
before they were to preach to the multitude:

"If they say to you: 'From where have you originated?' say to them: 'we have come from The Light, where The Light has originated through itself.'"

This is a remarkable comment, for in Genesis there is reference to Light. God says:

"Let there be Light."

And there was light and HE saw that it was good. It does not say God Created Light.

He said: *"Let there be."*

And there was Light. In other words, such is His Power He allowed it to happen. It Originated through itself, by His very words: *"Let there be."*

SO JESUS was telling His Disciples that they have come from God and were Originated from His Thoughts.

WE OFTEN THINK OF THE HEALINGS in this way; it is nothing we do as individuals; we 'allow' them to happen, instead of thinking they are not possible. Everything is possible with God, Jesus and The Holy Spirit; for He Created us in the first place; we only have to wait but this is difficult for humans, who want everything now!

ALLOW HIM TO TOUCH US; not surrounding ourselves with a barrier of doubt or even fooling ourselves that our science and understanding is superior; or we know more than He, because we do not. We only know what he has programmed us to know, this is why we are not aware of all the wavelengths of light which exist or hear all the sounds pulsating through our wonderful planet. Many other creatures see and hear more than we do.

ALLOW YOURSELF TO SEE THE LIGHT - real pinpoints of light and remember, Jesus said:

"His Father would manifest Himself and His Image is concealed by His Light."

He is here with us, concealed in the pinpoints of light and in the mauve shapes.

JESUS SAID:

"I tell my mysteries, to those who are worthy of my mysteries."

EVERYTHING WE HAVE WRITTEN ABOUT are His Mysteries, so we have to make ourselves worthy to receive them. You do not have to believe at this moment, He does not demand it of us, but do not ask to be allowed to receive Him as a test or a joke or even in sceptical doubt; be genuine; feel you want to know Him, this is real, allow it to happen, it will and it does.

LISTEN

JESUS SAID:

"Whoever has ears to hear, let him hear."

So listen for His Healing Wavelength in ONLY one ear, feel the warm breeze. Listen now while you are still reading, then listen when you are on you own and you will know you are not alone.

WE WERE TROUBLED that we would not be able to pass on what we have found to enough people to make a beneficial effect for mankind, because Jesus had already said:

"What thou shalt hear in thine ear and in the other ear, that preach from your housetops." (male-female)

Listen only in one ear.

FOR CERTAINLY our contacts, although thousands, are too few and it seemed too difficult for a one to one, hand to hand process to spread the word, as there is a magic figure, beyond which it perpetuates itself, but we could not reach this with our limited resources.

BUT THERE IS ANOTHER WAY and I am astonished we had not realised it sooner. It is here, not even hidden. It stands out like a beacon in one of Jesus' sayings, which everyone knows, but so few realise the implications. This is only just in time!

"Where two or more are gathered together in my name, there I am in the midst of them."

Now Remember, He told us, in our quotations, that He would Manifest Himself to us, (show Himself) but it has to be in His own way and the following is the message we are compelled to pass on:

**YOU ONLY HAVE TO ASK AND HE WILL MAKE HIMSELF KNOWN
BUT NOW YOU KNOW HOW HIS REPLY WILL BE.**

> *You may hear His Wavelength.*
> *You may feel the warm breeze*
> *Or the Touch on your forehead and cheeks,*
> *A single muscle twitch, in an arm or leg,*
> *Or see pinpoints of Light near a friend.*
>
> **NOW YOU KNOW WHERE TO SEEK HIM**
> (In The Midst Of Us)
> *In Ways Which Are No Longer Unknown.*

PREVIOUSLY we only knew it as a saying of Jesus, leaving it up to Him to make it so. But TO FEEL HIM IN OUR MIDST we need to do something about it ourselves, we have to reach out and ask Him to make Himself known, in one or all of the ways above.

THE LIVING WORD

UNBELIEVERS could not find him and believers could not help them to do so but now, if you ask, you know where to seek and if you genuinely mean that you want to know Him, He is here, He really is waiting for you and always has been.

NOW take it a step at a time, do not rush at it, enjoy it and marvel at the beauty of the moment. He will be with you forever. As a warm breeze, as a cobweb touch on the face, as a single twitch in a muscle, as a beautiful chord in only one ear and pinpoints or shapes of light.

ONCE YOU HAVE MET GOD, JESUS AND THE HOLY SPIRIT, *you will always know them and always be together.*

WE HAVE TO CONTACT JESUS and not just read about Him in The Bible, for it is Jesus Himself who said:

"You search The Scriptures, because you think, that in them you have eternal life; and it is they that bear witness to me - yet you refuse to come to me that you may have life."

NOW YOU CAN COME TO HIM, for He has told us how to do it and, most of all where to look and how His Presence will be experienced.

SO NOW IT IS UP TO YOU but it is very simple and easy to establish a real practical relationship with our Creator, for He is One and The Same with Jesus; then move on to unknown wonders.

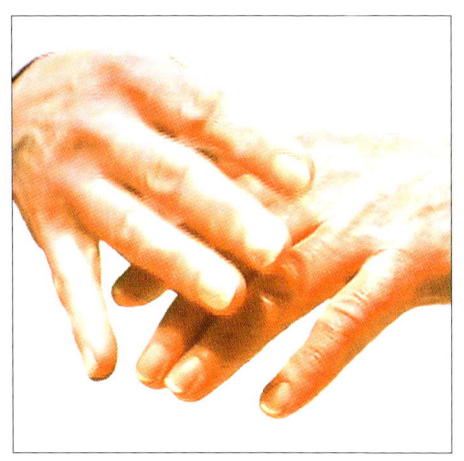

SIT QUIETLY with some like-minded friends, think peacefully of beautiful flowers, sunsets, cherry blossom trees, do not concentrate on them, just let your mind flow from one to another, think of nothing if you can or have a vase of flowers near you. Mention to your friends briefly what the book concerns or, preferably, they should read it themselves before making this ultimate communication with God's Presence.

PLACE YOUR HAND about an inch above the hand of the nearest person to you and let them do the same with someone else close by; to feel the warm breeze blowing between you. This is not a ritual or procedure; no need to sit in a circle or with hands on a table or anything similar; just be near enough to someone to be able to place your hand about one inch above theirs; be comfortable.

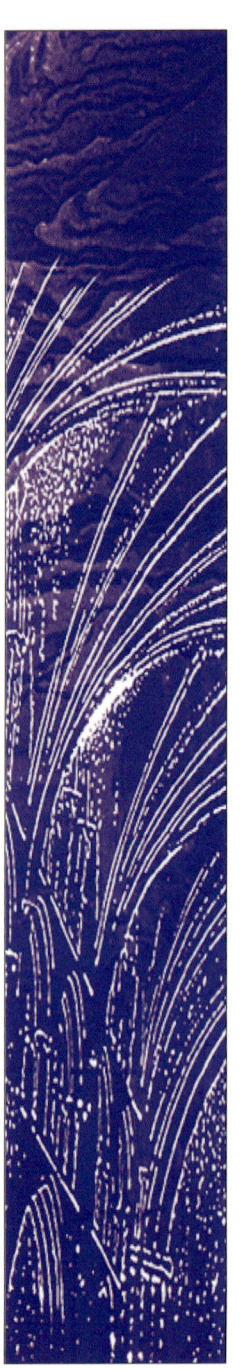

Do not switch the lights off, there is nothing 'spooky' about this, it is a normal and natural way to feel Jesus' Presence in our midst.

THEN ALL TOGETHER, LISTEN OUT INTO DISTANT SPACE WITH ONE EAR

(Left if male)   (Right if female)

Ask God, Jesus and The Holy Spirit to be allowed to receive them.

Do not be impatient,
Avoid intense desire,
Do not doubt.

He will take His own time - it will be in His own way. It may not be today, although usually it is, but you can be sure that the moment of contact, of realisation will be absolutely right for each one of you.

PEOPLE HAVE always asked Jesus to be with them and not known how His reply will be. So they have often wondered if He had responded at all but now you know, because He told us in The Biblical Texts:

The warm breeze,
The lovely high pitched chord in only one ear,
The pinpoints and shapes of Light,
The single muscle movement
in an arm or leg like a twitch,
The tickling sensation on your forehead or face.

This is worth repeating from page to page, so you know exactly what to expect.

REMEMBER JESUS SAID:

"I will give you what eye has not seen, what ear has not heard, what hand has not touched, and what has not arisen in the heart of man."

THESE LAST FEW WORDS are the ultimate message, for having experienced even one of the above sensations, something very special has arisen in your heart. YOU KNOW He has made contact with you and your new life is only just beginning.

IT CAN BE ONE OR ALL of these sensations; you can now see, feel and hear His reply, because you know where to seek. You are not left wondering if He has heard you.

BE STILL AND KNOW THAT HE IS GOD
HE HAS MADE CONTACT WITH YOU

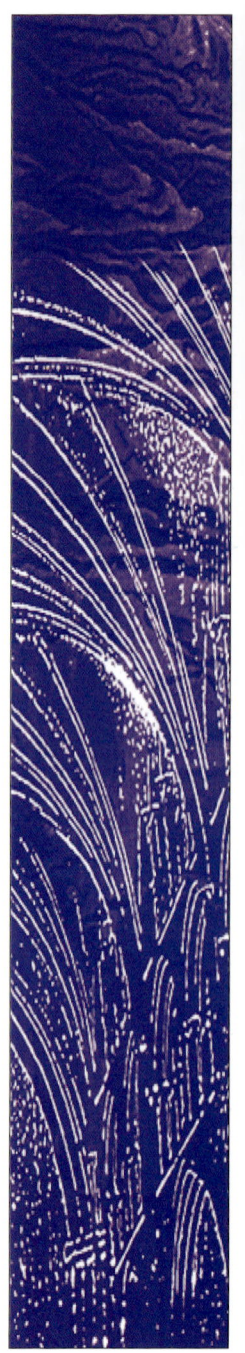

THIS ADDITIONAL MATERIAL will help with any difficulties which may have occurred in your first attempts to Feel His Presence.

USEFUL EXTRA DETAILS

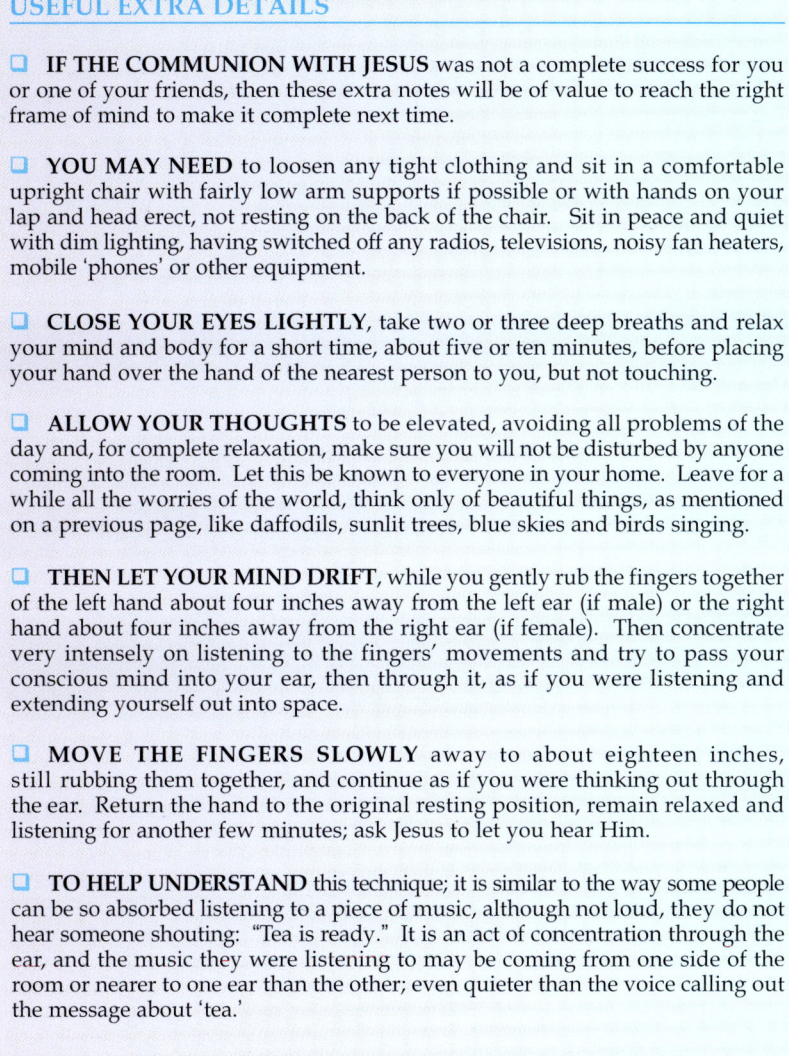

❏ **IF THE COMMUNION WITH JESUS** was not a complete success for you or one of your friends, then these extra notes will be of value to reach the right frame of mind to make it complete next time.

❏ **YOU MAY NEED** to loosen any tight clothing and sit in a comfortable upright chair with fairly low arm supports if possible or with hands on your lap and head erect, not resting on the back of the chair. Sit in peace and quiet with dim lighting, having switched off any radios, televisions, noisy fan heaters, mobile 'phones' or other equipment.

❏ **CLOSE YOUR EYES LIGHTLY**, take two or three deep breaths and relax your mind and body for a short time, about five or ten minutes, before placing your hand over the hand of the nearest person to you, but not touching.

❏ **ALLOW YOUR THOUGHTS** to be elevated, avoiding all problems of the day and, for complete relaxation, make sure you will not be disturbed by anyone coming into the room. Let this be known to everyone in your home. Leave for a while all the worries of the world, think only of beautiful things, as mentioned on a previous page, like daffodils, sunlit trees, blue skies and birds singing.

❏ **THEN LET YOUR MIND DRIFT**, while you gently rub the fingers together of the left hand about four inches away from the left ear (if male) or the right hand about four inches away from the right ear (if female). Then concentrate very intensely on listening to the fingers' movements and try to pass your conscious mind into your ear, then through it, as if you were listening and extending yourself out into space.

❏ **MOVE THE FINGERS SLOWLY** away to about eighteen inches, still rubbing them together, and continue as if you were thinking out through the ear. Return the hand to the original resting position, remain relaxed and listening for another few minutes; ask Jesus to let you hear Him.

❏ **TO HELP UNDERSTAND** this technique; it is similar to the way some people can be so absorbed listening to a piece of music, although not loud, they do not hear someone shouting: "Tea is ready." It is an act of concentration through the ear, and the music they were listening to may be coming from one side of the room or nearer to one ear than the other; even quieter than the voice calling out the message about 'tea.'

RECEPTIVE senses

WE DESCRIBED EARLIER how God is a constant background against which everything is experienced. The human brain seems to be programmed to ignore continuous gentle stimuli, so it can be ready to respond to danger by not being preoccupied with all the information imposed upon us, every moment of the day. It is within this framework we have spent our lives ignoring God, so now we have to renew our receptive senses to His Presence, to Jesus' Presence. Do not just wait for it to happen; encourage your mind to make it happen.

YOU MAY AT THIS STAGE hear The Healing Wavelength or experience a fluffy cotton wool effect (slight impairment of hearing) in your ear, as if there were something in the way and you had to listen through it. It is a quiet and beautiful chord consisting of three predominant notes, which are quite close together and because they are so high, an octave above top 'A flat', beyond the top end of the piano keyboard, they are difficult to separate, and would probably be a disharmony if played near the centre of the piano.

IT IS OCCASIONALLY experienced slightly above the ear and inside the head and, once you have become accustomed to hearing it, seems to remain audible above external noises but without getting any louder. Then it fades if you are distracted.

YOU MAY ALSO FEEL tickling sensations on the face or a small twitch in an arm or leg, just to let you know that, although you may not be hearing His Wavelength yet, He has made contact. So remain totally aware of your whole body and how you feel.

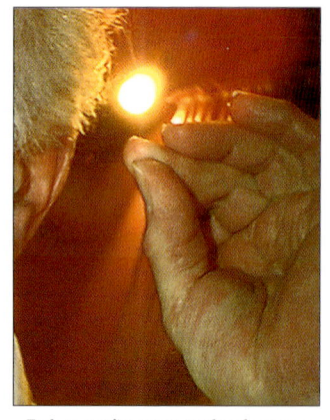

Rub your fingers together by your ear and become accustomed to listening outwards.

WE MUST POINT OUT here, you are not casually observing an experiment; you are participating, you are the experiment and your sole intention is to hear The Wavelength or feel The Warm Breeze. Some groups of friends, working on this for the first time, report the feeling of being somewhere else, while enjoying the state of peace and tranquillity that engulfs us all when reaching out to Our Creator. Remember, you are not testing Jesus to determine if He will make Himself known; you are making yourself available, because you want to hear Him.

WE HAVE MEMBERS of the Medical Professions, who hear The Chord when visiting us and quite regularly at other times, while at work or at home, and have experienced Healing within themselves, along with the Time Displacement phenomenon, but they are unable to explain them or dismiss them.

SOUL AND SPIRIT COMPONENT

A PHYSICIST WHO IS ALSO a mathematician has experienced these and finds it impossible to make them fit into the physical parameters of life and the universe and he may have to change some of his life long theories. He has explored ideas that there may be part of our brain, responding in a manner which is quite independent of time, space and matter and is capable of influencing the physical world by thought. We may be absorbing God's energies for specific purposes, if our belief system has not been overcome by the negative gene. In a round about way the professor is identifying our soul and spirit component, without actually admitting their presence.

FOR INSTANCE we may be Healed, if we ask. But there is no point in asking, if you do not have some form of belief, for you only get what you expect. But someone who does believe can intercede for you, because they care, even without you knowing, and thereby you will be healed. The unbelievers may say they would have got better anyway!

DISTANT HEALING OCCURS in this manner; it only needs one person somewhere to care sufficiently to ask God for Healing, for a person who may be on the other side of the world, and they get better. The first time we were asked how is this possible, I had to pause to think and Heather saved the day by saying: "Because we are all the same distance from God."

THIS IS absolutely true. So even thousands of miles away we can all strengthen a relationship with Jesus, with God, for someone who was lost, just by asking and believing it to be so.

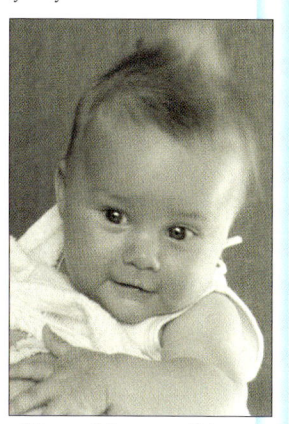

BABIES ARE REMARKABLE in the way they respond. One minute they would be yelling and screaming, then hold them in your arms and with a little silent prayer The Wavelength is with them and they become peaceful and often go to sleep.

We are all the same distance from God.

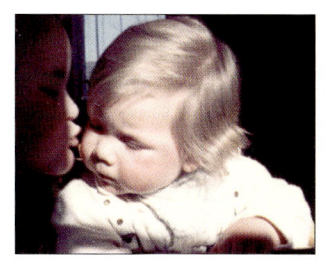

Bond between brother and sister.

FREQUENTLY gentle wisps of steam can be seen rising from the baby's head as the healing progresses.

IT IS WONDERFUL to see God at work, for there is no need of conversation or explanations for a baby. They would not understand anyway but know what is taking place. They feel it by being with you in God's Presence.

AT BIRTH all babies are nearer to God and enjoy His Contact in those early years and the mother bonds this union with our Creator.

THIS IS WHY a happy mother-to-be, has a wonderful radiance while the child is developing within her. She Is Not Alone and this is visible to others, even if she is not aware of it herself.

UNFORTUNATELY, without guidance, children seem to grow away from Him.

Radiance of motherhood.

LOST without knowing

SO EXPECT TO HEAR HIM AND YOU WILL. HOW COULD IT BE OTHERWISE?

YOU ATTRACT towards yourself what you wish, what you expect. He is here, so you only have to listen, to make yourself aware of what you have been ignoring for so long. Then you will be complete again, as a mature person with understanding, having brought something natural with you from your infant days, which you had lost without knowing what it was.

WHEN YOU HEAR JESUS' PRESENCE, His Healing Wavelength will stay with you as long as you wish, then gradually resume its place in the constant background, not noticeable at all. Although He will always be with you, as He has been in the past, now you know and you can renew the communion just by listening for Him, by the conscious thought of doing so or saying in your mind; may I hear you. Instantly, He will be there for you.

WHEN YOU HAVE to be involved in work or life's activities again, The Wavelength fades. He does not impose upon you but is your constant companion. He may give a short 'chord' or 'bleep' in one ear, if it is necessary for you to pause a moment in your thoughts or in what you are doing; or you may see a pinpoint of light. You are being guided. Take notice!

YOU SHOULD TAKE a pause here and always acknowledge His Presence, knowing He has changed the rest of your life by that fraction of a second. Thank Him, for there will have been a beneficial purpose for Him to impinge upon your mind. Although we think we hear it in the ear, it is of course an interpretation by the brain.

THIS HAS HAPPENED to us many times and always with beneficial results. Each night I check that everything electrical, which should be switched off, is switched off. One night while checking, I saw a pinpoint of light near a wall socket, in which many electrical items are plugged from time to time. I had switched it off, so as always I acknowledged His Presence and went to bed knowing all was well.

THE NEXT EVENING, on my way round the house, I noticed two pinpoints of light near the same wall socket. It intrigued me and I thanked Him for His Presence, as I always do, knowing the momentary pause had influenced my life.

A DAY LATER by the same socket there were four pinpoints of light and they were not just a brief appearance, they stayed there. This was serious, I had missed something. He was not about to let me get away this time. I pulled up a little stool and sat by the socket, it seemed to be in perfect condition.

A SIMPLE THOUGHT came to me, so I checked the plugs of all the items used in it and one of them, a lamp, if it had been pulled out of the socket without first switching off, could have been lethal, as both wires were frayed. I repaired it and slept well, knowing all His wisdom and knowledge was up to date, although the experiences of Jesus' time would only be with lamps using cold pressed oil from the olives.

SO IF HE COULD WARN ME in this way, then He is here in today's world. We are not alone.

Pinpoints of light were seen near faulty plugs.

POSITIVE thoughts

WE HAVE SEEN so many Miracles, which are seemingly impossible but they happen with us every day. We are compelled to write this book to help people reach out and feel His Presence.

IF YOU ARE in need of help, when you listen for His Healing Wavelength, make it known to Him what your wishes are. None are too small or too great but be prepared to wait. He is even helping while you are waiting, because something else concerning you may have to be attended to first to make your wishes possible.

IF YOUR HEALTH is poor at the moment, do not give in, be determined to become fit and well again. You are no longer alone; healing energies are working with you, so meet Him at least half way with positive thoughts.

DO EVERYTHING possible to be happy and contented, receive each improvement in your health with thanks, no matter how small. Look for and see only the best in everyone you meet; discover the beauty and perfection of our Creator in everything around you and remember, He dwells in all living things. It is His Presence which separates all the particles in every atom, hence the liberation of vast amounts of energy when an atom is disrupted.

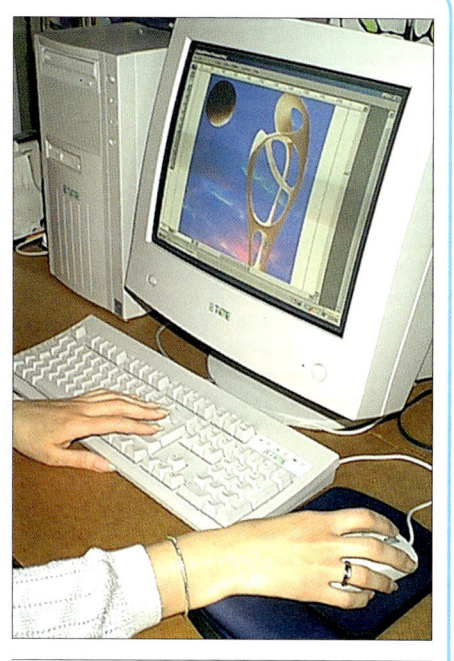

Creating this book has brought many revelations. We have been guided throughout its preparation.

VIBRATIONAL LEVELS

VISUALISE YOURSELF IMPROVING; think what you will do when you are well again. Enjoy The Healing Wavelength; experience the quiet high-pitched chord in one ear and the elation of knowing changes are taking place.

GOD'S PRESENCE stimulates all creative activities in human life. It may be that, when you accept His Presence, new cell conditions arise in the brain, liberating or allowing access to information which, prior to their formation, was not available. This may be due to an extrasensory ability to communicate on vibrational levels, which are not detected by the five normal senses. For He has access to our consciousness and influences our activities, so we may develop in ways that were uncharted for our soul and be of value for His beneficial purposes, while maintaining our freewill, because it is our choice to be with Him or 'go it alone.'

A CREATIVE STATE OF MIND ARISES, which may be applied to any sphere of human endeavour and may change your whole way of life. You could become capable of solving apparently impossible problems and creating original ideas in your own particular sphere of activity and expertise or in any other area you may choose. We have experienced this in our own primitive way, with the sculptures, paintings, poetry, Healings and other activities for which we had very little previous talent.

CREATIVE THINKING

ONLY IN LATER LIFE did I realise that my childhood experiences deeply depended on our Creator's Presence. To me Creative Thinking began in a very simple way, as a child learning to swim. I believed I could swim; it seemed to me that if other people were doing so; then why not I?

I BEGAN TO CRAWL along the surface of the sea water with one hand on the sand, one after the other, until a gentle wave came in; the water became deeper, my hands no longer touched the sand and for a few strokes I was swimming.

My brother Jimmy

I'm still fascinated by flowers

IT HAS NOW become obvious to me that if you believe, then you achieve in proportion to the strength of your belief (with a little help from the tide). In this respect, two individuals can learn the physical movements necessary to be able to swim but only the one who believes will succeed, the other will sink or flounder and yet there would be no difference between what they were doing, only in their minds.

FLOATING IS NATURAL; you do not have to do anything to float, only relax; even if a little belief is needed. It is similar to the healing work, by allowing it to happen, but the mind can make you sink or swim. We know that The Healing Wavelength is a natural part of our Creator's communications and many choose to ignore it or have not noticed it by making the world what we think it must be. As the swimming shows, we can make it what we wish, if we believe and allow it to happen and do not interfere with normality by imposing our negative thoughts upon it.

RIDING A TWO WHEEL CYCLE looks impossible to a child; you cannot explain the physics of it, to one so young like balance, speed and a gentle wobble of the front wheel and so on. But once he has experienced the complete process of doing it, he can always do it, without even understanding how it happens. So it is with Healing and hearing The Healing Wavelength. Once you have acknowledged the possibilities of Healing and the presence of The Wavelength, it becomes part of you and you can access both without any work or ritual. Even without you knowing how it happens or how it works, God, Jesus and The Holy Spirit have made contact and will be with you for ever, just as they have always been but now you can experience and enjoy their contact, living your life together.

CHILDREN RESPOND very rapidly to new ideas, far more readily than adults, who have rigidly learned thought patterns. With children, thinking creatively comes easily. There is no need to overcome the adult resistance to new ideas. A child does not always require proof but is prepared to believe, then attempt your method or suggestions and, when they find they are successful, it is sufficient. Many adults declare an idea is impracticable or impossible without even trying. Thus they limit their mental growth by the erroneous impression, that they are superior. With the humility and belief of a child, much more will be achieved.

YOU ARE YOUR ONLY LIMITATION!

IF THE MIND IS ABLE to help the body to achieve success almost by thought alone, then there would seem to be no limit to what the mind could achieve within itself, without any physical limitations your body may have placed upon you, either by birth or accident. Not only would it become possible for the body to find ways of doing things which previously it could not do but the mind could produce original ideas and solutions from previously unassociated information and even acquire missing details from extrasensory sources, which we will experiment with shortly, under the Telepathy heading. It seems obvious that everyone should be able to use their mind in this way but very few bother to do so.

AS YOU BECOME MORE AWARE of God's Presence within the framework of creativity, you could prepare yourself to recognise when spontaneous original information is coming through into consciousness, as it may present itself in a disguised form and may occur at any time of the day or night. Always have a little note book and pen with you to jot down any intuitive passing ideas, for they will have gone a moment later. Many people restrict their ability to do this by being bound by rules limiting their thought, thus viewing things in a fixed manner, often discarding ideas without giving them a chance to mature.

ALLOW YOURSELF the thought that something may be possible, instead of often dismissing it, because it does not fit into your knowledge of the physical scheme of things. You could know a set procedure for completing a certain task and, if you have always done it in one way, you may feel it is the best and only way of doing so but there could be several alternatives; some may be even better.

PREPARE YOURSELF

MANY PSYCHOLOGISTS believe and have stated the view that errors and mistakes in any expressed form are due to inhibitions, frustrations and repressions of the individual. Also faulty actions, faulty thoughts and erroneous recollections of facts and details are similarly initiated but we find this is not correct on every occasion. It would be easier for this to be understood in the following example.

YOU MAY BE PLAYING a piano or guitar melody, one which is well known to you, perhaps a passage you have played perfectly many times, and you may find you have performed one or two incorrect notes or slightly changed the rhythms. Some of these errors could be due to incorrect learning but several of them will be original material coming through from the subconscious, while the mind is almost in a state of reverie or 'on automatic pilot.' Each and every one of them should be thoroughly investigated and, if possible, when an error of this kind is made, you should stop and try to analyse the state of mind at the moment it occurred.

KEEP A NOTE OF THESE

DON'T SIT waiting for the future make it happen

Creativity Psychologist Alan Fraser Bell explains his method of

CREATIVE THINKING

to CHRIS KELLY and talks about Spontaneous inspiration on television

Altered states of consciousness
Vibrational bonding of Man, Plants, Animals & Matter.

Alan, surrounded here by his sculptures and works of art, discusses with Chris Kelly how all mankind could reach superb achievements if we would only try to experience our Creator's Presence.

Moments of spontaneous inspiration would then occur, with worldwide significance for peace and prosperity.

FUTURE RESEARCH

WE HAVE continued our research while writing the Book, covering new ideas and phenomena, and attempting to determine the sound frequencies of The Healing Wavelength, to check if they carry messages, maybe in a special way that can be interpreted by the brain, which if speeded up may sound like a high pitched note. Also we have to understand the warm breeze to measure its temperature, and even this may be the effect of a low frequency. Research into the MAUVE shapes and pinpoints of light will require unusual techniques as some are only fleeting occurrences lasting a fraction of a second.

AS NEW SCIENTIFIC methods evolve we hope to write a leaflet from time to time, or if all goes well another book. Although the cost of such research is probably too high for our resources.

SPONTANEOUS inspiration

CONTINUING THE IDEAS expressed on a previous page; when you are talking to someone, you may inadvertently reverse the words or drop a letter or superimpose another letter in its place, so an error is produced. Some of these errors may be due to the conditioning already mentioned or a dislike of the person to whom you are talking and these can be easily identified as such. Some may show a fragment of truth emerging when you are trying to hide something but a few of them will be due to spontaneous information coming through from the subconscious or coming via the subconscious from extrasensory sources.

EACH ERROR should be thoroughly investigated; try to sense the state of mind existing at the moment when the error was produced.

INSPIRED THOUGHTS OR FAULTY ACTIONS

(No! Not Fawlty Towers) Although some of these actions may remind you of such moments, in which your hands do not quite do what you originally intended them to do.

ON THESE OCCASIONS, the hands are under the control of the subconscious and you are not thinking consciously about what you are doing; and we all have memories of many incidents, embarrassing and otherwise, where we have knocked something over by an apparently careless action, which is usually perfectly performed.

HOWEVER, in the realm of the mind, this was necessary, although you had not thought about it, as it bypassed your conscious editorial processes. And, yes! some of them may follow from the above psychological diagnosis but several are original.

MANY OF THESE will be found to be most interesting, as situations will often arise, which would not have come about in any other way. Here also you should analyse your feelings and state of mind, when the errors and faulty actions occur. Ask yourself: are you happy, sad, irritated, tired or 'pushed for time?'

UNEXPECTED

EVENTUALLY, after continual practise along these lines, you will readily be able to place your mind in this creative condition, when, instead of faulty actions occurring in what you are trying to do consciously, a continuous stream of activity or thought, will occur, which is complete and perfect, in itself, but not of your own origination.

IT MAY not be complete in the early stages of this experiment, there may be small fragments over a period of time, which when joined together, create the whole item, as in a painting or sculpture for example, or a poem or written words such as this book.

Jesus taught the multitude, saying: "Beyond the icy peaks of struggle, lies the peace and beauty of The Infinite Garden of Knowledge."

FRAMEWORK

A MOMENT ARRIVES which is very fascinating, when you know the poem, painting, sculpture or other work, is complete. Beyond this point in our own research, we have been unable to add another spot of paint or another word, for it would spoil it to do so.

IT THEN BECOMES very apparent that what you have been doing is not within your control; you have been inspired or moved in some way to do it.

The final touch completes it.

YOUR MIND has frequently travelled somewhere else, as we spoke of earlier. Many musicians may briefly feel the soul of the composer, which would make their playing brilliant.

WE HAVE witnessed this state of mind in many of the private performances of my wife, since our research work into Creativity, within God's framework.

GOD'S Work

THE HEALING WORK is similar. You do not perform The Healings yourself, you are moved to act in a certain way to allow them to happen. The moment arises when your work is complete and you have helped someone to float in God's Hands, as they experience drifting into another place of peace, time and tranquillity, in His Presence.

IT IS GOD'S WORK, not ours, and we are privileged to be so close to these Miracles.

UNSEEN help

YOU MAY EVEN BE MOVED to walk a few steps behind someone who is in physical or mental distress and they will be touched by Jesus from your prayerful thoughts. This may be very rapid, you can see them take a deep breath and more joyful steps as you walk past.

SADLY in the present world we cannot stop or pause or indicate to them that they are not alone - God is with them. For it would be considered an intrusion into their personal life and disturbing for them that anyone had noticed their need of help. In times of accident or great suffering, these barriers are bridged and we can openly offer Healing.

YOUR MIND could be ahead of you and may itself initiate an action of a self survival nature had it first anticipated you were in danger, without you being consciously aware of it, and only afterwards realising, you had paused or performed an action, which was not deliberate. These are spontaneous or intuitive and of great value to the survival of your fragment of mind material, which was protecting your body, and of course, its own temporary home. God had touched you in your moment of need.

DON'T LET THESE WORDS *drift past you without absorbing their real significance. Study the last few paragraphs again, for they give an insight into what may be missing from many lives and thereby allow a two way communication between The Trinity and yourself. It soon becomes easier to hear The Healing Wavelength, to receive their Presence and experience their many ways of contact.*

UNIVERSAL mind

TRY TO PLACE yourself in the same frame of mind that occurred when you were presented with an error, as many of these will be found to be part of an original creative process awaiting completion or you may discover the solution to a problem which has been bothering you for a long time. You will also have allowed yourself to be more aware of God's Presence.

MAYBE we are all experiencing small fragments of a Universal Mind (Our Creator's) and our individual conscious mind interferes with the reception of Universal Mind material. This would occur by having to cope with physical stimuli and information received by the five normal senses, the intensity of which is too strong.

WE NEED moments of absolute quietness, peace and tranquillity to benefit from the subtleties of His Presence, to help us to reunite with our existence before we were given physical form.

JESUS SAID to His Disciples: *"Thy Father in Heaven hath loved thee, before The Foundation of The World."*

WHAT A WONDERFUL MESSAGE. We have all existed since before we were given physical form. This one thought alone gives absolute confirmation that we will continue to exist in Spirit form, even when the physical body ceases to be useful to us. Because everything God creates is complete and its future is known to Him, so He has no need to bring anything or anyone to an end.

"Thy Father in Heaven hath loved thee, before the Foundation of The World."

IN LIFE, He has given us the chance to touch and move real physical things, to appreciate His joy of being creative for ourselves, to be able to reproduce ourselves, so He no longer has to continue creating another Adam and Eve every day, giving Him more time for new works of exquisite form and function to place upon the earth. Even a white cross in the centre of an Honesty flower at Easter, should not go unnoticed.

WHILE IN ANOTHER CORNER of His Wisdom, and at the same time, He continues to tear empty space apart to create equal and opposite charges and keeps them separate to form a few more atoms of Hydrogen in outer space, to replenish elements which have given up their energy during radioactive disintegrations. Not destroyed; but converted into radiant energy.

OUR CREATOR alone can bring all things into being just by saying: *"Let There Be."* We can only change their form, once they are here, and only He can bring His Creations to an end. So, having Created us in Spirit form, even before He Created The Earth, we will continue to exist until He has the thought to say: *"LET THERE BE AN END."*

BUT HAVING CREATED such perfection from His thoughts, there is no scientific sign of any of His Great Works coming to an end, only changing. Why should there be, as everything He created is complete and He knows their futures? We should all be deeply worried if it had not been so.

KIND THOUGHTS and deeds

THIS IS AN ASPECT of living so often neglected, as many people spend their time doing, thinking and saying unpleasant things, by way of 'paying back' for suffering inflicted upon them on a previous occasion.

THESE THOUGHTS and actions are completely alien to Creative Thinking, Healing and communicating with our Creator and must cease as soon as possible.

AT ALL TIMES you must extend pleasant, kind, happy thoughts to everyone and, although this is difficult, even

Jesus spoke of The Infinite Garden of Knowledge: *"Here in the centre of its forest stands The Tree of Life, Mystery of Mysteries."*

to the people who are unpleasant and unkind to you. You must not wish them 'far enough,' or any other situation that comes to mind. If they treat you in an unpleasant way, this is not an excuse or a reason for treating them in a similar manner. You must extend kind thoughts to everyone, not only to your friends. *"Turn the other cheek."*

IT SHOULD BE APPARENT to you from your observations of life generally that those people who are constantly thinking evil thoughts about others and inflicting unpleasant 'tricks' on them, always suffer more than those to whom the thoughts are being directed. Therefore never be unkind or harm anyone, even if it is only for the simple reason that you will always do more harm to yourself, than to the person about whom you are thinking unpleasant thoughts.

YOU MUST ALWAYS aim at communicating happily with everyone and all living things. The principle of kind thoughts and deeds should be extended to include all animals, plants and insects. Never let the sun set on an argument; always make peace before sleeping.

Jesus said:
"There shall be no peace among peoples till there be one garden of the brotherhood over the Earth. For how can there be peace, when each man pursueth his own gain? . . . .

. . . . He who hath found peace with the brotherhood of man, hath made himself the co-worker of God."

THE PURPOSE of all these little stories is to show how God reveals Himself to each one of us in our own lives, in different ways. So look for him in yours and be prepared to be surprised.

GOOD WORKS

"I come because you need me"

Jesus said this to those who sought His help.

BRIAN QUINN M.B.E. has been honoured by The Queen for his good works in rehabilitating young offenders, with whom he has achieved remarkable success.

HE KNEW our little Healing Sanctuary was falling into a state of disrepair, having been put together many years ago by myself in a do-it-yourself manner, to keep the costs low.

BRIAN, HIS WIFE and children have been our great friends for a long time. He arrived one day with a collection of materials to rebuild The Sanctuary, and with him came two of the rascals he had moulded and encouraged to return to honest pursuits. He gave them a chance to show their hidden kindness and return more to society than they had taken away by devious means.

SINCE THEN, these two have continued Brian's work by helping others to reform and they frequently speak of their experiences in The Healing Garden.

Brian Quinn has always sought the best in every soul.

THIS IS YET ANOTHER example of God's guidance, through Brian, of how it has been made possible for our life's work to continue, just when we were in difficulties. Years after Brian and his rascals had made such a lovely job of The Sanctuary, the floor fell through. It was the only part we thought was in good condition.

ASTONISHINGLY, within a few weeks, a Formby friend of long-standing, Alex Wilson, rebuilt the floor and refurbished the walls and roof, which by this time were rapidly deteriorating, as we did not replace them all when Brian was here; we thought they would last a little longer.

Alexander Wilson rebuildingThe Sanctuary.

THIS IS REMARKABLE, for we had been helped, yet again, as by this time we had started on the book, so we were also able to continue with our Healing work. Both would have been severely disrupted if we had rebuilt The Sanctuary ourselves.

GOD'S GUIDANCE and Presence always brings us inspiration, which we hope to pass on to you.

Seek the best in everyone you meet.

Above: Refurbishment completed
Left: The original room

HEART broken, but not the spirit

SEVERAL YEARS ago two drunken lads came into The Healing Garden and started to roll the sculptures around, finally crashing one onto the paving stones, destroying it.

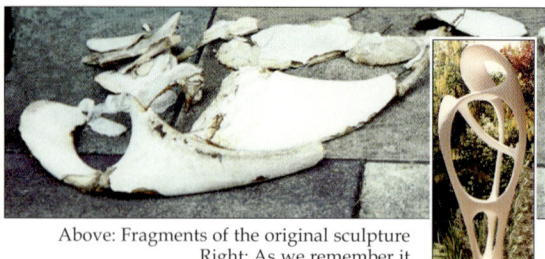

Above: Fragments of the original sculpture
Right: As we remember it

IT WAS a very sad moment, as the sculpture captivated many people and the lads should have known better, as they came from respectable wealthy families, who would have been appalled if they had known. But it was not in our nature to make a fuss and would have served no purpose in alleviating our loss. Nor could they have restored it, for it was not within their souls to have done so, as it came about after prolonged meditation in God's Presence and my hands were guided over every inch of its construction.

IT LAY ON THE GROUND for several years as we were too involved in helping people, to have time to make another sculpture. Then one year we were invited to give some Healing in The Isle Of Man for a couple of weeks.

MY WIFE and I went over to stay with Beatrice Qualtrough of Port St. Mary, who very generously looked after us during our stay at Mallmore Hotel. We were all her friends and it was a sad moment when she retired. She is greatly missed.

Heather re-creates and captures the inspiration of the original sculpture.

Sculptor's corner, beauty out of chaos!! Hard to believe, Dad created some of his best work in this mess.

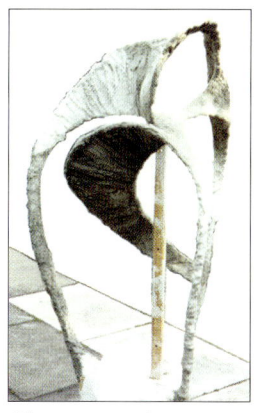

HEATHER REMAINED at home to look after everyone here, although we had not made any appointments for that period, as we liked to work together. However, we never knew who may arrive in need of help and she had a break later.

WHILE WE WERE AWAY Heather was moved in some manner to lovingly rebuild the sculpture with her friend Ron. They used some of the shattered remains to copy the shapes and a few photographs we had of its beauty.

The reconstruction process.

A LOVELY SURPRISE awaited us when we returned home, not just a reunion of all the family but the vision of a regenerated work of art. Heather had re-created the soul of the original sculpture from God's Presence; the same source as my own inspiration. We Are Not Alone.

Then freedom, the sculpture stretches out its leaves to welcome the start of spring.

Above: Even the horse chestnut tree seemed saddened by the destruction of the sculpture and produced little ones of its own.

Ron helping to reshape with loving care.

Completed with the same soul as the original.

167

TELEPATHY

THERE ARE MANY CREATURES like the horse, the dog and dolphin, who seem to know what you are thinking, often before it becomes a truly conscious thought of yours. They seem to feel the origination of your thoughts or we may have sensed a telepathic image from them, perhaps telling *you* it was time to go for a walk!

EVEN OUR humble guinea pig would know when you were about to cut him some grass and the rabbit would let you know it was time for something, by tapping underneath the seat of your chair with his head and strangely buzzing like a bee.

HAVING EXPERIMENTED with the rotating cylinder, mentioned earlier, you will find it very easy to communicate with a relative or friend by telepathic mind contact.

Friends Benjie and Bunge

ALL WE REQUIRE is a table with a dividing screen across the top, paper and two pens. If squared paper is used, then number the squares down the left hand side: 1 to 20 for yourself and your partner. Sit comfortably at the table either side of the screen, in such a way that neither of you can see the other person or their paper.

YOU MAY WISH to have a third member present, as a witness, to observe that no normal communication takes place, but only if you need to prove telepathic contact was established. The witness must not see the symbols and is only required to enforce simple safeguards to avoid any talking other than a prearranged 'OK', indicating the next transmission. Care should be taken with any phrase used such as 'OK'. It must be used on every occasion and not only when a zero has been written in the square, thus reducing the chance of an arranged code.

WITH MODERN TECHNOLOGY the whole experiment can be recorded on video to check upon perfected procedures. This prevents taps on the table or dropping the pen or any other hidden way of communication taking place.

I am thinking of the number 1

I'll list the number I see in my mind

Each person will have different abilities.

THESE are a few ideas. You could explore many more for added safety.

Mother and son can be very receptive to each others thoughts.

MANY BOOKS have been written concerning the interpretation of such experiments but, for our purpose, if over **70%** of the results are the same, then you have established mental contact with your partner.

USING ONLY TWO SYMBOLS **1** and **0**. One of you should act as a transmitter and one as a receiver. The experiment should proceed as follows:

LOOKING AT the piece of paper, the transmitter would write in the square against Figure 1 either a **1** or **0** and then say 'OK' to the other person (the receiver). You could perform these first twenty squares as a passive one, not even trying to send the symbol to your partner. When the receiver has written in their first square what they think the symbol is, similarly say 'OK'. Now in the square against Figure 2, the transmitter places another symbol, either a **1** or **0** and the receiver responds as before.

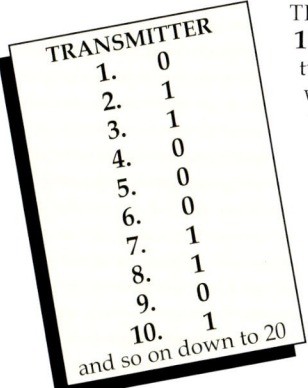

THIS IS repeated until the symbol **1** or **0** has been placed against all twenty squares. Then each of you would have figures in front of you that may look similar to the columns on these two pages.

NOW CHECK all your results and make a note below each line of how many of the symbols received were identical to the ones which were transmitted. In the case here there were six.

TRANSMITTER
1. 0
2. 1
3. 1
4. 0
5. 0
6. 0
7. 1
8. 1
9. 0
10. 1
and so on down to 20

RECEIVER
1. 0
2. 0
3. 0
4. 1
5. 0
6. 0
7. 1
8. 1
9. 1
10. 1
and so on down to 20

AS YOU BECOME more accustomed to working together, the results very often improve as the situation becomes more natural and less strained and less attention is given to the experimental procedure, with more concentration on the communication. So now it is time to try different ways of sending images to your partner. Try and visualise it, perhaps with eyes closed, or use a new coloured ink; do not look at any of the others, even cover them all, except the current symbol, you are in the process of transmitting.

YOU WILL FIND a peak may be reached of say 17 or 18 out of twenty, then there may be a rapid falling off in the results. You may be getting bored or tired and if you continued for an equal number of experiments that it took to reach the peak, then by analysis it may be possible to prove that the results were just what would have been predicted by chance alone and therefore telepathic communication did not take place. But if boredom or tiredness occurs, the results are equivalent to a mechanical procedure, as no mind effort or excitement exists.

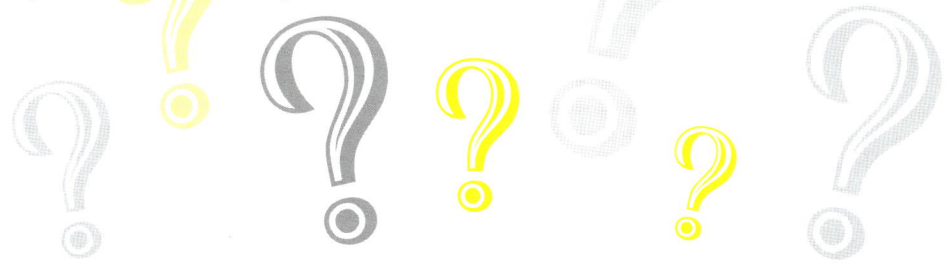

YOU'LL NEVER believe it until you try it

DEVELOPING
THE MARGINS OF THE MIND

THE IMPORTANT POINT we are making here is to stop while the results are still quite good, in other words before you become distressed. Pause for a few minutes, then meditate, as described later, or stimulate the mind with some music or beautiful natural scenes. Then repeat the experiment and it will rapidly peak again, say up to 17 identical symbols.

HAVING USED the symbols **1** and **0** for some time, you should then try irregular shapes, objects, colours and extend the experiment in any way you wish to keep the mind stimulated.

REMEMBER, you are not a passive observer; it is you and your partner who are making the results whatever they turn out to be. If you believe it is possible in the first place, then your results will be superior to those who do not think it is possible. When a disbeliever finds that telepathy can occur, even their results improve.

DO NOT become too involved with set procedures, experiment yourselves; the most important aspect of this research is to be absolutely honest with each other. There is no place for cheating in developing the attributes of the soul.

TRY TO ANALYSE your sensations of mind, when you have had a successful run; were you happy, sad, expectant, doubtful or were there any other feelings? Did you feel hot or cold on the top of your head or lightheaded or were you in a dream like state for those particular experiments? If possible try to re-create the same beneficial situations when you repeat the procedures.

Here are some examples of unusual shapes for transmission.

YOUR ABILITY to hear The Healing Wavelength should increase after each experiment.

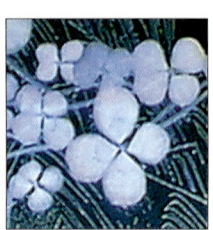

MARGINS OF THE MIND
Television
Alan Bell with Brian Inglis
TUESDAY, 7th MAY 1968

Formby chemist Mr. Alan Fraser Bell appeared on the television programme "Margins of the Mind" last Tuesday evening.

The television programme in which Mr. Bell, who is an experienced investigator into psychic phenomena, took part was concerned with telepathy. A considerable degree of success was achieved in the programme, but Mr. Bell explained to the Formby Times that a television studio, with all its incumbent distractions is not the best place for people to achieve a high degree of concentration.

Mr. Bell is hoping to take part in more television programmes concerning phenomena in the near future.

COMMUNICATION with plants

BULBS ARE PERHAPS the easiest plants to use for these experiments, as they can be grown readily indoors, where most of their conditions of growth can be easily controlled.

Above: Hyacinth
Left: Amaryllis

TAKE THREE HYACINTH bulbs (or three amaryllis, crocus, tulip or bluebell bulbs), the same size and colour and all in equally good condition. Set each bulb in a separate pot, using bulb fibre from the same bag. Place them all on one indoor windowsill about six inches apart, each resting on a separate dish or saucer, and add an equal amount of water to each. Label them 1, 2 and 3. Cover to keep them without light for a few weeks or until they have sprouted about two or three inches.

UNCOVER them and, do as follows each day or every time you pass.

PLANT No. 1: Encourage this one by thinking . . . .
'You are a fine strong plant; what a beautiful bloom you will have in a few weeks time.'

PLANT No. 2: Only pass the time of day with this one, without any encouraging thoughts at all.

Mauve crocus

PLANT No. 3: Should be completely ignored. Some people working on this experiment, have actually thought unpleasant words about the third one but this is not a good idea and should not be used in your experiment. You should only have kind, pleasant thoughts or none at all. Plant number 3 should be neglected in thought only but must be given the same treatment as the other two in every way. That is, water all three at the same time, with the same quantity.

THEY MUST HAVE equal light and warmth and if chemical food is given, it should be dissolved in the water so there are no differences between them.

THIS EXPERIMENT may be repeated many times, perhaps with other bulbs and plants. On every occasion the results will be similar if your thoughts have been accurate and not allowed to wander; plant number 1, will be superb, plant number 2, will be fairly good or normal, and number 3, rather poor.

Experimental Tulips No's 1, 2, 3.

Bluebells

TWO WAY communication

THE EXPERIMENT may be extended to the successful production of roots on cuttings and to horticulture in general. All life forms benefit from loving care and kind thoughts but mostly from the delight they stimulate within us. It is a two way communication; they are not just species of nature growing in isolation.

SOME OTHER refinements could be set in place to prevent another person interfering with the results, by thinking the opposite to you each time they passed. Having a witness is a problem, because they invariably influence the outcome, but it is your relationship with the plants that matters and what effect it has on your soul. Just be honest with yourself and the benefits to you will be superb.

Each day while we were writing the book we passed this Crassula plant on a windowsill, it flourished, growing very large, producing a group of small flowers and as we have become accustomed to expect, one of these was a perfect white cross amongst all the others which had their usual five petal shapes.

ALSO HAVE A FEW control bulbs planted in the garden, where no one will see them or even be able to look at them inadvertently, until the end of the experiment. Check to see which one they resemble, bulb number **2** or **3**. If they resemble number **1** or are better than this, then your garden has a hidden Angel, who has been saddened by your lack of thought for numbers **2** and **3**.

WE KNOW this does not sound very scientific but there is more to living organisms than we are prepared to admit and this experience may give a further insight into life's purpose, as well as the communication some plants also have with one another. There are many well documented experiments, which confirm that a plant nearby can 'feel' any damage inflicted upon a neighbour.

IDEAS HAVE BEEN EXPRESSED, from time to time, that constantly searching for a four leaf clover in the same place may stimulate its occurrence!!

PYRAMID SHAPES!

IN OCTOBER 1995 we had harvested and eaten many of the pears from the tree next to the robin's apple branches, where he sang every day. There was one remaining pear left on a shelf in the kitchen, where all the others had been. It was firm and hard and had not even begun to change colour. We looked at it each week to see if it was ripening. New Year had come and gone and so had all the other fruit.

WE SUDDENLY realised it was the middle of March and we have never had a pear last so long; it was not in a bag or waxed or greased in any way, just straight from the tree. It was still firm but by the 25th of April 1996 started looking golden; so we photographed it.

THE COLOUR and skin were good, not even wrinkled, but still firm, it had no perfume and did not seem ready to eat. The shape was slightly different from all the others; wider and a little shorter from stalk to base. In fact it reminded us of the Cheops pyramid, with slightly flattened sides, and seemed to have about six instead of four sides like a real pyramid, when viewed from above.

Pear blossom. This tree gave the pyramid shaped pears.

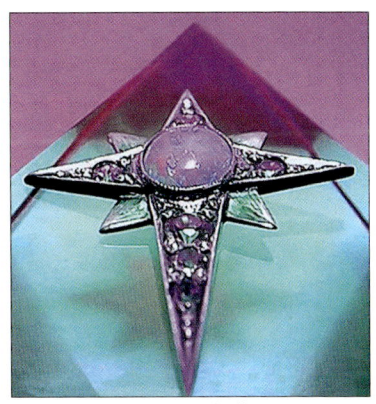

The Pyramid effect.

IN FACT it would fit inside a Cheops pyramid shape made of cardboard, according to the measurements given in Lyall Watson's book "Supernature."

THE REAL SURPRISE came on the 5th of May. The pear was slightly soft, we cut it in half but there was no taste or perfume, no real texture. Similar to a well boiled floury potato, it could only be described as soft, except for a thin layer of white firm tissue around the seed core. The seeds were beautifully preserved, without a trace of mould anywhere in the whole fruit.

WE MEASURED the position of the core in relation to the stalk and the base. It was about a third of the distance from the base, which is the area where you would place an object in a pyramid to be preserved.

WE HAD ANOTHER pear a similar shape a couple of years later, having eaten all those which were edible. We stored it on the same shelf in the kitchen, untreated, uncovered for as many months as the other one that lasted so long. But it did not ripen or become mouldy or soft, just very wrinkled, smaller and smaller, very hard and almost impossible to cut open. I regret we have no record of it containing any seeds. I wish we had, it could have been significant. We will have to wait for another year.

Pyramid pear top view, showing six sides.

Pyramid pear vertical view, showing proportions.

PLAYING MUSIC TO PLANTS

SOME OF THE MUSIC I composed and played while experiencing God's Presence, The Healing Music, has been used in our plant experiments. I have played tape recordings to several individual plants and to groups, and invariably find they respond by producing superior blooms and healthier foliage. You may wish to subject your plants to other types of music to check whether they benefit or become retarded; you may be amazed!

IT HAS BECOME OBVIOUS to us that the music we listen to has a profound affect on the ability to hear The Healing Wavelength and to feel God's Presence, and these are worthwhile areas for investigation if you have the time. We will leave this open, so as not to influence your findings, because in some cases it is what you expect that has more effect than the actual music. Furthermore some types completely over-ride anything you may be thinking and, in the plant experiments, they may not grow at all.

OCCURRENCES DO NOT happen by chance alone but are often responses to a thought; everything has its existence in a mind first, before it finds expression in or as part of the physical world. No matter what we may think, all things exist in God's Mind first.

STILL time

MANY OF US GO THROUGH LIFE absolutely unaware of God's Presence. You may be able to think of Him as a clock ticking on the mantlepiece, as we touched on earlier, but you do not hear the ticking, it is just a background noise to be ignored. You only know that something has occurred when it stops and it may take a while to realise what the change is, because you have become so accustomed to hearing it but not listening to it. So it is with God; He is here but we are not listening to Him, as we should.

WHAT DEVASTATION would follow if God suddenly ceased to be here. We would know something had happened (only briefly) but have no knowledge what it was; we may feel a terrible loss, before also ceasing to exist as physical beings. We must get to know Him now.   There Is Time.

Time Stood Still
at the Moment of The Crucifixion.

IT IS ONLY BECAUSE OF GOD'S PRESENCE THAT WE CAN EVEN THINK ABOUT WHETHER HE EXISTS OR NOT.

SUCH PERFECT CREATIONS COULD NOT HAVE ARISEN BY CHANCE ALONE, THE TENDENCY IS TOWARDS CHAOS.

HE IS NOT HIDDEN or hiding; He is very obvious, yet many intellectuals have become too involved in deep thought, trying to decide upon these matters. Whereas, if they paused a moment longer, they would know this cannot be understood by reasoning alone.

SOME ARE SO BRILLIANT that, to a certain following of people, they have explained Him away but at the bottom of their hearts wished they had not done so. For already they have an uncomfortable feeling of losing something special, which they all needed, and yet have never known, for they always deny His Presence.

THERE ARE MANY other situations which cannot be understood, because

♪ Music of the Heavenly Harps.

of the limitations God has placed upon all our minds, such as the knowledge that space beyond our universe continues on and on, in all directions, without end. It has no meaning to us, as we always need a beginning and an end to everything, but this is nevertheless the way it is and we find it disturbing to contemplate such thoughts.

JUST BECAUSE something cannot be understood, in no manner interferes with its existence. We are unable to understand God as a Creative Intellectual Wisdom, which is only a human limitation and does not negate His Presence, because He made us this way, but when His Time is right, He may allow us to have the knowledge.

5th Dimension

What if God = Gravity the force between

MANKIND has always known that we live in a THREE dimensional world, of up and down, backwards and forwards and left to right. Although we all experience the passage of time and have always been aware of the influence it has on our lives, it was Einstein who firmly spoke of time as being the FOURTH dimension.

THERE IS ALSO A FIFTH, a soul dimension, which we hope this book will help everyone to experience and it could be simply thought of, as the distance between good and evil. So, like the other four dimensions it becomes a measurement, by being either minutely small or infinitely large. It is the Presence of our Creator, who prevents the very small particles in every atom from touching each other, yet larger than cosmic space itself, extending in all directions, without beginning and without end. Electromagnetic frequencies (WAVELENGTHS) separating pairs of opposites, for whatever He creates, an equal but opposite also arises. There may be many more dimensions not related to physical material at all. (Cosmic strings)

IT IS HIS NATURE to make a perfect balance, for if these forces were to come together - there would be nothing left at all. It is as if He had torn empty space apart and from the void created two equal and opposite forces, negative electrons and positive protons. We exist because He keeps them all apart, and reality only seems to occur because of HIS ACTIVITY in between the particles, reality is not the particles themselves. For we can never find a proton, electron or any others, only where they have been, by what they leave behind, or by a disturbance in the surrounding space as they rotate within their orbits.

Many scientists do not seem to realise that what we study in all our research are various aspects of The Creator's Presence, not the little bits of opposites on either side of Him, which make up all the atoms. Scientists believe that these are real, but each atom is only present because every particle within it has an opposing entity forcing it to exist but, keeping its distance, so we fail to observe His Presence in between, keeping them all apart.

THE HUMAN SOUL is aware of our Creator's Contact, because we all possess a fragment of His Presence. The soul does not depend on matter.

Jesus said: *"The Father hath loved you before the foundation of the earth."*
(Before He made us from the earthly materials.)

The soul and spirit inhabit our complex physical body instilling it with life, consciousness and enabling us to think, influencing the physical world by thought and by moving things. For truly this is all that we can do!

Jesus said:
"The sign of your Heavenly Father in you, is a movement and a rest."

HIS FORCE is gentle, yet very strong, for we can lift a small stone from the surface of the earth to place it somewhere else with no apparent effort but, we are held firmly upon the ground and immense force is required to leave the earth to travel into space. Although we can feel the pull required to separate even two small magnets.

MEDITATION

WE HAVE INCLUDED THE FOLLOWING IDEAS TO HELP IN YOUR SEARCH FOR HIM

■ THE ROOM you have made available for yourself in which to practise, work and develop should have adequate daylight and must be well illuminated at night when studying, but dimly lit when meditating. It should always be well ventilated and as sound proof as possible, but if this is not practicable, then it should be as quiet as you can make it.

■ YOU SHOULD BE ABLE to sit each day for half an hour or more with your own thoughts, completely undisturbed by any physical stimuli. Do not sit there listening to the radio or watching television, even with the sound turned down, or playing tapes and records. Just sit quietly without any coffee, tea, drinks or cigarettes and retire within your mind. As mentioned earlier, dismiss all the worries of the World, think only of beautiful things, let your mind move from one to another, do not concentrate on any particular one; perhaps extend a mental wish to help someone.

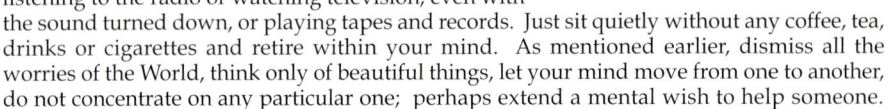

■ MANY WORDS have been written and many more spoken about meditation. A considerable amount of unnecessary mystery has surrounded the subject for many years. We are pleased to simplify this from the beginning, so you will be able to use it in a practical manner.

■ MEDITATION is a simple method of reaching a state of mental relaxation, a state of beauty, during which spontaneous original pulses of thought come through into consciousness and this is all that need concern us at the moment. Although you are relaxed, you are not sleepy; your awareness is increased. If you are meditating with the purpose of hearing The Healing Wavelength, then it may come through during this time. In other words Jesus has made contact with you, because your mind is in a state to receive Him, in a state of beauty.

■ REPEATING A WORD. The most convenient method of attaining this state of beauty is by continuously repeating a word or visualising a beautiful flower or scenery. Further mysteries exist involving the chosen word, with whispered rumours of secret sounds and special words designed for individual people. We feel it is a better way to choose one for yourself.

■ SELECT ONE, the sound of which suits you, the only requirements are that you have not heard it before, it means absolutely nothing to you and does not remind you of anything; create one of beauty for yourself.

■ THE WORD may be repeated out loud to start, gently, not too fast, then repeated within the mind, so it does not become a tiring procedure. Note here: When the word is repeated mentally, there should be no attempted movement of the lips, tongue or throat or restriction of breathing, as if the word were being spoken out loud. Then slow it down, as if in slow motion, and perhaps change the rhythm of it a little, still going slower.

Find a quiet area for your meditation.

■ WHEN YOU HAVE REACHED a state of beauty, allow the mind to rest, cease the repetition or release the mental image. You can identify this moment as being one free from any thoughts. Now listen 'out' for The Healing Wavelength in the left ear if a male or in the right ear if female. You may have already experienced His Presence before you ceased the mental repetition, so stop there and enjoy His Communication. NOW REST.

■ THE MIND ACHIEVES a deep sense of beauty within itself, not by 'observing' beauty via any of the senses, but by becoming beauty. You now have internal peace and tranquillity, time diminishes, the physical body ceases to be so important, you are joyful, rejuvenated; a happiness exists which comes upon you from itself, without a cause.

■ OUR PERSONAL explanation of this phenomenon has served our students well over the years in their understanding.

■ WITH A PENCIL draw a curved line on a piece of paper, similar to a parenthesis. It possesses a certain beauty of its own, due to its thickness, its colour and curve. Now draw another line in the same manner, with the same curve, but about one eighth inch from the first. These two curved lines now take on a slightly different beauty. They are in fact more beautiful than the first solitary line. Now add a third line underneath or on top of these two, in the same way, and a fourth and fifth if you wish. Each new line increases the experience of beauty, particularly if you make slight changes to each one, such as thickness, distance apart, widening, shortening, curving or swirling at the ends. These superimposed subtle changes are equivalent to variations in your tone of voice and the rhythms of the spoken word of your choice.

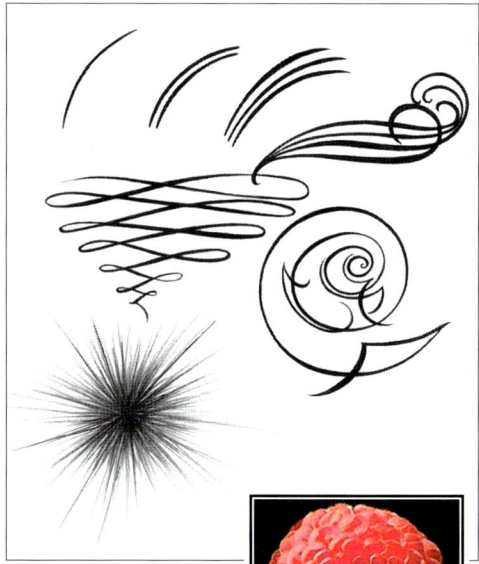

Abstract shapes with beauty

■ THEREFORE WHEN you continuously repeat a word, as in a meditation, your mind experiences beauty and becomes beauty. This idea may be extended to the beauty of a flower, with the repetition of the shape of its petals, some paler in colour or smaller and shaded, in circles and so on. It not only looks beautiful to us, it is beauty. It is one of His Creations and we experience something

Another perfect creation.

within us which is impossible to describe. For example, the beauty of a sunset moves us inside in a miraculous manner, experienced down the centre line of the body; attributed to, but not necessarily of, the heart. Hence the various expressions: heartfelt, heart-warming.

■ THIS IS PERHAPS an over simplification but it is more obvious when we mention this also occurs with music, where a note or chord may be repeated many times, with slight variations of the time distances between them or with the sustained chord of a symphonic finale or organ solo, when the whole body experiences the music and not just an auditory mental enjoyment.

PREPARE
to be moved

Jesus said: "The Kingdom of the Father is spread upon the Earth, and men do not see it."

▫ YOU SHOULD MEDITATE every day. During these periods you will find the persistence of the physical world diminishes and, in this state of mental relaxation, the beauty experienced has a stimulating effect on the mind. It enables communication to take place on different levels, that prior to the meditation was not possible.

▫ THE EXPERIMENTS in most of these areas of creative experience produce slightly imperfect and different results to those which would occur naturally. As it is a natural approach we are always seeking, then somewhere along the line at some time they must all cease to be experiments and should become part of your natural life. Then creativity blossoms and the results are perfect.

▫ COMMUNICATION is vital to all forms of life. No species should be isolated from its fellow members and an inter-relationship between all other species is essential. Love is the strongest outgoing emotion and also the strongest to receive; it allows and encourages all species to grow to perfection.

▫ EVERY DAY THROUGHOUT MY LIFE I have been guided. What I had termed Creative Thinking in my early school days and before was so much more. In my childlike way I had already experienced God's Presence

Laburnum

Copper Beech leaves

Left: Variegated Crocus.

Below: Aquilegia and Lilac

His touch of genius is in every shape.

and so has everyone else, perhaps without realising it. Years of investigation and research followed. The overwhelming feeling was that Jesus' messages are REAL and should be passed on hand to hand, generation to generation . . .

☐ IT SEEMED AS IF all this was in preparation for our most Miraculous Discovery. Jesus has made contact with us and now we can help other people to know how this will be and that we are not alone, HE IS IN OUR MIDST. This is a reality not just a hope.

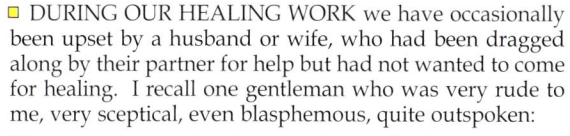

NOW WE KNOW WHERE TO FIND HIM
TO ASK A QUESTION & RECEIVE AN ANSWER

☐ DURING OUR HEALING WORK we have occasionally been upset by a husband or wife, who had been dragged along by their partner for help but had not wanted to come for healing. I recall one gentleman who was very rude to me, very sceptical, even blasphemous, quite outspoken:

"You can't do anything for me, it's all ridiculous nonsense. If there really is a God, I wouldn't be like this in the first place."

☐ I EXPLAINED I do not actually do anything; it is all God's work and He does it in His own way. I mentioned it was not important whether he believed. I have seen so many Miracles, I know we are not alone, we are together in His Presence. " It is beyond belief, it's knowing." I left myself wide open to further criticism, to which he responded:

"Yes, you're right, it is beyond belief."

☐ AT LEAST I established the fact he was listening to me, so I continued that all I do is arrange the situation in which we can receive God's Healing. We have a little Sanctuary, it is warm and comfortable, there are no rituals, no procedures, I say a little prayer in my mind, asking for healing and I would place my hands on his head.

Iris

Above: Alkanet   Below: V. Crocus

BLACK and white
Negative world - sceptical doubt

HIS RESPONSE was almost immediate. The pains left him, there was freedom of movement, he was making steps, forward and backward. There was a hint of a tear in one eye and when he left the Healing Room he was a changed person, his rudeness had gone, he was beginning to believe, he was on the way to regaining his lost faith.

A negative state of mind is like a world with no colour and without sound.

WHAT WAS ALSO of great interest to him, was the fact that he could see I did not actually do anything. But he could feel the warm breeze blowing between us and so could his wife, when she passed her hand between my hand and the top of his head.

I EXPLAINED. What they felt was not something I was doing or giving to them but we were all sharing God's Presence.

HEATHER AND I are just ordinary human beings and we get troubled when someone is rude to us. We are sensitive people because of the research and work we do. We had difficulty with these situations.

WHY IS IT that God heals someone almost instantaneously who is so rude and blasphemous, when a nicer person may have to wait for some time?

I HAD TO PRAY ON THIS for many days and no inspired thoughts explained it to me; I searched The Bible Texts to see if I had missed something. In distress I prayed again, I needed to know, so we could cope on future occasions, for there had been others. I knew I should not be thinking, why does God Heal such a person when another has to wait? I was obviously feeling he did not deserve to be healed and I knew it was a thought I should not be having.

THIS IS ANOTHER example of the closer you become to being a Christian, the harder it gets.

I PRAYED AGAIN and much to my surprise I heard a voice, not in my ears but in my head. It was not my voice, not my thoughts and they were not my words.

THIS WAS as startling as the moment we saw the mauve diamond shape and heard Jesus' Healing Wavelength:

"You should have known this my child."

He had lived in Formby all his life but saw no beauty or colour, only empty space and desolation.

IT WAS A BEAUTIFUL VOICE, kind, gentle, caring, even to this day I could not say whether it was male or female. That is all I heard. I waited and asked:

"What should I have known?" There was no reply.

I KNEW WHERE THE VOICE CAME FROM and thought it was a lovely phrase. He was not talking down to me, telling me off for not knowing, it was like Father to son, with encouragement to think again, to sort it out for myself, as more understanding and wisdom would be gained if I did.

BUT IN MY SCIENTIFIC IMPATIENCE I prayed again: "What should I have known?"

No reply.

I slept on it that night, after asking for guidance during my usual prayer but not asking the same question, and tried again later the next day.

TO MY EXCITEMENT an answer came, in the same gentle voice, showing no irritation at my persistence, as I was troubled, saying: *"Is it not so?"*

THEN A PAUSE, as if still giving another chance to work it out for myself, even encouraging me to agree with Him. Not talking down to me, not answering but asking for my response, in His phrase:

"Is it not so?"

THEN THE COMPLETE ANSWER:
"Is it not so that he who is rude and sceptical is in need of more help than one who already believes?"

IT IS A PERFECT ANSWER, not just a reply, and so obvious when you know, and of course absolutely correct; I should have known.

SINCE THAT DAY we have been able to help rude sceptical people without being troubled by our thoughts. There have been other occasions when God has replied with wonderful answers and His Miracles continue.

BEFORE time began

"For thy Father in Heaven hath loved thee before the foundation of the world."
This is another of Jesus' remarkable comments.

JESUS IS TELLING us that we were all in existence before being given a physical form, before even the world was created, identifying that each one of us contains His spark of life, a fragment of God Himself. We are hidden within the earthly materials of our body.

Jesus was saddened, for He said: *"Man is born to walk with the Angels, but instead he doth search for jewels in the mud."*

He said:
"Mankind should build the Kingdom of Heaven on earth."

BUT MAN has built the kingdom of man on earth, by cloning another living creature from genetic material, and now we are only one step away from cloning man himself. What made the scientists use an 'electric discharge' (a spark) to initiate life within their laboratory manipulated cell? Was it an inspired guess or the misuse of a Biblical message, as they searched for jewels in the mud? For a clone of man would be a jewel in terms of financial gain but an abomination in the mud of time.

Jesus continued later:

"The mind of the idle is full of the weeds of discontent; but he who walks with The Angel of Work, has within him a field always fertile, where corn and grapes and all manner of sweet-scented herbs and flowers grow in abundance."
God's Creations.

THE MINDS OF MODERN SCIENTISTS are certainly not idle but are full of the weeds of discontent. Are they not satisfied with God's Creations and His methods of fruitful reproduction, within the loving relationship of a man and woman, while in His Presence and according to His Laws?

WHAT SORT of spark will they use to induce a spirit and a soul to occupy this empty Temple of their creation?

How will THEY answer the questions of a cloned being:

"Where did I come from?"
"Where do I belong?"
"Who am I?"

WE MUST ALL PRAY FOR THEIR ENLIGHTENMENT, THAT THEY BE TOUCHED BY HIS TRUE AND ONLY WISDOM.

THEIR SCIENTIFIC EXPERTISE DOES NOT GRANT A GIVEN RIGHT TO DO IT.

Jesus said:
"As ye sow, so shall ye reap. The man of God who has found his task, shall not ask any other blessing."

WE MUST WORK with God, not try to take His place. Mankind has a special blessing, for we know that through the sayings and messages of Jesus He has made contact with us, allowing a two-way communication.

WE ONLY NEED to reach Him within ourselves to perfect The Temple. Then all our actions will be correct, becoming part of His framework, and we will not be making new forms of human life just because it can be done, without yet understanding who or what we are.

$E=mc^2$

NOW THE SCIENTISTS HAVE completed the Human Genome Project, are they closer or further away from our Creator? They know every gene of the human genetic makeup. One thing is certain, God knows exactly what they are doing and HE is the only ONE who also knows the complete outcome of their actions. He can intervene in a instant, if necessary; so all will be well with the world.

He Has His Mind Beyond The Pulse Of Human Life.

THE BLINDING LIGHT concealed God's Presence at the Birth of Jesus. Flashes in the storm-tormented skies as He rejoined His Creator, followed by The Resurrection, left the mystery of His photographic image on The Shroud. These are all related to the energy of electrons, protons, photons of light, the quantum building blocks of atoms, molecules and of life.

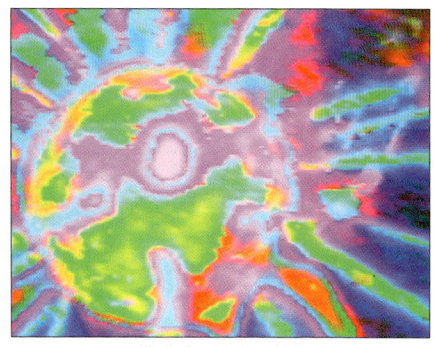

ENERGY: $E = mc^2$

(E) is the energy equivalent in the amount of matter (m) multiplied by the speed of light (c) squared.

WHY THE SPEED OF LIGHT SQUARED or even the speed of light at all? We feel that Einstein must have been in touch with a higher wisdom to have realised this relationship, although he had to demonstrate it mathematically.

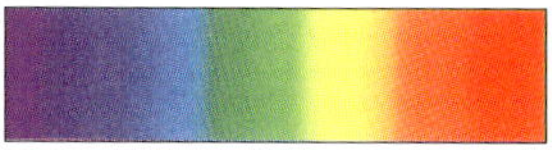

"Let there be Light."

Spectrum of visible wavelengths.

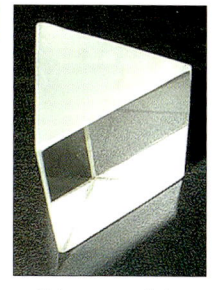

THIS WAS in the beginning, before science, which after all is only the study of things that already exist. Can scientists be expected to understand what occurred before our Creator's thoughts took on physical form and became reality?

NOT ONLY DOES LIGHT have speed and wavelengths of various frequencies i.e. colours, but it is also corpuscular in nature (particles), by which it induces some materials to emit electrons, when radiations fall upon them; (Selenium is one) and in this process light is looked upon as a stream of photons, a quantum process of little bits of light.

Prisms reveal the secret of His light.

EINSTEIN ALSO had an equation for its expression but, if light can be created by saying *"Let there be"* and at one and the same time have a wavelength, a speed and a corpuscular nature, why can it not also have another component, a constant background carrying God's Presence, which cannot be detected in any scientific experiment, but can become apparent to the human brain or mind. We are the natural receivers of His Presence and sound may be the same.

THIS IS GROSSLY over simplified and beyond the scope of our book but Einstein had a feeling at the back of his mind of Unification, perhaps of all things being related and belonging to each other, not by the separate little bits of electrical charge, but by what it is that holds them all together.

HIS IMAGE
is hidden by His Light

EINSTEIN MUST HAVE KNOWN that God exists but always wanted a demonstration in one equation; maybe his Grand Unified Theory. But the closer we get to such thoughts, the more difficult it becomes, because scientists always leave GOD out of the equation. Or is He hidden in one of the Constants they so often use?

THE CONSTANT BACKGROUND! Constant: G . . . perhaps!

WHETHER SOMETHING exists as a wave or corpuscle seems to depend upon what you are looking for at the time, as the detection of one appears to exclude the detection of the other. The problem is of course ours, not our Creator's. Are we ready to receive His wisdom? During our Healing work we are looking for Him, not excluding Him by expecting something else.

EVEN ELECTRONS, PROTONS and other 'particles' in ATOMS also seem to possess wave properties.

Crookes Radiometer

RADIOMETER

J. CLERK MAXWELL discovered that light exerts a pressure when it falls perpendicularly upon a surface, equal to the amount of energy in a particular colour. For example blue light has nearly twice the energy of red light.

SIR WILLIAM CROOKES tried to demonstrate this, which led to his invention of the Radiometer. This instrument has four freely rotating vanes, each black on one side and polished to a mirror finish on the other, contained in a glass vessel which has most of the air removed.

THE BLACK SIDE absorbs the light which falls on it and the polished side reflects it, so there is more energy in the space in front of the polished side and therefore a greater pressure. If light is shone on the Radiometer it rotates but it goes round the WRONG WAY to demonstrate the pressure of light. The pressure is so small it is overcome by the black vane warming and agitating the remaining air molecules, pushing the black side away. The complete process is a little more complicated than this. *THE PRESSURE OF LIGHT WAS EVENTUALLY MEASURED BY IMPROVING THE RADIOMETER, SO THE EFFECT OF WARMING THE AIR WAS ELIMINATED.*

THERE ARE OTHER factors of interest here. For instance, if the polished mirror side of each vane is aluminium, and ultraviolet light is used to illuminate the improved Radiometer, a high percentage of the u/v light is reflected. But if polished silver is used as the mirrored surface, only about 10% of the u/v is reflected. It is a difficult experiment to interpret, so we have kept the science to a minimum, but it is worth thinking about all these details, if you have the time.

IT YOU HAVE ACCESS to a Radiometer and your attitude of mind is creative and positive, then attempt to make it rotate by placing your hands either side, as in the Cylinder Experiment. Which way round would you expect it to rotate, or would you be able to make it move either way as if it were receiving 'photons' of energy and reflecting them from its polished mirrored sides? What would it be detecting if you make it produce the photon effect?

"HERE AND NOW is the mystery revealed"

IT-WILL NOW be the concern of future scientists to identify the Creative Presence in all matter, not as a proton, electron, muon, meson and so on, but perhaps we could postulate a Creaton. Not as a particle but as The Presence between them all, performing an equal and opposite function of keeping them apart, yet preventing them all from separating completely.

SCIENCE AND TECHNOLOGY are remarkable. Human life would be primitive without them, but we should have our Creator with us every moment of this journey and pray for His Wisdom to be upon us. For He alone knows the outcome of all our actions and will share this Power with us, if we would pause long enough to listen to His instructions.

MANKIND IS LIMITED in its understanding of the ramifications of our actions. We are able to perform wonderful scientific procedures but still have no way to accurately predict the complete future outcome of them. We always have to think in terms of 'damage limitation' or 'what is the worse case scenario,' but our Creator already knows and has an open line of communication. So help is at hand, if only we would have Him with us during our scientific procedures.

HE WILL INTERVENE, if necessary, to show the way and reinforce the messages Jesus has brought with Him to this present day. He has told us He will show Himself and many who have read these passages will have already met Him.

It is no longer a belief; you actually know Him, you are together, you can see, hear and feel His Presence.

REACH OUT AND GAIN HIS PASSING WISDOM

For Jesus said:

"Do not wait for death to reveal the great mystery. If you know not your Heavenly Father while your feet tread the dusty soil, there shall be naught but shadows for thee in the life that is to come. Here and now is the mystery revealed, here and now is the curtain lifted. Be not afraid, O man! Lay hold of the wings of the Angel of Eternal Life."

IN THIS PHRASE Jesus speaks of the life that is to come, He is talking of a continuity of life; here and now is the mystery revealed, here is the curtain lifted. He is telling us in all His Messages how we can experience His Presence in today's world.

SPECIAL moments

AFTER CONSIDERING all the fascinating scientific work we have been involved in, it became apparent, that all the lovely sensations which occur during Healing with prayer, are the most remarkable revelations we have ever experienced. They are identical with the sayings of Jesus. What makes them so remarkable, is the fact; we did not discover His lost sayings until a long time after the healings had started.

THEY WERE VERY SPECIAL MOMENTS when we realised that Jesus had already spoken of each and every one of our experiences.

IT CLEARLY SHOWS Jesus will make Himself known to you, wherever you are, there is no need to move or go anywhere; you only have to ask, then wait for His reply. Be still and know He is with you. There is no necessity to travel the world, searching for the unknown, what you are looking for, is here, everywhere.

Garden of Healing

LIVING SAYING

I SPENT THE FIRST few years of our return north, as a Director of a firm of Chemists near Liverpool, and then acquired another Chemist Shop, Dispensary and Sub-Post Office of our own, on the edge of Formby Village, towards the sand dunes and pine forest.

THIS WAS A VERY OLD building and had a wobbly cast iron spiral staircase which always reminded me of the structure of DNA, carrying messages from one cell to another. We had one of the first thirty telephone numbers which needed a rotating handle to make a call, but that is another story. I have to frequently remind myself, not to digress from our purpose.

Spirals of thought

HERE, where the countryside slopes gently down to the sand and shore, where it meets the sea and sky, I came upon another one line phrase of country folk, to add to those I had already written down many years ago. This one continues with the same atmosphere of the others, by relating to its location near the sea and to the people who place their lives in God's Hands to go about their daily work.

IT WAS WHISPERED QUIETLY by a very elderly local fisherman and shrimper, long since retired, which he would say to his friends as they went out to sea in their frail craft:

"May the wind safely fill your sails, and may you return in happiness and peace of mind."

He said this to me as I was leaving the shop to deliver some urgent medications for a sick child. It was a windy day, but I was only walking, and not going very far. It was his nature to be concerned. I asked if he knew any others? He did, but that was unusual for most folk knew only one line.

He replied:
"And for the fishermen returning to the land, after their night's work, I would say, 'Until we meet again, May The Lord walk with you always hand in hand.'"

"May the wind safely fill your sails..."

"PEACE! Be Still!"

WE CONTINUED to be intrigued by these lovely phrases, no one seemed to know where they came from, they were to their best recollections, passed on from mother and father to son and daughter, through the generations. They so clearly identify Mother Earth, but this last one speaks also of The Heavenly Father, and both were always in the mind of Jesus.

WE WONDERED about the origin of these beautiful words, which are so similar to the sayings of Jesus. For He would frequently refer to the Angels of Mother Earth and The Heavenly Father, to the fruits and crops, to honest toil, and water to make the soil fertile. He would talk of eating all the fruits except those which have bitterness, He told His stories always with reference to the land, the sea, the fish; to natural and real situations. His Disciples spoke of feeding the five thousand, and to the calming of the storm. "Peace! Be Still!"

HE SPOKE to the multitudes concerning the Angels of Mother Earth, and Communion with The Angel of Work, which identify with these phrases of country folk in their occupations and safety, and of being aware of God's guidance, in what they do of benefit for humanity, and all life on earth.

IN THE GOSPEL OF THE ESSENES Jesus said:

"For the honest work of humble hands, is a daily prayer of thanksgiving, and the music of the plough, is a joyful song unto the Lord."

"For in God we live, and move and have our being. In truth, we are his sons, and He is our Father."

Jesus also tells us: The Heavenly Father is in us, and we are in Him.

WE WERE DEEPLY MOVED by the similarity of these sayings of country folk, as if they had been derived from those of Jesus.

ONE DAY WE collected together all those I had written down on odd scraps of paper, during the past fifty years, and wrote them all on one piece of paper. Suddenly realising they seemed to belong to each other, probably as below, starting with the first one I ever heard when guarding a crashed aircraft in the middle of a field.

> *May the road ahead rise up to greet you,*
> *May the sunshine warm your face,*
> *May the breeze blow always from behind,*
> *And the wind safely fill your sails,*
> *May you return in happiness and peace of mind,*
> *May the rains fall gently on your fertile land,*
> *And your family's health and wealth abound,*
> *And until we meet again,*
> *May The Lord walk with you always,*
> *Hand in hand.*

Morning Glory spiral reaching for the dawn.

LIFE'S journey

Fertile land

His message in the tide

Sunshine smile of Celandine

Cherry blossom and below a fern

IT SEEMS COMPLETE; it speaks of having God's Presence, about the family's health and wealth, of fertile soils, fishing and agriculture. Then returning home in peace and happiness, living and working with nature's breezes at your back, sunshine on your face, gentle rains on your land and even being greeted into life's journey on the rising road ahead.

ALL COUNTRY FOLK are so close to the natural earth, the elements and the seas. They intuitively experience God's Presence, from His seasons of fresh growth, the blossoming of vegetation, harvesting, then resting dormant through the winter, preparing for the new Spring.

WHILE WE WERE COMPILING our book, trying to express our research and experiences in words, we came across some old Celtic Blessings and there, amongst all the others, was A Blessing on Setting Forth (See page 210). Six lovely lines, showing many of the phrases used by all the country people, from whom I had collected their similar one line sayings during a period of fifty years.

WE SEEM TO HAVE NOTED more than the six lines of the Blessing on Setting Forth and feel those I had written down during my life's journey were special. Each one showed how the people who spoke them had adapted their particular phrase to belong to their own natural occupation and to their part of the country, be it meadow or near the sea. Strangely, and this is intriguing, they only seemed to know one line.

WE STILL FEEL OURSELVES waiting for another; we are sure there is one; maybe it has not yet been spoken. But our suggestion would be:

**MAY YOU HEAR WITH ONE EAR
THE WISDOM OF THE LORD.**

SOME OF OUR FRIENDS, who had the original draft of our book to check for errors, made many comments, such as:

"What a superb way forward..."

"I enjoyed it..."

"Wonderful..."

"It will carry His Message..."

THERE WERE many more. Some heard The Healing Wavelength without even trying. Then we asked each one if they had performed any of the experiments and tested their own abilities to experience God's Presence? No! They had not but they had read it all the way through and one had read it twice.

"BUT WHY?" we inquired.
"Well, I was compelled to turn each page, it was too interesting to stop, and by the time I reached the end I just had to start again. I'll do the experiments next time. I've heard The Wavelength, now I hope to experience the others."

THE WAY FORWARD

AND ONE SAID: "It's a way forward. The book isn't a novel or a story, or an autobiography to pass the time, it's a new life. Wonderful to know we're not alone and I'm looking forward to the experiments and the experiences. These are things I've never known but I always felt there was something missing. Now the reality of Jesus' messages will make my life complete. I know there is someone with me all the way."

WE MENTIONED that, if the details in the book are not put to good use and passed on to many more of your friends, it would almost be like learning how to cook for your family but always 'eating out.'

IT IS A WONDERFUL MOMENT WHEN WE KNOW we are not alone; we are His Creations and are cared for and guided through every second of each day. Our Creator has made contact; and it is for us to be aware of His Presence.

IT IS OUR HOPE that you feel God's Presence from time to time, or all the time, in the same way we do, so you can start experiencing and living your own book of life, within His framework and guidance. Just like a 'Eureka' moment; you have found Him and will always be together.

THEN, LOOKING BACK over your time, you can identify those wonderful occasions when God touched you. There are many such moments in everyone's life but they are often forgotten or explained away by other people as being of no significance.

Sunshine on your face

Gentle breezes

Peace of mind

A moonlit walk with you hand in hand

JESUS said:
"The body is the Temple of The Spirit, and The Spirit is the Temple of God."

So we have to make ourselves worthy to receive Him and become aware of His Presence within.

And The Disciples asked Jesus:
"When will The Kingdom come?"
He replied:
"The Kingdom of The Father is spread upon the earth and men do not see it."

Jesus had already said: *"God wrote not the laws in the pages of books, but in your heart and in your spirit."*
"The words of God are written in His works."

Tranquillity of the Bluebell woods

ABILITY to move

YOU AND I and all His Creations are *"Spread upon the surface of the earth."* We are His Works. The Father is within us all and we must grow to recognise His Presence. Jesus told us how to do this and we have revealed His Message in the way that He reached us.

He also said:
"Everyone who is of the truth, hears my voice."

SURELY THIS MUST BE The Healing Wavelength we hear in only one ear. It was not a message intended only for the people of His time but for everyone today who wants to know Him. It is a communication from Him, The Father and The Holy Spirit, speaking directly to each one of us.

PLEASE DO LISTEN OUT FOR HIM

IN CREATIVE THINKING, Healing and being aware of God's Presence, science and religion come together, as the requirements of each are almost the same. Yet some are arrived at by scientific experiment and observation of natural phenomena, not by the application of The Ten Commandments, during which the experience of His Presence would occur naturally, when our soul is ready to receive Him.

MANKIND COULD HAVE ARRIVED at a more creative point in evolution by following the Ten Commandments and other Biblical references but we seem to be too preoccupied with scientific demonstrations and allow ourselves only minimal belief.

WE HAVE TENDED to develop the physical world using what is glaringly obvious and have neglected the subtle forces that brought about life itself; electrochemical animation. Remember, without God's Presence we would not have arrived on earth at all, and without our ABILITY TO MOVE, which is the sign of His Presence, evolution would not have taken place.

For Jesus said:
"The sign of your Heavenly Father in you, is a movement and a rest."

We would not move at all without Him.

The butterfly's life shows a movement and a rest with shape changing transformations and dancing like airborne petals between flowers.

SHROUDED in mystery

HAVING RESEARCHED the Shroud of Jesus for some time, I experimented with pieces of wood in contact with cloth to determine what stains occur in the presence of rain water, condensation and perspiration. Many patterns and shapes formed over a long period of months in the presence of strong sunlight but without the use of any chemicals, paints or pigments.

THE WORK is still continuing, so this is only a short note because of our astonishment when we decided to photograph one of the stains on the cloth, produced by being partly in contact with wood, metal and water condensation.

AFTER STARING at a print of the photograph for a few minutes, a very clear face became visible, which I had not noticed there while taking the pictures. I returned to view the piece of stained cloth, to check if the face was real but there was no face there in the stain.

I PHOTOGRAPHED IT AGAIN, printed it again, but the face had gone. It only exists on the first series of prints. We show one of those prints below. See if the face is visible to you. Over the page is the same photograph with a pencilled outline of its position, as we see it. (Ignore the horizontal tears in the cloth.)

THE CLOTH of Jesus' Shroud would have been hand woven but the samples we used were machine-made cotton and had been washed several times previously. One sample had been on a sunlounger and was slightly contaminated with perspiration; but this is not as obscure as it may seem.

THE STAINS AND IMAGES were formed on our fragments of material because of the water soluble compounds and vapours from the wood samples in the presence of moisture, sunlight and metals.

WOOD of the DOGWOOD TREE was said to be used to make the Cross for Jesus, which He had carried on His back over a long journey, while in great pain and suffering, accompanied by His companion, the robin. The stress

Before you turn the page - can you see the face

chemicals of pain, released through His skin in the perspiration, reacted with the resins of the wood and metal nails to imprint His Image on The Shroud by the brilliant intensity of The Father's Light, at the moment of Their reunion.

THE IMAGE

WHEN THE RESURRECTION took place, His tissues were cleanly separated from The Shroud before any deterioration had occurred and in a manner unknown to mankind, even in the realm of modern forensic science.

OUR PHOTOGRAPHS BAFFLED US by the appearance of a face that is not really there. We will need to research this and pray for understanding. It had not been anticipated or sought but was a scientific result in our study of staining cloth by the effects of nature, during our research on the Mystery of The Shroud.

AS ALWAYS we seem to have raised more questions than we have answered but each time we hope to gain in wisdom. There is more to life than we will ever know and our minds remain open for His further Communications.

The face outlined on the photograph in pencil, as it appears to us.

HEAVEN SCENT

A FEW DAYS LATER, while I was sitting by the open window reading a book about The Shroud of Turin, I was overjoyed by the perfume of Jasmine flowers drifting past. Pausing for a moment to view their beautiful little white shapes of five petals, some rounded at the tips and some pointed, I noticed one that was quite different.

A LOVELY FLOWER with only four petals, two long ones and two short; yet another Cross.

Jasmine normal five petal clusters

THE PHOTOGRAPH shows the perfection of each petal, with no place for a fifth. So now we seem to spend our days searching for Jasmine plants to determine how frequently this occurs, but we have only come across one flower with six petals and none with four. We hope to hear from horticulturists, who would know more about this than we do.

Jesus said:
"The Father knows what you need before you ask Him."

SO IT WOULD SEEM we are always searching for a Cross or a sign of His Presence and they are always there for us. He manifests Himself, as Jesus said, and makes His Presence known. But you may never feel the mysteries, if you only see what should be there.

Jasmine flower cross

DIRECT communication

WE NEED TO ASK, would Jesus have left a relic, like The Turin Shroud, on Earth to be found at a later date? Knowing, as He would, that one day science could be sufficiently developed to prove it was in fact His Shroud. It had miraculously become separated from His body at The Resurrection, leaving a perfect imprint of the suffering He endured to save the human soul.

HE HAD never written anything down to leave for us to read in later centuries. He knew He would be able to reach each one of us in a spiritual manner and all at the same time, if He so desired or if the need arose. He is within us all, so any words He may have written would not carry the message with the same intensity as His direct communications have with us all today.

THE SHROUD is unique; it is a proof far stronger than any written words could be that He died for us and was Resurrected by The Father. All the scientific forensic evidence confirms the narratives of The Gospels but the unbelievers still require more tests.

JESUS WOULD NOT want The Shroud to be worshiped as a religious relic and has enlisted the scientists to work with Him, even if it takes time, to indicate to those who need more proof that The Bible accounts are correct in every detail and that Jesus lived and died to save us all, to help us find The Kingdom of God. We Are Not Alone.

LIVING words

EVEN NOW our book seems to have taken on a life of its own. It has a growth and development from outside us. Each day, before we continue with another page, we say a little inward Prayer for God, Jesus and The Holy Spirit to be with us and move us, so the words become as near as humanly possible as Jesus would wish them to be. We are definitely guided in its preparation and pray that others truly find the way in which He reached us, in this present day. Let it lead into your Book of Life.

AS WE WERE arranging page 63 with the Passionflower Cross above the grey clouds and Dogwood flowers, the sky outside our window was darkening; the day had gone cold and the rain was making noisy squalls. Then the robin sitting in an apple tree, only a few feet from us, gave three very sharp shrill screeches, which we had not heard from him before, and after a while continued with his lovely little songs.

A MINUTE OR TWO later there was just one very loud clap of thunder but no prior flash. It echoed for a while and the birds were silent for a few seconds, only to resume with delicate mutterings. They probably knew and tried to tell us what was coming but there was only one loud crash. A storm did not develop. This was mid-September 1999.

THEN IN September 2000 he returned with more shrill sounds but this time it was reversed, there was one flash of lightning but no thunder. We are again baffled! Is there something special about September in the life of Jesus, unknown to us? What have we missed?

HE LIVES today

FROM THE VISION OF ENOCH, God Speaks to Man:

"I speak to you, through the thunder and lightning. Be Still, Know I Am God."

THIS SEEMS TO BELONG HERE, as the wood from the Dogwood tree was used to make The Cross for Jesus and the robin was with Him all the time, until the storm tormented skies were torn asunder, as Jesus rejoined His Creator.

THE BRILLIANT LIGHT surrounding Jesus at His Birth may also have occurred at the moment of reunion with His Father, and the intensity of the radiations from the flash may have fused His Image into The Shroud.

WHILE SCIENTISTS and intellectuals argue and fuss about its authenticity, they have missed His message, that He Lives and is with us all today, and as Jesus said:

"Not in The Scriptures," but, "In your heart and in your Spirit."

MAY WE ADD, not in The Mystery of The Shroud, although genuine, He left this behind Him at His Resurrection. But He is in the joyful wisdom of His communications with us all today, which continue, because He brought them with Him. These are real; you may have already experienced them or soon will.

Remember, Jesus said to His Disciples:

"Have you then discovered the beginning, so that you inquire about the end?"

JESUS NO LONGER had a physical body, it was the end of one sequence but the beginning of another. His new way of reaching us all instantly, and all at the same time, is with His Spiritual Presence.

MAY THE SCIENTISTS continue with their quests, but as Jesus said:

"The Kingdom of The Father is spread upon the earth, and men do not see it."

THEY ARE LOOKING in the wrong places. The Spiritual Presence of God and Jesus are not in the remains of things or in relics, they are here now, within us all.

THIS SHOULD NOT be an argument or discussion or an intellectual process. It is a leap of Faith for us but spontaneous for a new born baby.

Jesus said:
"I COME BECAUSE YOU NEED ME."

Just meet Him here today and leave the past where it is. Jesus wants to take us all into
THE FUTURE, THE NEXT 2000 YEARS.

We are privileged to have met Him and to have the chance of sharing our research with you.

**THE FUTURE IS IN YOUR HANDS
SEEK GOD'S WISDOM TO MAKE IT GOOD**

Meet Him at least halfway

**DISCOVER THE BEGINNING,
BEFORE YOU INQUIRE
AFTER THE END . . .**

**may you HEAR with ONE EAR
THE WISDOM OF THE LORD**

LISTEN . . .
NEW EVIDENCE *of* THE SCIENTISTS
who stepped back in time to discover your future

Recent research has revealed that certain types of music and sounds can increase the growth of neurons in the brain.

Also, with modern magnetic resonance equipment, it can be shown from brain activity that the human male hears with the left side of the brain and the female hears with both sides.

This has prompted our thinking that the beautiful chord (The Healing Wavelength), which we hear in only one ear when we ask to receive Jesus, could be our Creator developing His Presence in all mankind. So that we may become more like Him . . . **JESUS SAID:** *"You will become as I"*. . . Perhaps we should be less involved in the material desires of the present world. He may be growing special cells, helping us to be more receptive to Jesus' Message and preparing us all for a wonderful overshadowing with many miraculous happenings, for those who are prepared to meet Him. **NOT THE END - THE BEGINNING...**

THE SAYINGS OF JESUS

*See list of Parallel Sayings from The Bible on page 202

These Quotations are mainly from the Gospel of Thomas and the Gospel of The Essenes.

Jesus said: Page No. in this book

* (1) *"You hear with one ear"* 124, 129

(2) *"I will give you what the eye has not seen,
what the ear has not heard,
what hand has not touched,
and what has not arisen in the heart of man."* 5, 129-131, 152

(3) *"Whoever has ears to hear, let him hear."* 7, 131, 150

(4) *"Cleave the wood and I am there,
lift the stone I am there also."* 9

(5) *"If they ask you: 'What is the sign
of your Heavenly Father in you?'
say to them: 'It is a Movement and a Rest.'"* . 10, 34, 36, 95, 132, 175,190

(6) *"The Kingdom of God is like a little leaven* (yeast)
hidden in a lump of dough." 11

(7) *"Eat of all the fruits,
except those which have bitterness."* 11, 187

(8) *"If you do not first understand water,
you know nothing."* 11, 12, 43

(9) *"There is nothing hidden which will not be revealed."* 13

(10) *"I tell my mysteries to those,
who are worthy of my mysteries."* 26, 149

(11) *"What thou shalt hear in thine ear,
and in thine other ear, that preach
from your housetops."* 27, 38

(12) *"Have you then discovered the beginning,
so that you inquire about the end?"* 31, 104, 142, 194

(13) *"For where the beginning is, there shall be the end."* 104

(14) *"The world is a bridge, become passers by;
but build not your dwelling here."* 8, 34

(15) *"Let the fields be joyful, let the floods clap their hands;
leave off your moans and lamentations."* 39

(16) *"Everything that happens is good."* 39, 49

(17) *"Why do you wash the outside of the cup?"* (the body)
*"Do you not understand that He who made the inside,
is also He who made the outside?"* 43

197

THE SAYINGS OF JESUS

*See list of Parallel Sayings from The Bible on page 202

These Quotations are mainly from the Gospel of Thomas and the Gospel of The Essenes.

Page No. in this book

*(18) "I marvel at how this great wealth, (God's Soul and Spirit) has made its home in this poverty." (The Human Body) 51

(19) "My soul was afflicted for the sons of men." 51

(20) "The Kingdom of The Father is spread upon the earth, and men do not see it." 51, 178, 189, 195

(21) "There is no power save that from The Heavenly Father; all else is but a dream of dust." 51

(22) "He will manifest Himself   (The Father) and His Image is concealed by His Light." 53, 54, 127, 129, 149

(23) "With the Angels of The Heavenly Father, will you learn to see the unseen." 54, 121

(24) "While we are children, we will see the rays of the sun, but not the Power which created it." 54

(25) "Even the hairs of your head are numbered." 62

(26) "All things are possible to him who believes." 77

(27) "Commune with The Angel of Air, who spreads the perfume of sweet smelling fields." 94

(28) "Holy Wisdom, The Understanding that unfolds continuously, as a Holy Scroll, yet does not come through learning. All Wisdom cometh from The Heavenly Father." 95

(29) "He who is without wisdom, his words are empty, and his deeds harmful." 95

(30) "With The Angels of The Heavenly Father, will you learn to see the unseen, to hear that which cannot be heard, and to speak the unspoken word." 54, 118, 121

(31) "My Heavenly Father is in all things, and He will manifest Himself." 119

(32) "Peace be with you." 54, 127

(33) "All living things are nearer to God than the Scripture, which is without life." (They are only written words) 128

(34) "God wrote not the laws in the pages of books, but in your heart and in your spirit." 128, 131, 189, 194

(35) "The words of God are written in His works." (His works are you and I and all His creations) 125, 128, 189

198

THE SAYINGS OF JESUS

*See list of Parallel Sayings from The Bible on page 202

These Quotations are mainly from the Gospel of Thomas and the Gospel of The Essenes.

Page No. in this book

*(36) "Whoever is near to me is near to the fire." 130

(37) "What thou shalt hear in thine ear,
and in the other ear, that preach from your housetops;
for no one lights a lamp and puts it under a bushel,
nor does he put it in a hidden place." 130, 150

(38) "He who loves me, will be loved by my Father,
and I shall love him, and shall manifest myself to him." 132

(39) "I will pray The Father (ask God) to send another
Counsellor to be with you forever."
(Then He breathed on them,
and they were filled with The Holy Spirit) 132

(40) "Where two or more are gathered together in my name,
there I am in the midst of them." 150

(41) "Within a man of light, there is light,
and he lights the whole world." 148

(42) "If they say to you: 'From where have you originated?'
say to them: 'We have come from the Light,
where the Light has originated through itself.'" 149

(43) "You search The Scriptures, because you think,
that in them you have eternal life; and it is they
that bear witness to me - yet you refuse to come
to me that you may have life." 151

(44) "I come because you need me." 165, 195

(45) "For thy Father in Heaven hath loved thee,
before the foundation of the world." 163, 181

(46) "Everyone who is of the truth, hears my voice." 190

(47) "Beyond the icy peaks of struggle, lies the peace and beauty
of The Infinite Garden of Knowledge." 161

(48) "Here in the centre of its forest stands
The Tree of Life, Mystery of Mysteries." 164

(49) "There shall be no peace among peoples till
there be one garden of the brotherhood over the Earth.
For how can there be peace, when each man
pursueth his own gain?" 164

(50) "He who hath found peace with the brotherhood of man,
hath made himself the co-worker of God." 164

(51) "Man is born to walk with the Angels,
but instead he doth search for jewels in the mud." 182

THE SAYINGS OF JESUS

*See list of Parallel Sayings from The Bible on page 202

These Quotations are mainly from the Gospel of Thomas and the Gospel of The Essenes.

Page No. in this book

*(52) "Mankind should build the Kingdom of Heaven on earth." 182

(53) "The mind of the idle is full of the weeds of discontent; but he who walks with the Angel of Work, has within him a field always fertile, where corn and grapes and all manner of sweet-scented herbs and flowers grow in abundance." 182

(54) "As ye sow, so shall ye reap. The man of God who has found his task, shall not ask any other blessing." 182

(55) "Do not wait for death to reveal the great mystery. If you know not your Heavenly Father while your feet tread the dusty soil, there shall be naught but shadows for thee in the life that is to come. Here and now is the mystery revealed. Here and now is the curtain lifted. Be not afraid, O man! Lay hold of the wings of the Angel of Eternal Life." 185

(56) "Turn the other cheek." 164

(57) "For the honest work of humble hands is a daily prayer of thanksgiving, and the music of the plough is a joyful song unto the Lord." 187

(58) "For in God we live, and move, and have our being. In truth, we are His sons, and He is our Father." 187

(59) "The heavenly Father is in us, and we are in Him." 187

(60) "The body is the Temple of The Spirit, and The Spirit is the Temple of God." 189

(61) "The Father knows what you need before you ask Him." 192

(62) "Six days shalt thou labour, the seventh is the day of thy God, keep it Holy." 40, 61

(63) "All the waters the Creator hath made are Holy." 106

RECENT RESEARCH has shown that certain types of music and sounds can increase the growth of neurons in the brain. This has prompted our thinking that the beautiful chord (The Healing Wavelength), which we hear in only one ear when we ask to receive Jesus, could be our Creator developing His Presence in all mankind. So that we may become more like Him . . .

(64) **JESUS SAID: "You will become as I."** . . . Perhaps we should be less involved in the material desires of the present world. He may be growing special cells, helping us to be more receptive to Jesus' Message and preparing us all for a wonderful overshadowing with many miraculous happenings, for those who are prepared to meet Him.

GOD SPEAKS TO MAN
Through Moses

*"I am the invisible Law,
without beginning and without end."*

"If thou keepest my commandments, thou shalt enter the Infinite Garden where stands the Tree of Life in the midst of the Eternal Sea."

*"The seventh day is the Sabbath: thou shalt remember it,
and keep it Holy."* (Biblical parallel in Leviticus 23:3)

*"For know ye that six days thou shalt work with the Angels,
but the seventh day shalt thou dwell in the Light of thy Lord."*
(Biblical parallel in Leviticus 23:3)

"I AM THAT I AM."

Genesis

God said: "Let There Be Light" 6, 149, 163, 183
(Genesis 1:3)

GOD SPEAKS TO MAN
Through The Vision of Enoch

*"I will speak to you throughout Eternity.
Be still, know I Am God."* 51-52

*"I speak to you, through the dew of the morning.
Be still, know I Am God."* 66, 98

*"I speak to you, through the thunder and lightning.
Be still, know I Am God."* 194

The Holy Ghost Descended Upon Jesus in The Shape of A Dove

And a Voice from Heaven said:
"Thou art my Beloved Son, in Thee I am well pleased." 134

After my own desperate Prayer, God answered:
"You should have known this my child."

Then continued:
"Is it not so?"

Later the complete answer:
*"Is it not so that he who is rude and sceptical
is in need of more help than one who already believes?"* 180-181

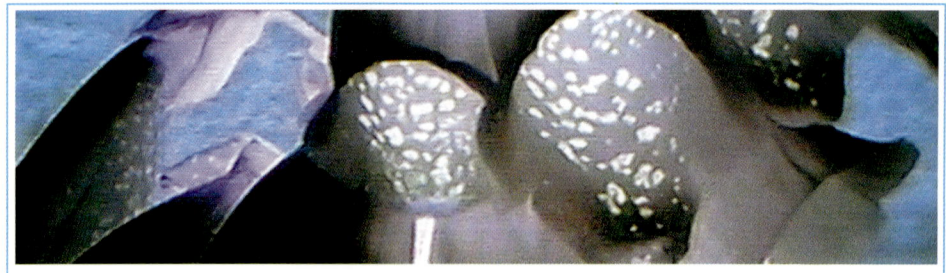

IDENTICAL OR PARALLEL SAYINGS FROM THE BIBLE (King James Version)
As Listed on pages 197 to 200 numbered (1) to (64)

(1)   Isaiah 30:21. One John 4:6. Proverbs, possibly 10:8.
(2)   One Corinthians 2:9. Two Corinthians 4:18. Matthew 13:15 and 17. Isaiah 64:4. Luke 10:24.
(3)   Mark 4:23. Matthew 11:14 - 15, 13:9 and 43. Mark 14:9 and 23. Revelation 2:7, 13:9.
(4)   Colossians 1:16 - 17.
(6)   Matthew 13:33. Luke 13:20 - 21.
(8)   John 3:5 - 6. *"Peace Be Still"* Mark 4: 39.
(9)   Mark 4:22. Luke 8:17, and 12:2. Matthew 10:26.
(10) Mark 4:11 - 12; 4:34. Matthew 13:11. Luke 8:10.
(11) Matthew 10:27. Luke 12:3.
(12) Matthew 24:3 and 36 - 44. Mark 13:4 and 31 - 33. Luke 9:27 and 21:7 - 27. Revelation 21:6.
(16) Romans 8:28.
(17) Luke 11:39 - 40.
(18) One Corinthians 6:19. Galatians 5:17. Romans 8:6 - 9.
(19) One Timothy possibly 3:16.
(20) Luke 17:20 - 21. Mark 1:14 - 15.
(22) Two Corinthians 4:4 - 6. One John 3:2.
(25) Matthew 10:30. Luke 12:7.
(26) Matthew 21:22. Mark 8:23 - 25.
(31) Luke 17:21.
(32) John 14:27.
(33) One Corinthians 6:19.
(34) Luke 17:21.
(35) Luke 17:21
(36) Mark (possibly) 12:34. Deuteronomy 4:11 - 12, 33, 36, 5:23 - 24.
(37) Matthew 5:14 - 15, 10:27. Mark 4:21 - 24. Luke 8:16 - 18, 11:33, 12:3 and 12.
(38) John 14:23.
(39) John 14:16 - 17, 14:26, 16:7 - 11, 20:21 - 22.
(40) Matthew 18:20, 28:20.
(41) Luke 11:34 - 36. John 8:12. Matthew 6:22 - 23.
(42) John 8:12 - 16, 12:35 - 36. Ephesians 5:8. Genesis 1:3 - 4.
(43) John 5:39 - 42.
(44) John 14:18.
(45) John 17:24, 1:1 - 2, 1:14.
(46) John 3:8, 18:37.
(47) Revelation 22:2.
(48) Revelation 22:2.
(52) Luke 17:20 - 21.
(55) John 5:24 - 25.
(58) Romans 8:16.
(59) One Corinthians 6:19, 8:6.
(60) Luke 17:20 - 21. One Corinthians 6:19.
(61) Matthew 6:8.
(62) Leviticus 23:3, see also Leviticus 25:3 - 4.
(64) John 4:14, 7:37.

202

FOR FURTHER READING
Concerning the Sayings of Jesus and other material

King James Version
THE HOLY BIBLE
CONTAINING THE
OLD AND NEW TESTAMENTS
TRANSLATED OUT OF THE ORIGINAL TONGUES AND WITH
THE FORMER TRANSLATIONS DILIGENTLY COMPARED
AND REVISED BY HIS MAJESTY'S SPECIAL COMMAND

APPOINTED TO BE READ IN CHURCHES

THE DEAD SEA SCROLLS UNCOVERED
BY
Robert Eisenman
(Professor at California State University)
& Michael Wise
(Assistant Professor at the University of Chicago)
ELEMENT BOOKS LTD

THE GOSPEL ACCORDING TO THOMAS

COPTIC TEXT ESTABLISHED AND TRANSLATED
BY
A. GUILLAUMONT, H.-CH. PUECH, G. QUISPEL,
W. TILL AND †YASSAH 'ABD AL MASĪḤ

THE OXYRHYNCHUS LOGIA
AND THE
APOCRYPHAL GOSPELS
BY THE
REV. CHARLES TAYLOR, D.D.
MASTER OF ST. JOHN'S COLLEGE, CAMBRIDGE

THE GOSPEL OF THE ESSENES
THE UNKNOWN BOOKS OF THE ESSENES
&
LOST SCROLLS OF THE ESSENE BROTHERHOOD

The Original Hebrew and Aramaic Texts
translated and edited by
EDMOND BORDEAUX SZEKELY

The Gospel of Peace of Jesus Christ by the disciple John

The Aramaic and Old Slavonic
Texts compared and edited by
Edmond Szekely. Translated by
Edmond Szekely and Purcell Weaver

THE APOCRYPHAL NEW TESTAMENT
BEING THE
APOCRYPHAL GOSPELS, ACTS,
EPISTLES AND APOCALYPSES

WITH OTHER NARRATIVES AND FRAGMENTS
NEWLY TRANSLATED BY

MONTAGUE RHODES JAMES
LITT. D., F.B.A., F.S.A.
PROVOST OF ETON.,
SOMETIME PROVOST OF KING'S COLLEGE, CAMBRIDGE

EGYPT EXPLORATION FUND
GRAECO-ROMAN BRANCH
NEW SAYINGS OF JESUS
AND
FRAGMENT OF A LOST GOSPEL

FROM OXYRHYNCHUS
EDITED WITH TRANSLATION AND COMMENTARY,
BY
BERNARD P. GRENFELL, D. LITT., M.A.
AND
ARTHUR S. HUNT, D.LITT., M.A.

Index

A

Ability to move - Without Him we would be still 190
Absolutely confirms Jesus' Presence 104
Acetone 92
A chance event? 53
Acidic rain 110
Action necessary 84
Active herbal compounds 84-85
Aflatoxins 100
After image of the eyes 21-22
Air Force years 25
Alan with Gordon Burns on Television 146
Alex Wilson's kindness 165
Allergy Specialists 108
Allsorts - Alan on Television 36
Allow it to happen 149
Aluminium, to be avoided 92, 108
Amethyst "Lift the stone" 9
America - National Enquirer - News story 144
America - National Examiner - News story 145
Amino acids 104
Analysis 81, 107-108
Angel of the flowers 12, 172
Angels of The Heavenly Father 118
Angels - Walk With Them 182
Animals are telepathic 168
Answer came in a Gentle Voice 181
Antibiotics 42
Antibiotic resistance 115
Anticancer well known herbs 82
Antiparasitic herbs 102
Arnica cream 97
Aromas from the past 56
Aristocracy 42
Asbestos 92
Astonished - by the appearance of a face 192
Atoms 15, 28-31, 184
Aura during Healing shown on TV 146
Aura - normal 146

B

Babies - wisps of steam during Healing 155
Baby Food - Chemical free 108
Background - Constant Presence 21-24, 154
Baffled - "In the heart of man" 131
Being somewhere else 154
Barrier of Doubt 149
Beauty of the mind in meditation 177
Beautiful chord in one ear 131
Beautiful Voice Spoke inside 181
Before The Foundation of The World 181
Beginning and End 142
Belief 149
Belief has weight 69
Belief helps Telepathy 170
Believe 77, 151
Beneficial Compounds in Herbs 82-91, 99
Benzene 92
Berries 114
"Be Still" 51-52, 66, 152, 194
Beta-carotene 90
Biblical Texts/others 117-134, 148-152, 163-165, 181-195
Biblical Times 19, 41, 50, 62-63, 156, 187, 203
Bill Bailey 16
Bioflavonoids 90
Birds singing with the music 134
Birth of Heather 37
Birth of Paul 39
Birth of humans - near to God at birth 155
Birth of Jesus - Unseen 132, 194
Blackberries and wild ponies 114
Black side of Radiometer 184
Blinding Light at Jesus's Birth 132, 183, 194
Blue bloods 42
Bob Wooler at the Cavern 139
Bonding - mother and child 155
Bonds between children 155
Bones - broken - regeneration - minerals required . 103, 115
Bones - rapid healing with Silver 103
Bracken - unsafe - toxic 96
Brain 133
Brains hidden 32
Breathing on them - The Holy Spirit 132
Breathing deeply 115
Brian Quinn's Good Works 165
Broadcast of Television Garden Party 108
Broccoli and other beneficial vegetables 91
Building blocks of life 112
Bumble Bee does not know he cannot fly 49
Burnt foods and Barbecues 94
Bushel 130
Butterfly's life 49, 190
Butterfly phenomenon 49

C

Cabbage 91
Calder High School 21
Cancer prevention 78-91, 99-103
Carbon filters 107
Cauliflower 91
Causes and effects 105
Cavern, Mathew Street, Liverpool 139
Celery 92
Celtic Blessings 188, 210
Chaos and chance 174
Chemicals to avoid 93
Chemists 108
Cheops Pyramid 172-173
Cherry blossom 151
Children 9, 155, 158
Children are already in touch with God 9, 158
Chillout room - musical experience 139
Christian difficulties 103
Choirs and music 26, 38, 123
Chord - high pitched 121-123, 129-131, 152-154
Chris Kelly with Alan on Allsorts TV 36
Chris Kelly - Creative Thinking 160
Cigarettes .... , 92, 115
Circuit diagram of Frequency generator 101
Citrus Fruits 91
Clap of thunder - Flash One Year Later 193
Clay 32
Close to Mother Nature 188
Cobweb Touch on face or cheeks 125, 132
Coffee and Tea 93
Colloidal Silver 37, 42-48, 89, 97, 100, 103, 115
Colloidal Silver Preparation of 46-48
Coloured squares-after image-Constant background . 21-22
Come Into The Garden - Sunday People 143
Commandments - The Ten are relevant today 190
Communion with Jesus 120-134, 140-153
Communication with plants 171-173
Companion molecules of benefit 99
Compelled to write this book 157
Composing inside the piano 139

204

Index

C continued

Compounds of benefit to health	78-91, 99
Concert at Quarry Bank	17-18
Conscious Mind	133
Concealed - God's Image	53-54, 127, 129, 149, 198
Constant background	21-24, 154, 184
Constant - G - a new one perhaps	184
Constant sounds	24
Contact with you	120, 152
Contaminants	60, 108-109
Cookware	92
Copper	30-31, 48, 74, 102, 108, 111, 112
Copper (Cu) in table of Elements	30, creations - 31
Counsellor - Holy Ghost	132
Country sayings	27, 33, 37, 186-187
Country sayings joined together	187
Cranberry Fruit	97
Crash guard	25
Creative Intellectual Wisdom	174
Creative Thinking	65-66, 158-160
Creative works-paintings, sculptures, music, poems	134
Creaton? - not a particle	185
Creator - *See* : ....God's Presence - His Presence - Jesus Our Creator - On almost every page
Cross in each grain of starch	62
Cross in Crassula flower ... 172, Honesty flowers ... 62, 119
Cross in Jasmine	192
Cross in Passionflower - (also page 1 miniature)	63
Cross in The Dogwood Legend	63
Crutches discarded	143
Crystal set '2LO'	85
Crystals - containing hidden water	111
Cured... By a Top of The Pops Disc	143
Cylinder Experiment	70-73

D

Daily Post - Newspaper Pure Water story	109
Damage limitation - What if scenario?	185
David Carradine (Heather's drawing)	67
David Soul (Heather's drawing)	67
DC current	48
Deaf, but now Hears	143
Demob'	33
Demonstration on Television	108
Denominations	142
Dental Surgeon - now plays tennis	144
Derek Nimmo	18
Desert sand ripples - and the Seashore	111
Details of value to help to Hear Him	153
Detecting hidden items	74-77
Detrimental health effects	92-94
Diet and foods	112-115
Dimensions The Fifth	175
Disbelief - outspoken	179
Distant Healing - "All the same distance from God"	155
Distillation	110
Divine Healing	104
DNA	13, 62, 95, 186
Doctors	108
Doctors Confirm Miraculous Powers	144
Doctor hears The Healing Wavelength	144
Doubt into Knowing	120
Doubt not	152
Dove Descending	134
Dowsing or Divining	75, 104-105
Drawings	16, 65-66, 159, 177, 211
Drawings (Heather's)	67

E

$E = mc^2$	183
Eamonn Andrews - with Alan's research	65
Ear has not heard	5, 129
Ear left	121, 122-124, 129, 133, 150, 152, 154
Ear right	121, 124, 129, 133, 150, 152, 154
Eclipse of the Moon (2000)	111, 116
Eclipse of the Sun (1999)	53-54, 110
Einstein's comment	55
Electric spark in cloning	182
Electrical charge on silver colloid	45
Electrolysis - makes visible	108
Electrons	6, 15
Elements	6, 24, 28-31
Elevate your thoughts	153
Enamel	108
End and Beginning	104, 142, 163
Equal and opposite - Everything God Created	6, 23, 50
Erring parents	120
Escaping pain - rather than experiencing the truth	57
Events to bring us all together?	142
Ever changing - never ending - before the first atom	163
Evil	15
Exciting Sayings of Jesus	129-132
Experiences - Out of this world	121-125
Experiments - then a lecture to the tutors	20
Explain or dismiss - phyicist is baffled	154-155
"*Eye has not seen*"	5, 118-123, 129
Eyes closed - for a Special Event - useful details	153

F

Fainting - loss of sight and sound - last to fade	7-8, 124
Faith Healing - Foreword page (III)	35, 104, 117, 140-147
Fasciolopsis buskii - a parasite	99-103
Fats, carbohydrates and proteins	112
Faulty actions and thoughts	159, 161-163
Feel, Listen, Experience His Presence in our midst	150-152
Ferns are different from Bracken	96-97
Film music - special effects on Thumponium	139
Filters - carbon	107
Fingers - rub together and listen	153-154
Fire - Near to	130
Fish	115, 187
First and last	104
Floating with God	8, 141, 147
Floating in water	158
Floods	38-39, 49
Flower bulbs - mind experiment	171-172
Food colourings, avoid them	92
Food flavourings, avoid them	92
Foods and Diet	112-115
Food storage temperatures	92
Footsteps in the sand	7
Forces unseen	6, 148-151
Forensic evidence of The Shroud is unique	192-193
Forgiveness - Touched by His Wisdom	133, 174
Formby Times - Healing does Work - Story	35
Formby Times - Mulberry, Anticancer	80
Formby Times report on TV Telepathy	170
Four billion people - One vision	53
Four leaf clover - (also page 1 miniature)	61, 119
Foxglove flower	24, 119, 122
Foxglove - unusual flower	119
Free from Rituals - we know where to find Him	179
Frequency generator - antiparasitic	99-102
Fresh air - negative ioniser	60-61, 115
Fruitful reproduction - natural, not with a spark	182

205

Index

F continued

Fruits	11, 80, 90-91, 114
Fuchsias - odd shapes	119
Fungi	41, 45
Future is good - Remarkable Revelations	104
Future - glimpses of the unknown	105

G

Garden of Eden - in Psychic News	35
Garden Party Television - scientific demonstration	108
Garden Sculptures, also see Sculptures	118
Gateway to Thinking - TV Alan with Chris Kelly	160
Geiger counter	109
Geller, Uri	56-57
Gene - self destruct, and genetic modifications	13
Gene Religious	50
Germanium - also in Brazilian Suma root	85
Germanium (Ge) in table of Elements	30
Ghosts	104-105
Ginkgo leaf	78, 96
G.M. foods	13, 94-95
God - A personal relationship	142
God stimulates Creativity	134, 157
God Has Made Contact - real phenomena	121-133, 152
God's Garden	26-27, 33, 61, 78
God's Image - concealed	7, 53, 127, 129, 184, 194, 198
God's Kingdom	100
God's Presence	115, 117, 140, 146, 151, 160
God's Presence - TV Alan with Gordon Burns	146
GOD'S SAYINGS	51-52, 66, 98, (128), 134, 149, 183, 194
GOD'S SAYINGS, also on Special Page	201
God reached out ahead of us - our path was guided	140
God Speaks to Man	51, 201
God Speaks directly to each one of us	190
God The Father - Jesus makes Himself known to 'man'	132
God Touched you	115
God Touched them and made them well	61
God Wrote The Laws	128, 131
God's Seasons	188
God's Words	128
God's Writings	131
Good News Herbs	97
Gordon Burns - Live Issues -TV in Liverpool	146
Grapes	85, 90
Grape washing	90
Gravity	6, 110, 132
Gravity and the Fifth Dimension	175
Gravity of Moon on Tides	110
Green leaf tea	46, 87, 93
Grew 9 inches - Dentist grew 2 inches	121, 145
Guided by God	141, 145
Guide to Telepathy - TV Alan with Brian Inglis	170

H

"Hand has not touched"	5, 129-130
Hand to Hand	125
Hand over hand	148, 150-151
Hands about an inch above	151
Hands are guided - U.S.A. National Examiner	145
Happiness - Peace - Tranquillity	142
Happy Contact with all living things	164
Hazel twigs for dowsing	76-77
Healing in I.O.M. Beatrice Qualtrough's kindness	166
Healed Miraculously	121
Healers - we became	116-125
Healing - at a distance	155
Healing Garden	3, 35, 58, 118, 121, 135, 140-145

Healing Letters	140, 147
Healing Music	135-141, 173
Healing research	124
Healing Sanctuary - rebuilt	165
Healing Wavelength	35, **117-133**, 140, 142-144, 147, 150
	152, 154, 158, 170, 173, 177, 195
Health back in our own hands	82, 95
Health protection	92-93, 96
Hearing - the last physical sense to fade	8, 124
Hear That Which Cannot Be Heard	118, 121
Hear The Miracle	122
Hear with One Ear	124, 129, 150
Hear with One Ear - The Mysteries of The Lord	186, 195
Hear God's Presence	26-27, 38, 117-133, 181
Hear The Wavelength	35, **117-133**, 140, 142-144, 147, 150
	152, 154, 158, 170, 173, 177, 195
Heart of man	129, 131, 152
Health Consultants	108
Heaven	14, 147
Heavenly Choir	26-27, 38
Heaven on Earth	182
HE Has Heard You	152
HE Touches You	132-133, 148
Herbal facts	78-91
Herbal paradox	83
Herbal poultice	81
Herbal combination	81
Herbal research	81
Herbal Preparation equal parts of each	81
Herbal Preparation at home	88
Herb Barks	88
Herb Berries Fruits and Seeds	87
Herb Flowers	86
Herbs complete and Leaves	87
Herb names - binomial Latinised	86
Herb Robert	97
Herb Roots and Rhizomes	86
Herb Woods Gums and Resins	88
Herbs destroy parasites	100
Herbs inhibit cancer cells	100
Hell	14
Hello Earth	51
Here and Now is The Mystery Revealed	185
He Will Manifest Himself	132
Hidden? - God's Presence	129, 142-144, 150, 174, 184, 192
High pitched chord	See Healing Wavelength
Hinges moved - Uri Geller effect	57
History	19
Holy Ghost Descending	134
Holy Wisdom	95
Holy Spirit	7, 57, 131-132, 148, 152, 190, 193
Holly with three cotyledons	119
Homeopaths	108
Honest work	187
Honesty flowers with a cross	119
Horse chestnut made sculptures of its own	62, 167
Horsetail herb	29, 78
Hospital in a bottle	44
How the Herbs work	98-99
How To Feel God's Presence	**117-133**
Human bonding	155
Human brain - God's receptor	6
Humble hands	187
Hyacinth	12, 171
Hydrogen	6, 24, 110, 163
Hydrogen (H) in table of Elements	29
Hypericum species and St. John's Wort	94

Index

I

Ice - in nature ... 110
Ice cubes - clear ... 108
Images experimental in cotton ... 191-192
Image of God hidden by His Light 7, 53, 127, 129, 184, 194
Images - photographic ... 40-41
Image of spine in French polish on chair back ... 119
Image on Shroud of Turin ... 183, 191-194
Impatient ... 152
Infant school - awareness of soul ... 11-12
Infinite Garden - Mystery of Mysteries ... 164
Infusion of herbs ... 88-89
Intellectual ploy - still learning ... 68
Intense desire ... 152
Intensity of The Father's Light ... 191-194
Internet ... 82
Intervene - and show Himself ... 185
Invitation To Feel God's Presence ... 129
In your heart and in your Spirit ... 194
I prayed again for an answer ... 180
"Is it not so?" - The answer came ... 181
Isopropyl alcohol ... 92, 100
Items to avoid ... 92-94
It's a way forward ... 189
I Will Speak to you ... 52
I Wiill (a very unusual print-out) ... 52

J

Jasmine flowers - unusual four petals ... 192
Jesus - came forth by the ear ... 7, 132
Jesus Communicates ... 122-123
Jesus endured the suffering for us all ... 193
Jesus knows about today's world ... 156
Jesus Manifests Himself ... 132
Jesus really is with us ... 123
JESUS' SAYINGS, Written on Special pages ... 197-200
JESUS' SAYINGS 43, 49, 51, 54, 62, 95, 104, 118-119, 121
 .... 124, 127-132, 142, 148-152, 161, 163-165
 .... 178, 182, 187, 189-190, 192, 194-200
Jesus speaks directly to each one of us ... 190
Jesus - The Circle ... 104
Jeweller's creations ... 55
Jewellery stones - care! ... 92
Jewels in the mud ... 182
Jimmy Tarbuck ... 21
Joy of God ... 9

K

Kilohertz 30kHz - generator, inhibits parasites ... 101
Kind thoughts and deeds ... 164
Kingdom of The Father ... 178
Kirlian Image of hand ... 130, 146
Kitchen table technology ... 46
Know that He Is God ... 152

L

Latin binomial plant names ... 86-88
Laughter Experiment ... 65-66
Laying on Hands - also in the Foreword (III) ... 79, 104
Leap of Faith ... 195
Leaven - yeast ... 10-11
Left ear ... 121, 124, 129, 133, 150, 152-154
Letters from home and abroad ... 140, 147
Life changes ... 18
Life's secret - and the mystery ... 12
Life that is to come ... 185

Light - Diamond Shape (mauve) ... 121, 129, 152
Light - Of The Father ... 7, 127, 132, 191
Light - God's Image concealed 7, 53, 127, 129, 184, 194, 198
Light *"Let There Be"* ... 6, 149, 163, 183
Light pressure ... 184
Light - shapes and pinpoints ... 121, 125, 149-150, 152
Lignans ... 85
Like minded friends ... 151
Limitations placed on humans ... 174
Line out of order ... 142
Listen into space ... 152
Listen with One Ear ... 121, 124, 129, 133, 152, 150, 154
Liverpool Philharmonic Hall - Strange music ... 139
Living forever ... 14
Living space ... 115
Living Words - Jesus direct contact ... 193
Love encourages perfection in all living forms ... 178
Loving relationship ... 182
Lucky (No.13) ... 68
Lycopene in tomatoes ... 90

M

Make peace before sleeping ... 164
Make ourselves worthy to receive Him ... 189
Make your wishes known ... 157
"Manifest Myself." said Jesus ... 132, 150
Married ... 37
Margins of the Mind on TV - Alan with Brian Inglis ... 170
Mary overshadowed ... 7, 131
Mathematician ... 155
Mauve Diamond Shape ... 121, 149
May you Hear With One Ear ... 188, 195
Meaning of life ... 13
Medical Professions ... 154
Meditation room and mystery revealed ... 176
Mercury distillation ... 37
Metal mystery ... 55-56
Methanol ... 92
Michael Bentine ... 65
Midst of us - (Jesus) ... 150, 179
Migraines cured ... 143-144
Mind in an altered state ... 69-77, 158-163, 168-172
Mind sensitivity ... 105
Mind Contact ... 69-74
Mind Contact procedures ... 168-172
Mind drifting ... 153
Minerals ... 9 (amethyst), 32 (quartz), 104, 112-113
Miracle gene? ... 50
Miracles ... 117
Miracles confirmed - Letters ... 147
Miraculous Birth - Not seen ... 7, 132, 194
Moon 2000 Eclipse ... 116
More to life than we will ever know ... 192
Morning Glory - inside flower ... 126-127, 135
Mother's only remaining drawing ... 10
Movement and a Rest ... 10, 34, 36, 43, 132
Mulberry Fruit ... 10-11, 79-80, 87, 90, 114
Mulberry leaf ... 10, 78, 80, 87
Mulberry story in Formby Times ... 80
Muon, meson and so-on ... 185
Muscle movement - a twitch in arm or leg ... 133, 150, 152
Music for Healing ... 135-141
Music - Heavenly Choirs ... 26, 38, 130
Music - not part of this world ... 135
Mycotoxins ... 100
Mysteries - of Jesus ... 149
Mystery of meditation revealed ... 176

Index

N

National Enquirer U.S.A. Story ... 144
National Examiner U.S.A. Story ... 145
Nature's moving sculptures ... 59
Nature's Pharmacy ... 84-91
Nature's sculptures ... 58
Negative gene ... 50
Negative ioniser ... 115
Negative world of sceptics ... 180
New Dimensions The Fifth ... 175
New Zealand Magazine - Healing Story ... 140
Night choir from above ... 26, 38, 130
Nimmo, Derek ... 18
Nitrates and nitrites ... 93, 107, 114
Nitrogen oxides ... 110
No need to travel or search - He is here ... 186
No rituals or procedures ... 179
Not heard - Hear with The Father's Angels ... 121
Not of this world - music ... 135
Nothing 'Spooky' - it's natural ... 152
Now stands erect ... 144
Now you know how His reply will be ... 150
Nuts - avoid moulds in all foods ... 100, 115

O

Ocean tides ... 110
Offset circuitry of 'zapper' ... 101
Old Wives' Tales - come to life ... 86
Olive oil ... 93
Oils and Fats ... 93, 115
One and The Same - Jesus 'wrote' nothing ... 125, 151, 193
One Ear ... 121, 122-124, 129, 133, 150, 152, 154
One God ... 142
One hundred and twelve elements ? ... 29
One line sayings of country folk ... 27, 33, 37, 186-188
One Spirit ... 128
Only God knows the outcome of His Own Actions ... 6
Only God knows the outcome of all our actions ... 185
Opera and rock'n'roll ... 64
Operations were crucial ... 120
Opposite ears ... 121, 130
Originated from God's Thoughts ... 149
Organic foods ... 91
Outspoken disbelief ... 179
Overshadowing of Mary ... 7, 131
Overshadowing - physical ... 54, 57
Overweight and under ... 112-114

P

Pain ... 57, 121
Paintings ... 5, 6, 8, 13-14, 17, 19, 26, 28, 32-34, 38, 50-51
 ... 54, 86, 88, 99, 100-101, 104-107, 112-113, 120-124
 .. 128-130, 133-134, 151-152, 161-164, 166, 170, 181, 194-196
Parasites - single cell ... 45, others 94, 99-102
Parents - guiding hands ... 55
Parsnips ... 92
Parsley ... 92
Passers by ... 8, 34
Pathogenic organisms ... 45
Patrick McGoohan (drawing) ... 65
Patulin ... 100
"Peace be with you." ... 127
"Peace! Be Still!" ... 12
Peace and Tranquillity ... 142
Peach - "Eat of all the fruits except...." ... 11
Peak performance in telepathy ... 169
Pear shaped pyramid ... 172-173

P

Peeling fruit ... 91
Pencil lines in meditation ... 177
Pencilled in The Face as we see it ... 192
Pendulum for dowsing and divining ... 76-77
Perpetuate itself - a special number ... 150
Pharmacy ... 35, 37-40, 44-45, 104, 141-144
Peter Levy has Alan's Healing Music on Radio City ... 139
Phenomena we have experienced .. 26, 35, 57, 104, 117-125,
 ... 129-133, 146-150, 152
Photographs baffled us ... 192
Photography - the silver saga ... 40-45
Photons of light ... 183-184
Physicist - baffled ... 155
Piano legs missing at the Philharmonic ... 139
Piano - through the floor ... 39
Pinpoints of Light ... 125, 129, 149-150, 152, 156
Plant experiments - mind effect on their growth ... 171-172
Plastics ... 20, 33, 56
Playing music to plants ... 173
Poem - Early Morning (Heather's) ... 66
Poem - Which Peach - with Chris Kelly ... 36
Pollutants ... 60-61
Pollution free process ... 98
Poltergeists ... 104-105
Pottery - clays carry memories from the past ... 32
Prayers - special needs ... 79, 120, 180-182
Prepare herbal infusion ... 88-89
Prescriptions ... 143
Pressure of light ... 184
Prisms reveal His secret of white light ... 183
Privileged to see His Miracles ... 162
Privileged to have met Jesus ... 195
Professions - Medical ... 120, 143-145, 154
Psychic News Newspaper - Story ... 35
Psychic News - see World Press and TV ... 211
Pulse of Life ... 98
Purified water ... 106-111
Purification of Body, Temple, and Soul ... 106
Pyramid Shapes and the effects - (pear) ... 172-173

Q

Quarry Bank High School ... 16
Queens Drive ... 21
Queueing to be healed ... 143
Quentin Crisp - After 92 Elements and beyond ... 28-29
Questions answered ... 179
Quinn, Brian - Honoured by Queen - Foreword (II) ... 165

R

Radioactive materials - avoid them ... 92-93
Radiance of motherhood ... 155
Radiations from you ... 148
Radio City program - plays Healing Music Record ... 139
Radio crystal ... 85
Radiometer - Sir William Crookes invention ... 184
Radium ... 30, 93
Reaches us all instantly - Jesus Spiritual Presence ... 194
Reader's brief comments ... 188-189
Realisation of your special moments ... 186
Recordings ... 135-141
Recycling ... 33, 34
Religious Gene ... 50
Remission ... 84
Repeated word in meditation ... 176
Resins Herbal ... 88

Index

continued

Resins synthetic plastics	20, 33
Resveratrol	79-80, 90, 114
Resurrection Sculpture	8, 19, 34, 117, 118, 123, 128
Reveille - Story - Magic hands	141
Revelations	104, 117-124
Reverse Osmosis	106-107
Right ear	121, 124, 129, 133, 150, 152-154
Ripples on the desert sands	111
Robin	33, 61, 193
Rock'n'roll and Opera	64
Rods for dowsing	75
Ronald Tortoiseshell works with loving care	167
Rosemary herb	78, 87, 96
Rotating cylinder	70-73
Rotating cylinder in a glass vessel	72-73
Rub fingers together and listen	153-154

Salt Marsh	59
Salts in human body fluids	110
Sand writing	7, 125
SAYINGS of GOD, see God's Sayings	201
SAYINGS of JESUS - Special pages	197-200
SAYINGS of JESUS - see Jesus' Sayings index	-207
SAYINGS of JESUS - Identical or parallel to Bible	202
Scientific Constant - G - perhaps	184
Scientific literature	82
Sculptures	3, 8, 12, 15, 19, 34-36, 58, 63, 95, 116-118
	123, 128, 133, 139, 145, 160, 166-167, 180, 186, 196
Sculpture - Mary and Baby Jesus	3, 34, 35, 58, 63
	116, 145, 166-167, 186
Sculpture re-created	166-167
Search The Scriptures	125, 151
Seasons of Our Creator	188
Sea water - mystery of the minerals	110
Secret of Colloidal Silver - Keep it moist	41-48
Seeing the Future	105
Seeking pleasure - Escaping pain	57
See the unseen	54, 121
Selenium	91
Selenium (Se) in Table of Elements	30
Shroud of Turin - Image Formation	183, 191, 193-194
Shroud of Jesus - research	191
Silhouette of Jesus	126
Silver and Colloidal silver	37, 40-48, 184
Silver - Spoon and pusher	41
Silver and Gold	31
Silver more precious than gold	40-48
Silver (polished) reflects only 10% U/V light	184
Silver wires in bone healing	103
Sit quietly with friends	151
Six sided pear pyramid	172
Small flower Willow Herb	84, 97
Smoke alarms - Disposal care!	92
Snails - ponds and parasites	99
Solvents avoid them	92
Somewhere else	8, 154
Soul	106, 155, 170, 193
Soul and Spirit component	155
Sound proof or as quiet as possible	176
Sparks from Jesus' Head	123
Spark of Life	9
Spark in cloning - Electric?	182
Speed of light	183
Special Invitation	129
Spectrum of visible light	183
Spelling Goldberg Letter	67

Spike Milligan	65
Spinal condition (Heather's)	120
Spine image on chair back	119
Spirit - Is The Temple of God	189
Spirit - One only	128
Spooky? - No!	152
Sports	16
Sprouts	91
Squeak in one ear	121
Stains on cotton cloth - unexplained	191
Station X	32
Steam - visible vapour state of water	110
Steam rising from babies heads	155
Still time - and see Back Book Cover	174
St. Georges Hotel - Uri Geller	56-57
Strings - Cosmic in Space 5th Dimension	175
Suffering endured to save the human soul	193
Sunday People - Stories	143
Sunday People - see also World Press and TV	211
Sunsets move the Soul - 177, and Sunrise	126-127
Sunsets	27, 59, 98, 131, 151, 177, 189
Surgeon's comments	144
Sycamore with three cotyledons	119

Taller by 2 inches - Dentist	145
Taller by 9 inches - Heather	121
Tarbuck, Jimmy	21
Tea and Coffee	93
"Tea is ready"	153
Telepathy and TV see (211)	104-105, 168-170
Television - Telepathy aids sensitivity of The Soul	170
Temperatures for food storage	92
Temple - human	106
Temple - of The Spirit	189
Ten Commandments are relevant today	190
Test - never Test God or Jesus	133
The Future	104-105
The Way	124, 128
Theories may need changing	155
Things unknown to them	189
Think	16, 25, 55, 158, 160, 173
Thoughts elevated	153
Thought exerts a force	68-73, 160
Thorium	30, 92
Thorium in Table of Elements (Th)	30
Thumponium - play on the strings	139
Thunder and lightning	193-194
Ticking clock	24
Tickling sensation	125, 150, 152, 154
Time - displacement	27, 122-123, 154
Time - In His Own Time	152
Time slip	122-123
Time stands still	27, 123, 174
Time tunnel - from the past	128
Tinnitus - Meniere's - or is it?	124
Toast	92
Tobacco	92
Tomatoes are special - Lycopene	90
Top A flat - Healing Wavelength is an octave above	154
Touch of our Creator's Genius	9, 53-54, 95, 119, 179
Touch like a cobweb on cheeks or face	133, 150
Toxic compounds removed	108
Toxins in foods	92-94, 106
Toxic Lifestyle - isopropyl alcohol and parasites	100
Trace Elements in diet	112-113

209

Index

T continued

Tranquillity and Peace 142, 154, 177
Trees - rapid growth rings 110
Troubled 3, 150, 179-180
Tumour Necrosis Factor 100
TV - Audience Feel God's Presence 146
TV - Telepathy Alan with Brian Inglis 170
Twitch 125, 133, 150, 152, 154
Two or more - "*I am in the midst of them*" 150

U

Ultimate Message 152
Ultimate Purpose 140
Ultraviolet light 30, 59-60, 92, 107, 184
Unified Theory? 184
Universal Mind - Our Creator's 163
Uranium Glass and Pendant - Care! 30, 92
Uranium in Table of Elements (U) 30
Unbelievers find The Way 151
Unique Phenomena 104, 120-125, 129-132, 149-150, 152
Unknown wonders 151
Unseen - Angel - sounds that cannot be heard 121
Unseen Forces 148
Uri Geller 56-57
Useful details for increasing sensitivity 153
Use The Revelations wisely - "Written in His Works" .. 189

V

Vapour trails - not a natural cloud in sight 60
Vegetables 90-91, 112, 114-115
Vibration of molecules 98-99
Video frames 53-54
Vinyl disc (music) 140
Viruses destroyed by Colloidal Silver 45
Visible light spectrum 183
Vitamin C 89, 112-114
Vitamin E 91, 112
Vitamins 89-91, 104, 112
Voltage below 0.9V 103

W

Waiting for one more line 188
Walking sticks 143
Walk with The Angels 182
Warm breeze 125, 130, 150, 152, 154-155
Warmth 133, 155

W

Water - bottled 93, 107
Water content of the body 110
Water - the facts 110-111
Water hidden in many crystals 111
Water in meteorite 111
Water purification 106-109
Water ripples on sand 111
Wavelength .... see Healing Wavelength
Way - The Way 124, 128
Ways which are no longer unknown 150
"We are all the same distance from God" 155
We Are Not Alone 6, 19, 57, 115, 123, 146, 193
We existed before God Created The Earth 163, 181
We are privileged to have met Him 195
We have seen His Miracles - felt His Presence 121-157
Weeds 16
Weighing belief 69
We will know who it is 131
Where do I belong - Who am I? 182
Where to find Him 179
White light 183
Why Do You Not Hear Me? 51
Willie Rushton wishes me luck at the Philharmonic 139
Without end, but ever changing 104, 142, 163
Without knowing how it happened 49, 158
Wisdom 5, 31, 43, 95, 133, 174, 181, 185
Woman's Own Magazine - Story 142
Wood's metal melts at 71°C 56
Woody Allen - drawing 65
Words of God 128, 201
World Press Television and Radio Reports 211

X

Xylene and other toxic vapours - Methanol 92

Y

Yeast - beneficial 10-11
Yeasts - detrimental 41, 45
You Are Your Only Limitation 159
Your Decision 83

Z

Zapper 101-102
Zinc in diet 90
Zinc in Table of Elements (Zn) 30

We referred to these lines on page 188.

A BLESSING ON SETTING FORTH

May the road ahead rise to meet you.
May the wind always be at your back.
May the sunshine warm your face,
The rains fall gently upon your fields;
And, until we meet again, may
God hold you in the palm of His hand.

Source said to be: Traditional.

WORLD PRESS TELEVISION AND RADIO
Some Reports about our Research, for Further Reading

LIVERPOOL ECHO	Runcorn Psychic research in 1952
BURTON MAIL	Sunspot Activity - May 1958
TELEVISION	With Eamonn Andrews - Laughter research - December 1964
TELEVISION	Formby Times report - January 1965
LIVERPOOL ECHO	Research at Newton-le-Willows - March 1968
DAILY MAIL	Ghost research - Newton-le-Willows - March 1968
FORMBY TIMES	Psychic research - March 1968
TELEVISION	Alan with Brian Inglis - Telepathy - May 1968
FORMBY TIMES	Spontaneous inspiration unlimited - June 1968
TELEVISION NEWS VIEW	Plants respond to human thoughts - January 1969
LIVERPOOL ECHO	Creative Thinking - Our early research - April 1969
ALLSORTS TELEVISION	Chris Kelly talking with Alan about Creative Thinking 1969
LIVERPOOL ECHO	Understanding Palace Hotel Ghost - May 1969
SUN NEWSPAPER	Investigation of Psychic Phenomena in Birkdale Hotel - May 1969
DAILY TELEGRAPH	Psychic Investigation - May 1969
TELEVISION NEWS	Alan examines Moon Rock - January 1970
FORMBY TIMES	Human Mind is greatest scientific instrument - January 1970
IMAGE 28	Phenomena resolved, only accurate report of our research - July 1971
FORMBY TIMES	Creative? It's all in the mind - May 1972
FORMBY TIMES	Water purification - February 1972
FORMBY TIMES	Power of the Subconscious Mind - August 1974
FORMBY TIMES	'Healing Wavelength' confirmed by readers - August 1974
PSYCHIC NEWS	'Healing Wavelength' produces incredible results - August 1974
FORMBY TIMES	Big response to healing story - September 1974
FORMBY TIMES	Giving up Pharmacy-To Help The Sick - November 1974
FORMBY TIMES	"Whatever it may be, it works." - December 1974
RADIO MERSEYSIDE	New Year message from Heather and Alan - January 1975
FORMBY TIMES	Unharmed after car crash - February 1975
PSYCHIC NEWS	'Garden of Eden' saves suicide - May 1975
FORMBY TIMES	Woman says that healing method works - June 1975
FORMBY TIMES	Mysterious foxglove in healing garden - September 1975
FORMBY TIMES	Looking to time when healing will be part of everyday life - March 1976
SUNDAY PEOPLE	Come Into The Garden And Be Healed - 11th April 1976
FORMBY TIMES	Many benefit from 'Healing Wavelength' 1976
SUNDAY PEOPLE	Queueing To Be Healed - 18th April 1976
PSYCHIC NEWS	Photos of Healing Aura - April 1976
AMERICA NATIONAL ENQUIRER	Incredible Healer, Mysterious Chord - July 1976
PSYCHIC NEWS	Doctors Praise Healer's Cures - August 1976
REVEILLE	Man with 'Magic' Hands - October 1976
PSYCHIC NEWS	Healers Make News - October 1976
ESOTERA (German Magazine)	You Can Hear The Healing Waves - December 1976
FORMBY TIMES	Conservation-solar heating - April 1978
WOMAN'S OWN	Healers Psychic Directory - Alan and Heather - July 1979
SUNDAY PEOPLE	Healing Music Recording - March 1980
PSYCHIC NEWS	Creates Record with Healing Music - March 1980
RADIO CITY 194	Peter Levy plays 'Healing Music Record' on Air - March 1980
FORMBY TIMES	Healing Apparition changed his life - March 1980
NEW ZEALAND	Heralds of the New Age - A Healing Musical Chord - July 1981
EXCHANGE FLAGS TV	Exchange Flags Programme with Gordon Burns - November 1982
AMERICA NATIONAL EXAMINER	Amazing healing power - January 1983
FORMBY TIMES	Healer now spreads the word - March 1983
DAILY POST	Water Fresher than a mountain spring PURA-LIFE - September 1987
TELEVISION	Garden Party Programme - Water Purification/Health - September 1990
DAILY POST	Special Commission - Water analysis for The Daily Post - April 1990
GREATER MANCHESTER RADIO	Paul Schaefer interview - Pura-Life 1990
LIVERPOOL ECHO	Purified Water research - Alan and Paul - August 1993
FORMBY TIMES	Mulberries may hold cancer cure - February 1997

With a very special thanks to my wife Brenda, who has helped us every day throughout our fascinating journey of research and writing the book. I drew this little sketch to capture the happiness she brings to everyone we meet.